PRAISE FOR RESILIENT RISK MANAGEMENT

'In an environment defined by uncertainty and disruption, this book provides a practical and compelling blueprint for building resilient organizations. What I found particularly interesting is the focus on assessing whether information actually travels, challenge actually occurs and lessons are actually adopted. In practice, these are often the leading indicators of resilience.'
Frederic Gielen, Executive Partner, Reply

'Risk, resilience, crisis management and continuity are too often treated as separate disciplines, creating dangerous corporate gaps. As a CRO, I know firsthand that balancing resilience with business growth is a massive challenge. Drawing on deep academic and practical experience, Julien Haye delivers a thought-provoking, pragmatic guide to navigating this convergence and building truly agile, resilient organizations.'
Richard Fielden, Chief Risk Officer, Fidelity International

'Extensive, sharp and refreshingly bold – this is the resilient risk management book today's organizations need. It's rigorous in its research, confident in its conclusions and essential reading for any leader navigating complexity today.'
Angela McConville, Chief Executive, NCT

'A compelling work that places risk management at the heart of strategic thinking, not simply to anticipate risks but to build organizations that are more resilient, agile and capable of adapting, deciding and ultimately turning uncertainty into opportunity.'
Alexandre Goullier, Deputy Chief Executive Officer, Global Agrosupply Division, Groupe Roullier

'The term "resilience" is so frequently used that it risks losing meaning. However, in this fresh and challenging approach, Julien Haye argues that resilience is a meta-capability; an outcome, not a process. It is complex and multi-dimensional. Easy to discuss, more nuanced to implement. A competitive advantage, not a shock-absorber. This is a highly recommended read on the topic of the day.'

Jennifer Geary, author and Founder of the C-Suite Framework

'Julien Haye has written the practical guide risk leaders have been waiting for: how to anticipate change, adapt as conditions evolve and keep creating value when the assumptions everyone relied on are challenged. Insightful, clear-eyed and immediately usable.'

Roger Spitz, author, World's Top 15 Futurist and Chair of Disruptive Futures Institute

Resilient Risk Management

How risk leadership enables agility

Julien Haye

KoganPage

Publisher's note

Every possible effort has been made to ensure that the information contained in this book is accurate at the time of going to press, and the publishers and author cannot accept responsibility for any errors or omissions, however caused. No responsibility for loss or damage occasioned to any person acting, or refraining from action, as a result of the material in this publication can be accepted by the editor, the publisher or the author.

First published in Great Britain and the United States in 2027 by Kogan Page Limited

Kogan Page
Kogan Page Ltd., 2nd Floor, 45 Gee Street, London EC1V 3RS, United Kingdom
Kogan Page Inc., 8 W 38th Street, Suite 902, New York, NY 10018, USA
www.koganpage.com

EU Representative (GPSR)
eucomply OÜ, Pärnu mnt 139b–14 11317, Tallinn, Estonia
www.eucompliancepartner.com

Kogan Page books are printed on paper from sustainable forests.

ISBNs
Hardback 978 1 3986 2934 9
Paperback 978 1 3986 2932 5
Ebook 978 1 3986 2933 2

British Library Cataloguing-in-Publication Data
A CIP record for this book is available from the British Library.

Library of Congress Control Number
2026949901

Typeset by Hong Kong FIVE Workshop, Hong Kong
Printed and bound by CPI Group (UK) Ltd, Croydon CR0 4YY

CONTENTS

LIST OF FIGURES AND TABLES

ABOUT THE AUTHOR

Julien Haye advises boards, executives and risk leaders on strengthening governance, building organizational resilience and making better decisions under uncertainty. He is the Managing Director of Aevitium LTD, a boutique risk and compliance advisory firm, and serves as Fractional Chief Risk and Compliance Officer for Fennech Financial.

With more than 26 years of experience across global financial services, Julien has held senior roles spanning front-office trading, enterprise risk management, compliance and organizational transformation, including Chief Risk Officer and Global Head of Non-Financial Risk and Operational Resilience. This breadth of experience provides a distinctive perspective on how governance, culture, strategy and human behaviour shape organizational resilience and long-term performance.

Throughout his career, Julien has designed enterprise risk frameworks, strengthened governance, led complex regulatory and organizational transformations, and advised boards and executive teams through periods of significant change.

Julien is the author of *The Risk Within* (Risk Books, 2025), which explores the role of psychological safety in risk culture and strategic decision-making. *Resilient Risk Management* builds on that foundation, demonstrating how organizations can embed resilience into governance, develop organizational agility and transform uncertainty into strategic advantage.

Alongside his advisory work, Julien hosts the CPD-accredited *RiskMasters* podcast, where he speaks with senior executives, board members and thought leaders about resilience, governance and the future of risk leadership. He also designs and delivers executive education programmes for organizations, professional bodies and regulators, helping leaders translate complex risk concepts into practical capability.

An award-winning LGBT role model, Julien has been recognized among the world's leading thought leaders in risk management and governance. He is passionate about creating inclusive environments where diverse perspectives strengthen decision-making, innovation and organizational resilience.

He also serves as a trustee and independent audit and risk committee chair, supporting charities and non-profit organizations in strengthening governance and delivering sustainable impact.

Julien lives in London with his husband and their two daughters.

ACKNOWLEDGEMENTS

Every book is shaped by the people who influence the way we think, broaden our perspective and encourage us to see the world differently. *Resilient Risk Management* is no exception.

Over more than two decades, I have had the privilege of working with exceptional colleagues, leaders, clients and mentors across financial services and beyond. Every conversation, success, setback and shared experience has contributed, in some way, to the ideas explored in these pages. I remain deeply grateful to everyone who has been part of that journey.

The book has been enriched by the generosity of the leaders who agreed to share their experience, perspectives and lessons learnt. My sincere gratitude goes to Bruce McIndoe, Frédéric Gielen, Angela McConville and Emmanuel de Rességuier for their openness, generosity and willingness to question established thinking. Their insights have brought depth, practicality and real-world perspective to these pages. While the interpretations and conclusions are my own, they are undoubtedly stronger because of their contributions.

Richard Fielden deserves special recognition for his detailed review of several chapters, which helped stress-test the ideas and strengthen the overall narrative. I am also grateful to Bruce McIndoe and Melvina Metochi for reviewing sections of the manuscript and providing thoughtful observations, constructive feedback and valued encouragement. Your perspectives have improved both the clarity of the arguments and the practical value of this book.

None of this would have been possible without the support of the team at Kogan Page. From the earliest conversations through to the development of the manuscript, your guidance, professionalism and belief in this project have been invaluable. Publishing a book is a collaborative endeavour, and I greatly appreciate the expertise, encouragement and care that the editorial and production teams have invested throughout the process.

I also owe a debt of gratitude to the organizations I have worked with throughout my career. They provided the opportunity to test ideas, question established practices and learn from complex situations. Many of the frameworks and principles presented in this book have been shaped through practical application alongside dedicated professionals committed to making better decisions under uncertainty.

To my family, thank you for your patience, encouragement and unwavering support throughout the many months of writing. Your understanding during the evenings, weekends and countless hours devoted to this project made its completion possible.

To everyone who has read, discussed and challenged the ideas presented in *The Risk Within*, thank you. Your questions, experiences and encouragement helped shape the thinking that ultimately became this book.

Finally, thank you to you, the reader. By choosing this book, you have become part of a wider conversation about the future of risk leadership. I hope the ideas in these pages encourage meaningful conversations, inspire better decisions and help you build organizations that are not only better prepared for uncertainty but also more confident, more adaptable and better equipped to create lasting value.

Introduction

Does your organization belong to the two in five organizations lacking capabilities and resources to deal with the current unpredictable environment?[1]

LEGO, Microsoft and Ørsted have demonstrated the importance of resilience when organizations are forced to confront existential disruptions and the risk of long-term decline. These organizations, like many others across the commercial and non-profit sectors, have had to contend with a shift from a linear and predictable world to a highly complex and interconnected environment marked by rapid and frequent change. Traditional business model and risk management strategies are unsustainable in the face of interconnected disruptions. The adage 'adapt or die' seems more appropriate than ever.

Many businesses have developed some form of capability to scan and monitor their environment. Horizon scanning, scenario analysis, market intelligence and increasingly, AI-enabled tools provide valuable insight into emerging trends and potential disruptions. Yet visibility does not equate to preparedness.

The concept of a resilient organization counters many organizational norms of the past decades. Standardization, lean six-sigma, just-in-time supply chain, treasury and capital optimization, and other similar business optimization strategies have been the main tenets of business execution during the period with a clear focus on cost-cuttings and improving returns. The impact was simple: more profits and less slack. That worked for as long these organizations were not subject to a constant need for strategic or operational pivot, that might require reallocating resources from one area to another or deal with a major supply chain disruption. But when a business operates with just what it needs without an inch of margin, any unexpected issues can derail it.

Risk management has developed core capabilities to support executive and leadership in the management of uncertainty and to anticipate the next crisis. But these capabilities have also been to a large extent predicated on predictive linear models and cannot really deal with secondary and interconnected effects. Risk models, however advanced, rely on 'known knowns' or 'known unknowns' to quote former US Defense Secretary Donald Rumsfeld. As we have seen in 2008, in the financial services industry, these models can fail on a systemic scale with catastrophic consequences for the industry and the wider society if they are the main drivers for decision-making.

Financial resilience has long been treated as the primary way organizations protect themselves from major shocks, with a strong focus on ensuring they have sufficient financial resources to absorb losses and continue operating under stress. In regulated sectors, this has often required organizations to override short-term profit optimization in favour of building financial slack to withstand severe shocks.

However, recent experience has shown that financial resilience on its own is not enough. The UK bank TSB core banking migration in 2018 is a clear illustration. The bank remained financially sound, yet customers were unable to access their accounts for extended periods. Capital strength did not translate into service continuity. This has reinforced the need to look beyond financial buffers and address operational resilience and operating sustainability as core elements of organizational resilience.

Business, non-profit and governmental organizations must rethink how they handle this environment. This is no longer about adding to the list of signals that could impact them. There is now ample evidence that many crises of the past few years, whether at business level or in civil society, fall into the category of grey rhinos[2]: ignored 'known knowns', with warning signs visible on risk radar screens, but not collated or structured in a way that enables organizations to understand what is unfolding in front of them.

Moreover, having the right information at the right time sent to the right person is still not sufficient to trigger the right response. If the organization does not have the bandwidth to deal with the emerging problem, whether financial or operational, people and business alike will flounder when faced with unexpected events.

In the context of this book, I assume you already have the capability to source relevant information, even though I will revisit what is required to ensure your toolkit is fit for purpose. The focus here is on how organizations should respond to this situation by building resilience.

Why this book and what will it help you do

Resilience is a business strategic differentiator. In an environment marked by deep uncertainty and high interconnectivity, the need to permanently adapt is consistently increasing.

The concept of resilience is universal, applying as much to individuals as it does to organizations. Yet, despite its prevalence, it remains ambiguous and fragmented. For many experts, the term acts as a 'fuzzy' catch-all, leading to applications in business that vary wildly from narrow business continuity planning to broad cultural initiatives.

This lack of a unified definition often results in inconsistent approaches with differing success rates. Some organizations treat resilience as a defensive 'shock absorber', focusing on absorptive capacity to endure crises, while others view it as an adaptive meta-capability used to pivot and seize market opportunities. The gap between these approaches defines the leaders from the laggards.

Crucially, organizational resilience is now recognized as a mutually reinforcing system: it cannot exist without the personal resilience of employees, yet individual grit alone is insufficient if the organizational structure is rigid or lacks psychological safety.

Much of the existing literature treats resilience as a static process or a 'tick box' exercise in compliance and mitigation. I argue that true resilience is not a procedure to be followed; it is a strategic outcome. It is the measurable result of effective risk management acting as a 'command centre' and leadership acting as the cultural engine. When these two forces align, resilience ceases to be a defensive shield and becomes a competitive advantage that allows an organization to thrive amid disruption.

So, I felt that in the current environment, senior leaders and executives, chief risk and compliance officers, and board directors needed to equip themselves with a meta-capability framework integrating resilience, leadership and risk management to shape the strategic direction of their organization and drive performance.

This is not about standard competency lists. It is about a unified system that enables your organization to adapt its primary skills to changing environments. I worked for a long time in an industry that had a strong focus on financial resilience through higher capital and liquidity resource requirements. In the past few years, the regulators realized that it was critical to overlay operational resilience not only to maintain financial resilience but also preserve overall systemic and market stability.

This led me to reflect on my experience in the industry. While financial institutions are driven by profit, it is clearly in their interest to ensure their businesses are sustainable and able to withstand significant shocks. Over that time, I have witnessed multiple market crashes and major geopolitical events unfold, each triggering widespread disruption. Technological innovation has enabled rapid development of new products and services, while simultaneously driving a material increase in complexity and exposure to new vulnerabilities. From today's vantage point, it feels increasingly likely that these pressure points will continue to intensify rather than recede.

As I have been helping my clients with the concept of resilience and what it means to them, I also found myself focusing on one central question: How can we establish a resilient organization bridging the gap between leadership and risk management?

To answer this, I am looking to discover new mental and organizational models, and perhaps rediscover timeless principles of resilience. I want to move beyond the 'static plans' of the past and explore resilience as a dynamic capability that allows for composure and clear decision-making even with incomplete data. This book brings together lessons drawn from practice, research, interviews and reflection to explore how organizations build resilience as a strategic capability.

I set myself a handful of objectives and questions I would like to answer:

1. What is organizational resilience in practice?
2. How does it apply across business, non-profit and public organizations operating under sustained uncertainty?
3. What enables resilience, and how are those enablers unlocked at organizational scale?
4. How does resilience shape decision-making and response when uncertainty materializes?
5. How can risk management and risk leadership act as catalysts for organizational agility and resilience?

Is this book for you?

Thank you for your interest and getting a copy of this book. I have prioritized keeping the core content as accessible as possible. I have also structured this book to respect your most valuable resource: time.

So, if you need immediate, actionable insights, you can navigate directly to the 'Key takeaways' and 'Reframing forward' summaries at the end of each section. These are designed for rapid, evidence-based decision-making.

If, however, you are looking to rethink the foundations of your organization, I invite you to explore the deeper conceptual chapters. Through preparatory structural brainstorming of this book, it became clear that a truly resilient organization requires more than just standard protocols. To widen the potential for learning, I have enriched the content with more sophisticated conceptual frameworks. We will leverage antifragility[3] (i.e. learning not just to survive shocks, but to improve because of them) and the Jugaad Innovation framework, which provides a roadmap for flexible, resourceful problem-solving when traditional means fail, to name two. By integrating these 'higher-order' ways of thinking, we can move from defensive risk management to a state of competitive, adaptive strength.

Throughout the book, I examine resilience through a series of interconnected lenses, drawing on practical experience, research, case studies and insights from leaders operating in complex environments. Rather than presenting a single formula for resilience, the chapters that follow identify recurring dynamics. Certain leadership behaviours strengthen adaptability, while certain governance choices improve organizational awareness. Certain cultural conditions enable faster learning, better decisions and more effective responses under pressure.

My aim is to translate these dynamics into practical frameworks, questions and actionable insights that you can apply within your own context. Whether you are leading a digital-first start-up, a global corporation, a public institution or a non-profit organization, the concepts explored in this book are designed to help you strengthen your organization's ability to anticipate disruption, adapt under pressure and sustain performance through uncertainty.

The successful application of these ideas can transform how your organization understands the relationship between leadership, strategy, resilience and risk. By bridging the gap between strategic intent and operational reality, organizations can move beyond siloed compliance activities and develop the adaptability required to navigate an increasingly uncertain world.

Does it work?

Yes, it does. But adopting this mindset may feel unsettling. It requires moving from the comfort of predictable 'procedures' to the dynamic reality of a living system. Yet, you likely already possess the means to succeed. Think of resilience as your organizational immune system: a self-correcting network that senses emerging threats, limits the spread of disruption and accelerates recovery when shocks occur. It provides the adaptive capacity required to sustain performance, preserve trust and respond effectively when conditions change.

Too many organizations are still conflating resilience with mere business continuity planning (BCP). This siloed approach often leads to catastrophic failure. Take the example of firms during the 2025 Iberian grid collapse. Many had invested heavily in local power contingencies for their data centres, ensuring their servers stayed 'on'. However, they failed to account for their interdependence on telecommunication providers. Their data was safe and powered but entirely inaccessible. In our highly interconnected landscape, we are truly only as good as our weakest link.

Can you do it?

You may be wondering whether building this kind of resilience is realistic in practice. You may also be questioning whether it is worth the potential disruption and cost. The short answer is yes.

The more important answer is that it requires a shift in how organizations think about capability, accountability, leadership under pressure and how risk management is used to support timely decision-making when conditions change.

This is not about heroics. It is certainly not about asking individuals to be more resilient in systems that remain fragile. And it is not about expecting perfect foresight in environments that are inherently uncertain. Organizations do not fail because people lack effort or intent. They fail because the system within which people operate constrains their ability to act when it matters.

Building resilience starts with recognizing that it is an organizational property, not a personal trait. It is inherent to how decisions are made, how authority is distributed, how challenge is handled, and how quickly resources can be reallocated when conditions change. These are design choices. They can be examined, tested and improved.

Many leaders assume that resilience requires wholesale transformation, significant investment or radical restructuring. In practice, meaningful progress often comes from addressing a small number of structural and behavioural constraints that repeatedly slow response or suppress early action.

In my experience, organizations are rarely as far from resilience as they believe. More often, they are closer than they realize, but constrained by habits, incentives and governance patterns that have not kept pace with their environment.

This book does not assume unlimited time, budget or organizational attention. It recognizes that most leaders are operating under sustained pressure, with competing priorities and limited capacity for large-scale change. Thus, the focus is on leverage: identifying the points where relatively small changes in leadership behaviour, decision design, escalation pathways or risk governance can materially improve how the organization responds to stress.

You do not need perfect information to act with resilience. You need sufficient clarity, trust and alignment to make decisions when information is incomplete. You do not need to eliminate or control uncertainty. You need the ability to absorb it without paralysis or overreaction.

If you are willing to question some long-held assumptions about efficiency, control and predictability, then yes, you can do this. Not by adding more process, but by strengthening the organizational conditions that allow people to act early, adapt quickly and learn continuously. That is what this book is designed to help you do.

From psychological safety to organizational agility

In my previous book, *The Risk Within*, I explored how psychological safety shapes risk culture, escalation and decision-making. The central argument was simple: when people do not feel safe to speak up, early warning signals are suppressed, challenge is impeded, and risk accumulates under the leadership radar. What appears externally as a technical or governance failure is often rooted in human behaviour.

Yet, psychological safety explains why signals are raised or withheld. It does not, by itself, explain what happens next. An organization may encourage openness and still struggle to respond effectively if decision rights are unclear, governance is slow or resources cannot be reallocated under pressure. In such cases, safety enables voice, but the system lacks movement. This is where organizational agility enters the picture.

Agility is often misunderstood as speed or flexibility. In practice, it is the organization's capacity to translate insight into action without friction. It reflects how quickly information travels, how decisions are made, how authority is exercised, and how the organization adapts when plans no longer fit reality. Agility cannot be an operational add-on. It is an inherent property of leadership, structure and culture working together.

With that, psychological safety and organizational agility are tightly linked. Safety creates the conditions for truth to surface. Agility determines whether that truth leads to timely, coherent action. Without safety, organizations act too late. Without agility, they act too slowly or inconsistently.

In many organizations, these two capabilities are developed in isolation. Psychological safety is framed as a people or culture issue. Agility is treated as an operating model or transformation objective. This separation weakens both. When safety is detached from decision-making, it becomes performative. When agility is pursued without trust, it becomes brittle.

The shift explored in this book is from psychological safety as a protective condition to agility as a performance capability. That shift requires leaders to think beyond individual behaviour and examine how systems respond when uncertainty materializes. It requires attention to escalation pathways, decision thresholds, governance cadence and the distribution of authority under stress.

Research into team effectiveness, including the work popularized by Amy Edmondson[4], has shown that psychological safety improves learning, performance and error detection. What is less often examined is how those benefits compound or dissipate at organizational scale. An organization can be safe to speak in, yet slow to act. It can encourage challenge, yet default to centralized control when pressure rises.

Organizational agility closes that gap. It is the mechanism through which safety translates into responsiveness, adaptability and resilience. It determines whether organizations merely surface problems earlier or actually change outcomes.

This book builds directly on the foundations laid in *The Risk Within*. Where that work focused on why people hesitate, this one examines how organizations move. Together, they form a continuous logic: from voice to action, from culture to capability, from psychological safety to organizational agility. That progression underpins everything that follows.

How to use this book

This book is not intended to be read in only one way. Some readers will move through it sequentially, building a conceptual understanding of resilience before engaging with the practical applications. Others will approach it selectively, dipping into chapters that speak directly to current challenges. Both approaches are valid and the structure of the book is designed to support them.

You do not need to agree with every premise to find value in the analysis. The intention is to provide lenses that sharpen judgement, not doctrines to be adopted wholesale.

The key takeaways and practical playbooks at the end of each chapter are designed to translate insight into action without requiring full immersion in the underlying theory. They can be used as prompts for reflection, discussion at leadership or board level, or as inputs into ongoing risk, strategy or transformation work.

If you are looking to rethink how your organization approaches uncertainty more fundamentally, the earlier chapters provide the conceptual foundations. These explore how resilience emerges from the interaction between leadership behaviour, culture, governance and systems. They are deliberately reflective and are intended to challenge assumptions that may no longer hold in today's environment.

Practical application runs throughout the book. As the chapters progress, the focus shifts increasingly towards implementation, examining how resilience shapes decision-making, risk governance, operational design, leadership practice and organizational agility. Drawing on real-world experience across sectors, these chapters are designed to help leaders assess whether resilience is genuinely embedded within the organization or simply assumed to exist.

You can use this book individually, as a way to refine your own thinking, or collectively, as a shared reference point. Several chapters are suitable for group discussion, whether within executive teams, boards or risk and transformation functions. The questions raised are intended to surface differences in perspective and to support more informed conversations about trade-offs, priorities and capacity.

Above all, this book is not about achieving a final state of resilience. It is about building the capability to adapt repeatedly as conditions change. You may find that some chapters resonate more strongly at certain moments than others. That is expected. Resilience is not static and neither is the way this book is meant to be used.

Read it with curiosity. Use it with intent. Return to it when the environment shifts.

Enjoy the read!

Endnotes

1. PwC (2025) *Global Compliance Study 2025*, PricewaterhouseCoopers, www.pwc.com/gx/en/issues/risk-regulation/pwc-global-compliance-study-2025.pdf
2. Wucker, M (2016) *The Gray Rhino: How to Recognize and Act on the Obvious Dangers We Ignore*, St. Martin's Press, New York
3. Taleb, N N (2012) *Antifragile: Things That Gain from Disorder*, Random House, New York
4. Edmondson, A (2018) *The Fearless Organization: Creating Psychological Safety in the Workplace for Learning, Innovation, and Growth*, Wiley, Hoboken, NJ

Online resources for this book are available at:
http://www.koganpage.com/RRM

PART ONE

The foundations of resilience and risk

01

Rethinking resilience in an age of uncertainty

> **CHAPTER OBJECTIVES**
>
> - Challenge continuity-based views of resilience and their limitations under deep uncertainty.
> - Reframe resilience as a leadership and organizational design capability.
> - Establish the foundations for building adaptive capacity in uncertain environments.

Strength is the ability to resist. Resilience is the ability to yield. But true power is the ability to be transformed by the very forces that seek to break you.

In an era where 'once-in-a-century' disruptions now arrive at least annually, leaders must abandon the pursuit of predictive precision. They must instead design for deep uncertainty. Designing for deep uncertainty treats uncertainty not as a forecasting problem but as a permanent constraint on decisions, structures and authority. Under these conditions, resilience shifts from building systems that withstand stress to architecting organizations that adapt through the very volatility they cannot control.

Many leaders will recognize this logic and respond that their organizations already conduct stress testing and resilience planning. These practices matter but they are designed for known scenarios and bounded shocks. They test whether existing systems can withstand pressure, not whether decision authority, incentives and resource allocation can adapt when assumptions fail. Under deep uncertainty, the risk is that they anchor their organizations to yesterday's logic just as conditions change.

Some organizations have already moved beyond this mindset. Rather than treating resilience as a defensive capability, they treat uncertainty as a design constraint. They prioritize optionality, invest in modular infrastructure and distribute decision-making authority closer to emerging challenges. Water Corporation in Australia,[1] for example, maintains multiple 'shovel-ready' options for Perth's future water supply rather than committing to a single forecast. Similarly, BioNTech's modular BioNTainer manufacturing units[2] allow production capacity to be relocated rapidly as circumstances change.

Such adaptability depends on leadership. Satya Nadella's transformation of Microsoft from a 'know-it-all' to a 'learn-it-all' culture illustrates a broader shift required under deep uncertainty. When the future cannot be mapped with confidence, leadership is less about finding the correct path and more about building the capacity to adjust course. Resilience becomes a property of organizational design rather than individual endurance.

This requires leaders to move beyond the illusion of certainty. By encouraging challenge, learning and psychological safety, organizations become less dependent on past success and more capable of adapting to emerging realities. Resilience then evolves from a defensive cost into a strategic capability, replacing rigid optimization with flexibility, experimentation and preparedness.

Ultimately, resilient organizations build the structures, authority and recovery capacity needed to adapt collectively. Their advantage lies not in predicting the future more accurately than others but in remaining capable of responding when the future unfolds differently than expected.

Why we misunderstand resilience

In most boardrooms, resilience is discussed as a defensive cost, a 'break glass in case of emergency' insurance policy. It is framed as the ability to maintain continuity, recover lost ground or satisfy an operational preparedness checklist.[3]

In an era of deep uncertainty, this framing can become a source of fragility. When resilience is reduced to 'bouncing back', organizations are preparing for a world that no longer exists.

Resilience is not the ability to return to stability.[4] In a non-linear environment, continuity often anchors organizations to an obsolete past. True resilience is the capacity to endure uncertainty and discomfort long enough for a superior strategy to take shape.

CHECKLIST: CONTINUITY BIAS DIAGNOSTIC (BOARD-LEVEL)

- Do we define resilience primarily in terms of recovery and continuity?
- Do our performance measures reward stability more than adaptation?
- Are resilience investments justified mainly through compliance or assurance?
- Do we treat redundancy and slack as inefficiency rather than capability?
- When disruption occurs, is the dominant question 'How do we return to normal?'

If most answers are yes, resilience is being framed as protection rather than capability.

If the continuity model is so dangerous, why does it persist? Because it is reinforced by success bias, compliance-driven incentives and legacy risk models.[5] Past performance is mistaken for future readiness, while governance assurance creates confidence that may not reflect actual adaptive capability.

The failure of legacy models reflects environmental change, not leadership decline. In tightly coupled systems,[6] escalation is rapid and non-linear, while assumptions of abundant resources are eroding. Systems built for efficiency under stability are increasingly fragile under constraint.

Resilience must move from a technical concern to a governance responsibility.[7] It is a leadership capability rooted in organizational design, enabling systems to absorb disruption and adapt without systemic failure.

Risk reporting is not resilience

Many organizations confuse evidence of risk management with evidence of resilience. Heat maps, dashboards and risk reports may demonstrate visibility and oversight. Resilience answers a different question: can the organization continue achieving its objectives when assumptions change, dependencies fail or conditions deteriorate unexpectedly? (Adapted from insights shared during interviews conducted for this book.)

TABLE 1.1 The continuity trap vs adaptive resilience

Feature	The continuity trap	Adaptive resilience
Core assumption	Stability can be restored	Change is permanent
Organizational logic	Efficiency-first, just-in-time	Modularity, just-in-case
Leadership focus	Recovery and control	Adaptation and evolution
Risk framing	Discrete, solvable problems	Systemic, cascading effects
Governance posture	Compliance and assurance	Preparedness and learning
Outcome	Return to an obsolete state	Emergence of a new, fitter state

Table 1.1 contrasts the assumptions and behaviours that distinguish continuity-focused organizations from genuinely resilient ones. With that, my definition of resilience is as follows:

> Resilience is the dynamic capability of an organization to navigate volatility and pivot its strategy without fracturing its core identity. It is a generative design that surfaces latent strain, enabling leaders to make asymmetric trade-offs before pressure crystallizes into crisis. Truly resilient organizations evolve through disruption by design, strengthening coherence rather than merely surviving shock.

The new risk dynamics

In previous decades, risk was treated as largely containable. Events were assumed to be local, bounded and manageable in isolation. Today, that assumption no longer holds. Over the last quarter-century, organizations have become deeply interconnected. Software failures in logistics platforms, disruptions in semiconductor supply and shifts in monetary policy now interact within the same system. Risks that once appeared independent increasingly propagate across sectors and geographies.

As a result, resilience can no longer be managed at the level of a single entity. Organizations are exposed through dependencies they do not directly control, and boundaries that once separated industries and risks have become porous.

This exposure is compounded by speed. Digital transformation and algorithmic decision-making have shrunk reaction windows from weeks to hours and sometimes minutes. Risk no longer unfolds gradually. It escalates rapidly, often before leadership teams can convene or formal crisis protocols are activated. By the time a response is formally agreed, the situation has frequently moved into second- or third-order effects.

These conditions create systemic amplification. In the past, organizations benefited from buffers of time, inventory and slack that absorbed disruption. Efficiency-driven and highly connected operating models have largely removed those buffers. As a result, small disruptions are now magnified through automated processes, market reactions and confidence effects. What begins as a minor operational issue can quickly translate into financial, reputational or liquidity stress. Leaders increasingly operate in environments where interventions aimed at stabilization can unintentionally intensify tension elsewhere.

The core risk under deep uncertainty is not surprise but escalation. Because systems are tightly coupled, the transition from local issue to systemic crisis is rapid. Leadership failure in these moments is rarely a failure to imagine scenarios. It is a failure to respond at the speed required. Organizations remain structured to manage discrete incidents, not accelerating cascades. By the time escalation is formally recognized, momentum has often exceeded the organization's capacity to contain it.

At the same time, regulators and stakeholders are becoming less tolerant of preventable failures. Preparedness remains largely invisible, while failure is public and enduring. As a result, claims that crises were unforeseeable carry less weight than they once did.

Increasingly, regulators and stakeholders distinguish between genuinely unpredictable shocks and highly probable risks that were visible but unaddressed. As sensing and analytical tools improve, failure to prepare is less often treated as bad luck and more often as a failure of judgement and design.

Underlying these dynamics is a widening asymmetry between cause and effect. In linear environments, small errors produced limited consequences. In today's tightly coupled systems, minor disturbances can trigger disproportionate outcomes. When impact is so disconnected from the initiating event, resilience can no longer remain a recovery capability. It must become a design principle.

The intellectual spine: Understanding uncertainty properly

To navigate deep uncertainty, leaders must move beyond a single definition of the unknown.[8] Many corporate failures stem from a basic category error: applying tools designed for measurable risk to conditions that are fundamentally uncertain or unstable. These states are not interchangeable. Each requires a different response.

Risk sits at the most stable end of the spectrum. Outcomes are known, probabilities can be estimated, and historical data provides a reliable guide. This is the domain of risk registers, insurance and standard controls. Risk can be modelled, priced and managed because the underlying rules of the system remain broadly intact.

On the other end, uncertainty emerges when plausible futures can be identified but probabilities cannot be assigned with confidence. Scenarios replace forecasts. Success depends less on prediction and more on preparedness across multiple outcomes. Traditional optimization gives way to judgement, flexibility and optionality.

Deep uncertainty defines the current era. Here, decision makers cannot agree on the models, the probabilities or even the boundaries of the system itself. Climate instability,[9] geopolitical fragmentation and AI-driven disruption interact in ways that break prior assumptions. In these conditions, traditional risk management becomes a distraction. Designing for one 'correct' future increases fragility. What is required instead is resilience across many unknown futures.

CHECKLIST: UNCERTAINTY CLASSIFICATION CHECK

- Are we relying on historical data to assess a situation with no clear precedent?
- Are probabilities being debated where assumptions themselves are contested?
- Are escalation thresholds based on impact rather than speed of propagation?
- Are we increasing reporting precision instead of increasing adaptability?
- Are we treating disagreement as noise rather than a signal of deep uncertainty?

If so, the challenge may not be risk management but uncertainty misclassification.

Misclassifying these is a primary source of systemic fragility. When leaders apply risk tools to deep uncertainty, precision becomes a proxy for control. Heat maps and models appear reassuring, yet they filter out the very outliers that matter most in non-linear systems.

Boards presented with sophisticated heat maps and high-resolution risk models often mistake numerical clarity for underlying stability.[10] This is the illusion of control in its most technical form: the belief that quantifying a threat is equivalent to mastering it. Organizations appear well protected on paper while remaining exposed to shocks their models classify as implausible. By optimizing for the most likely scenario, they remove the buffers and adaptive capacity needed to survive the unlikely ones. The result is structural brittleness: systems that perform efficiently within a narrow range of conditions and fail when assumptions no longer hold.

Escaping this trap requires abandoning a binary view of risk as either 'safe' or 'dangerous' and recognizing that different forms of disruption require different leadership responses. Some events fall within established experience and can be addressed through operational discipline, redundancy and recovery. Others span multiple systems and demand greater adaptability, distributed decision-making and continuous sense-making. At the extreme are assumption-breaking disruptions that challenge how the organization creates value and require reinvention rather than optimization.

Table 1.2 illustrates how leadership priorities evolve across this spectrum of unpredictability.

TABLE 1.2 Responding to different degrees of unpredictability

Dimension	Narrow-band shocks	Broad-band shocks	Systemic ruptures
Nature of disruption	Within historical experience	Multiple systems disrupted simultaneously	Core assumptions break down
Leadership focus	Operational discipline	Sense-making and adaptation	Evolution and reinvention
Decision approach	Established plans and procedures	Distributed judgement and learning	Strategic reframing and redesign
Organizational capability	Robustness and recovery	Adaptability and agility	Transformation and renewal
Success depends on	Restoring performance	Sustaining effectiveness	Creating new strategic coherence

Viewing unpredictability as a spectrum allows leaders to apply the appropriate level of attention, authority and organizational energy to the nature of the challenge they face. It preserves cognitive and operational reserves for the moments when the ground truly begins to shift.

From robustness to resilience to antifragility

The notion of resilience is frequently invoked across diverse contexts and for a multitude of purposes. Within the framework of this book, it is necessary to establish a formal hierarchy of stability, moving from **robustness** to **resilience** and finally to **antifragility**[11] before we can understand how they intersect in an age of deep uncertainty.

For decades, organizational strength has been defined by robustness. The oak tree embodies this logic: resilience through resistance. In practice, it produces just-in-case buffers, rigid hierarchies and fortified silos built to keep uncertainty out rather than adapt to it.

Why do we default to the oak? Because for much of the late 20th and early 21st centuries, the world was 'complicated' rather than 'complex'. In a complicated system, the relationship between cause and effect is clear enough that you can predict and optimize. If you can predict the wind's maximum velocity, you can simply build a wall strong enough to stop it.

However, the fatal flaw of the oak is its linear limit. Robustness is a binary state: you are either standing or you are broken. Because the oak is too rigid to change, it snaps the moment a storm exceeds its design limit. There is no 'give' in a robust system.

In the current landscape, defined by the polycrisis and non-linear shifts, relying on robustness is a gamble on the limits of your own imagination. If you cannot predict the exact nature of the next shock, you cannot build a wall high enough to stop it. We see this in the 'just-in-time' supply chains that collapsed during global disruptions; they were optimized for a world that no longer existed, making them 'oak-like' in their inability to yield without shattering.

The willow: Resilience as a dynamic capability

We must move from the rigidity of the oak to the flexibility of the willow tree. Where robustness resists the wind, resilience yields to it in order to remain standing.

In an age of deep uncertainty, resilience is a dynamic capability, expressed at both individual and organizational levels. Individuals draw on emotional, cognitive and behavioural flexibility to navigate uncertainty and recover from setbacks. Organizations rely on structures, relationships, governance and decision-making processes that allow them to absorb disruption and adapt as conditions change.

At its core, resilience is not a fixed state. It is a dynamic capability. It enables people and organizations to maintain coherence while adjusting to changing circumstances. Despite this, resilience is often treated like a rubber band, valued for its ability to stretch and return to its original shape. This interpretation is increasingly inadequate in environments characterized by deep uncertainty.

When success is defined as recovery, organizations anchor themselves to the past. They optimize to restore what *was* rather than adapt to what is emerging. In doing so, they delay necessary change and increase exposure to future disruption.

Yet, resilience is not about returning to where you were. It is about remaining viable when returning is no longer possible.

THE BURNOUT OF SYSTEMIC FLAWS[12]

This misconception also shapes how organizations think about people. When resilience is equated with perseverance, structural challenges are often reframed as individual shortcomings rather than organizational conditions.

Resilience is not determined solely by how much pressure individuals can absorb. It is also shaped by the systems, relationships and operating environments within which people work. The interaction between individual resilience, organizational design and collective agility is explored in greater depth in Chapters 3 and 15.

At its core, resilience is about adaptation. Organizations absorb disruption, adjust to changing conditions and continue functioning without losing their identity or purpose. Yet adaptation alone is not the end of the journey.

The most advanced organizations do more than withstand uncertainty or recover from it. They use disruption as a catalyst for learning, renewal and capability development. This shifts resilience from a defensive capability to a source of strategic advantage and introduces the final concept in this progression: antifragility.

STRENGTHENING THROUGH VOLATILITY (ANTIFRAGILITY)

To move beyond the limits of robustness and resilience, organizations must embrace antifragility. Introduced by Nassim Taleb, antifragility describes systems that do more than withstand disruption or recover from it. They improve because of volatility, stress and uncertainty.

Where robustness seeks to resist disruption and resilience seeks to adapt to it, antifragility treats disruption as a source of learning, renewal and capability development. The objective is not simply to preserve performance under pressure but to emerge stronger because of it.

Achieving this requires a different organizational mindset. Leaders must move beyond protecting existing structures and instead create conditions that support experimentation, learning, adaptation and continuous evolution. Uncertainty becomes more than a threat to manage. It becomes a source of insight and opportunity.

This does not mean seeking disruption for its own sake. It means building organizations that can learn from stress, adapt as conditions change, and strengthen their capabilities over time. In environments characterized by deep uncertainty, this capacity to evolve becomes a powerful source of long-term advantage.

The practical implications of antifragility, including optionality, organizational design, decision-making and adaptive leadership are explored throughout the remainder of this book and revisited in Chapter 17.

Framing the scope of resilience: The three circles of influence

When leaders confront the magnitude of deep uncertainty, the most common response is a sense of overwhelm. If the world is non-linear, if a one-in-a-thousand-years event feels ever-present, and if traditional models of robustness are no longer sufficient, the natural question becomes: where do I even start?

The answer lies in recognizing that resilience is not a single lever to be pulled but a property of where leadership attention and energy are placed. To clarify responsibility in an environment that cannot be fully controlled, this chapter draws on the framework of the Three Circles of Influence[13] (see Figure 1.1).

The **circle of control** contains the areas over which leaders have direct authority, including structures, policies, technology and resource allocation. The **circle of concern** contains external forces that shape outcomes but cannot be controlled, such as geopolitical events, market volatility, climate disruption and regulatory change.

Between the two sits the **circle of influence**. This is where resilience is built. Trust, culture, incentives, communication and decision-making all

FIGURE 1.1 Framing the scope of resilience: The Three Circles of Influence

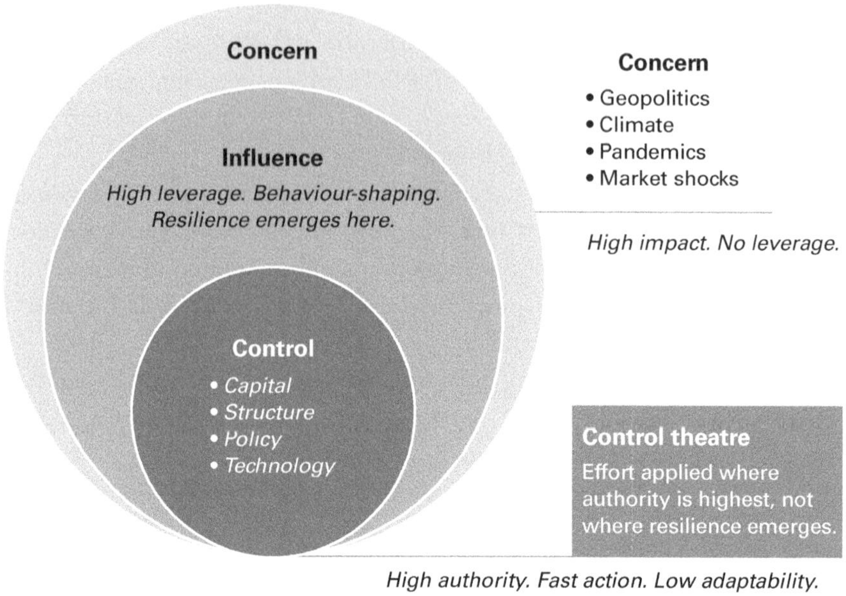

Resilience emerges where leadership shapes behaviour, trust and decision flow, not where authority is highest or uncertainty is greatest. Misallocating effort towards control or concern amplifies fragility rather than reducing it.

influence how effectively an organization responds when disruption occurs. Leaders cannot eliminate uncertainty, yet they can shape the conditions that determine how people adapt to it.

The distinction is important because organizations often overinvest in control while becoming distracted by concerns they cannot change. Under pressure, leadership attention can drift towards increased reporting, tighter oversight and reactive responses to external events. These actions may create reassurance without necessarily improving adaptability.

Resilience takes root when leaders focus their energy where influence is greatest. The objective is not to control every outcome, nor to react to every uncertainty, but to strengthen the conditions that enable effective adaptation. Many of the leadership, cultural and governance capabilities that shape this circle are explored throughout the remainder of the book.

The most liberating realization for leaders navigating uncertainty is this: resilience can be influenced even when circumstances cannot be controlled. By shrinking the energy spent on **control theatre** and concern-driven anxiety, and expanding the energy invested in the circle of influence, leadership moves from a defensive posture to an evolutionary one.

REAL-WORLD EXAMPLE

Covid-19: Adaptation under uncertainty

The Covid-19 pandemic tested resilience on a global scale. Health systems were confronted with rapidly changing information, uncertain transmission dynamics, shifting policy requirements and sudden surges in demand. The challenge was not simply absorbing a shock. It was adapting continuously as conditions evolved.

In the UK, the National Health Service (NHS) rapidly reconfigured how care was delivered. Digital consultations expanded at unprecedented speed, clinical staff were redeployed across traditional boundaries, and new approaches, such as virtual wards, enabled thousands of patients to be monitored remotely. Existing operating models were adjusted repeatedly as information emerged and healthcare pressures shifted.

Japan faced many of the same uncertainties. Rather than relying on a single predefined response, authorities continuously adapted public health measures, healthcare coordination and operational priorities as infection patterns and healthcare pressures evolved. Flexibility, communication and local adaptation became as important as formal plans.

Neither system possessed perfect information. Neither could predict the precise course of the pandemic. Success depended less on forecasting accuracy and more on the ability to revise assumptions, reallocate resources and coordinate action as circumstances changed.

Plans provide a starting point but resilience depends on the capacity to adapt when reality diverges from expectations. It is not possible to anticipate all possible scenarios, nor is it required. Organizations struggle because structures, decision processes and assumptions cannot adjust quickly enough when conditions change.

In environments characterized by deep uncertainty, resilience is demonstrated not through the accuracy of prediction but through the speed and effectiveness of adaptation.

Seeing the unseen: Risk foresight and behavioural blind spots

In the transition from robustness to resilience, the primary hurdle is not a lack of data but a failure of perception. To build systems capable of operating under deep uncertainty, leaders must move beyond spreadsheets and address the behavioural blind spots that cause organizations to walk knowingly into avoidable crises.

The bestiary of risk: Grey rhinos and black swans

Not all risks are difficult to identify. Some are visible long before they become critical, while others emerge with little warning. Distinguishing between the two is an important leadership capability.

Figure 1.2 contrasts two widely used risk metaphors. The 'grey rhino', a term introduced by Michele Wucker, describes a highly probable and high-impact threat that is clearly visible but insufficiently addressed. Climate change, ageing infrastructure, demographic pressures and accumulated technical debt are common examples. The challenge is rarely awareness. It is delayed action.

By contrast, Nassim Taleb's 'black swan' describes a rare and consequential event that sits outside normal expectations. These events matter and cannot be eliminated entirely. In that context, resilience requires sufficient adaptability to absorb shocks that cannot reasonably be predicted in advance.

The distinction matters because many leadership teams misallocate their attention. They devote significant effort to explaining unexpected events

FIGURE 1.2 The bestiary of risk: Visibility, not impact, determines leadership failure

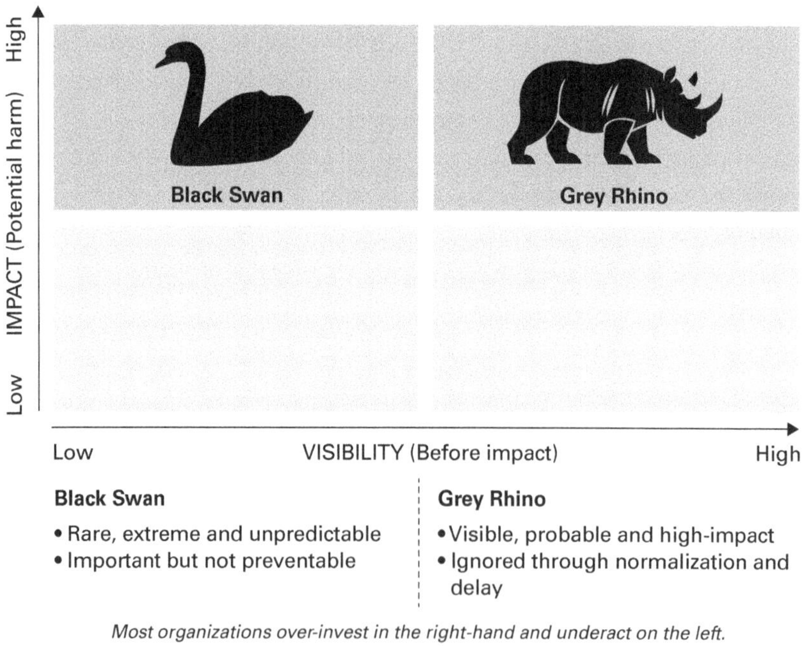

while underinvesting in visible risks that continue to grow in plain sight. In practice, failure is more often associated with neglected grey rhinos than genuinely unforeseeable black swans.

The challenge is not simply identifying risk. It is recognizing which threats are visible, which are uncertain, and where leadership attention is creating blind spots.

Why we stay blind: The behavioural drivers

Resilience fails in the boardroom long before it fails in the field. Most systemic collapses are behavioural failures that later appear technical. Three recurring dynamics sustain strategic blindness:

1. **Normalization of deviance**
   Small glitches and near misses are accepted because they do not trigger immediate harm. Over time, safety margins erode. What once demanded escalation becomes 'how things work around here', until the system quietly crosses a threshold it cannot recover from.
2. **Incentive distortion**
   Efficiency is rewarded visibly and immediately. Resilience investments are invisible until they are needed. In many organizations, leaders are incentivized to optimize for short-term calm while resilience is treated as discretionary cost rather than strategic capacity.
3. **Diffusion of accountability**
   In complex structures, responsibility for risk is often shared so widely that it effectively disappears. When everyone owns the risk, no one feels authorized to act. This creates the conditions for grey rhinos to advance unchallenged.

Bridges do not collapse solely because of engineering flaws. They fail because inspection warnings were rushed, budgets were trimmed under performance pressure, and early cracks were normalized over years. Seeing the unseen requires more than better dashboards or more data. It requires confronting how decisions are rewarded, how concerns are voiced, and how discomfort is handled long before a crisis materialises.

From foresight to attention

Foresight is about widening what an organization is willing to notice. Practically, this means leaders must:

- **Audit the rhinos**
  Ask explicitly, 'What is the obvious risk we all see but rarely discuss?'
- **Challenge incentives**
  Examine whether managers are penalized for building buffers or raising uncomfortable signals.
- **Reframe near-misses**
  Treat every close call as evidence of latent fragility, not proof that the system is safe.

Ultimately, the goal of risk foresight is not a crystal ball. It is the recognition that what organizations ignore often matters more than what they model. By identifying behavioural blind spots, leaders move beyond the mythology of surprise and towards cultures that are alert, honest and capable of responding early. In an environment defined by deep uncertainty, resilience begins not with prediction but with attention.

REAL-WORLD EXAMPLE

Grey rhinos in action: Germany's dependence on Russian gas

Germany's dependence on Russian natural gas provides a powerful example. Prior to 2022, more than half of Germany's gas imports originated from Russia. Policymakers, industry participants and energy analysts had long recognized the strategic vulnerability created by this concentration of supply. The risk was neither hidden nor poorly understood.

At the same time, the arrangement delivered clear economic benefits. Reliable supply, competitive pricing and established infrastructure supported industrial competitiveness and broader economic growth. Alternative supply arrangements, diversification initiatives and infrastructure investments remained under consideration, although the immediate incentives to accelerate change were limited.

The situation changed rapidly following Russia's invasion of Ukraine in 2022. A strategic dependency that had been debated for years became an immediate economic and operational challenge. Energy-intensive industries faced significant pressure, wholesale gas prices reached historic highs and governments across Europe were forced to accelerate investments and contingency measures that had previously been deferred.

The underlying vulnerability had been recognized long before the crisis emerged. The challenge was translating awareness into action while the consequences still appeared distant and manageable.

This is the defining characteristic of a grey rhino. The threat is visible, the direction of travel is understood, and the warning signs are widely recognized. Leadership failure occurs when familiarity reduces urgency and known vulnerabilities become accepted as part of the operating environment.

For leaders, the question is rarely whether a grey rhino exists. The challenge is acting while the costs of intervention still appear greater than the costs of inaction. By the time that calculation reverses, the threat has often become significantly more difficult and expensive to address.

Organizations as complex adaptive systems

In our pursuit of stability, we have long been taught to view organizations as machines. We speak of drivers, inputs, mechanisms and optimization. If an organization is a machine, resilience appears to be an engineering problem: identify the weak part, reinforce it and the system continues to run.

In the landscape of the mid-2020s, this metaphor is not incomplete. It is misleading. An organization is not a machine. It is a **complex adaptive system**. Understanding this distinction marks the difference between leaders who attempt to force resilience and those who learn to cultivate it.

A machine may contain many parts, but the relationships between those parts are largely predictable. Complex adaptive systems behave differently. Small changes can produce disproportionate effects. Feedback loops reinforce behaviours over time. The most important properties of the system, including trust, innovation, culture and resilience, emerge from interactions between people rather than from any single component.

Resilience cannot be installed like software or mandated through a policy update. You cannot engineer a team to be adaptive any more than you can engineer a garden to grow. You can only shape the conditions in which growth is possible.

Policies, controls and procedures remain necessary. They provide structure, consistency and accountability. Yet they are insufficient on their own. Excessive reliance on control can remove the agency, initiative and cognitive flexibility people need when confronted with novel situations. Writing a policy for every conceivable contingency does not produce resilience. It often produces rigidity.

True resilience is a latent property. It remains largely invisible during periods of stability and reveals itself only under pressure.

You cannot declare an organization resilient in a strategy document or leadership presentation. Resilience becomes visible when people must act without complete information, clear instructions or perfect certainty. In those moments, formal processes matter less than the conditions embedded within the system itself.

Do people feel safe enough to act and possibly fail? Do they understand the organization's intent well enough to adapt without waiting for permission? Does the governance structure allow local decisions to be made without creating wider systemic consequences?

These conditions determine whether the organization freezes or responds.

Understanding organizations as complex adaptive systems requires a corresponding shift in leadership. The role moves beyond directing activity and controlling outcomes. It becomes one of shaping conditions, reinforcing trust, creating clarity and enabling adaptation.

The most important insight is this: resilience is revealed, not declared.

You cannot command an organization to be resilient. You can only create an environment in which resilience is allowed to emerge. By understanding organizations as complex adaptive systems, leaders stop searching for the single fix and start paying attention to the conditions that matter most: culture, incentives, trust and decision-making under pressure.

Resilience is not built by tightening control. It is revealed when people are trusted to adapt.

Board and executive implications

Boards traditionally oversee resilience through governance structures, risk reporting and assurance activities. These provide visibility over whether controls, plans and processes exist. They do not necessarily reveal whether the organization can adapt when conditions change unexpectedly.

Oversight extends beyond preparedness and recovery. It includes understanding whether the organization can detect emerging risks, respond to weak signals and adjust decisions as assumptions evolve. Resilience becomes less about protecting a fixed plan and more about preserving the capacity to adapt when the plan no longer reflects reality.

For boards, this changes the nature of challenge. The focus shifts from reviewing resilience capabilities to examining the conditions that enable resilience in practice. This includes how information moves through the organization, how quickly concerns are escalated, and whether decision-making remains effective under pressure.

Observable patterns often provide stronger insight than formal reporting. Delayed escalation, excessive reliance on key individuals, repeated governance bottlenecks and the absence of constructive challenge may indicate fragility even when performance remains strong.

For executive leadership, resilience becomes a question of organizational design. Executives influence how authority is distributed, how decisions are made and whether structures support adaptation when circumstances change. The objective is not to eliminate uncertainty. It is to ensure the organization can respond effectively when uncertainty materializes.

This requires balancing efficiency with adaptability. Excessive optimization can remove the flexibility needed to absorb disruption. Effective leaders preserve the capacity to learn, adjust and reconfigure resources as conditions evolve.

For the Chief Risk Officer (CRO), resilience sits across both the circle of control and the circle of influence. Risk appetite, thresholds and escalation frameworks provide structural clarity. Culture, leadership behaviour, challenge and decision discipline determine how those mechanisms operate in practice.

Within the circle of control, the CRO helps define the structures that support resilience, including governance arrangements, decision thresholds, escalation pathways and risk monitoring mechanisms. Within the circle of influence, the role extends to reinforcing behaviours that support transparency, challenge, learning and timely action.

Resilience emerges through the interaction of these domains. Structure without behavioural alignment creates visibility without intervention. Behaviour without structural clarity creates inconsistency and reliance on individual judgement. Sustainable resilience requires both.

Many of the capabilities that support this shift, including leadership behaviour, culture, governance design, foresight and collective agility, are explored throughout the remainder of this book.

For boards, executives and CROs alike, the central question is simple: if assumptions changed tomorrow, how quickly could the organization recognise it, respond to it and adapt?

The answer to that question is often a better indicator of resilience than any recovery plan, dashboard or assurance report.

Practical playbook

Building resilience begins with a shift in how uncertainty is interpreted and how leadership attention is directed. The objective is not to predict every disruption. It is to strengthen the organization's capacity to recognize change, adapt to emerging conditions and respond before pressure becomes crisis.

Boards

Boards oversee whether the organization is prepared to operate under uncertainty rather than simply recover from disruption.

1. **Challenge assumptions, not just outcomes**
   Board discussions should examine the assumptions underpinning strategy, performance and risk reporting. Resilience weakens when assumptions remain untested for extended periods.
2. **Ask where adaptation would be most difficult**
   Boards should identify areas where the organization would struggle to change direction if conditions shifted suddenly. These often represent hidden concentrations of risk.
3. **Look beyond assurance**
   Reporting should provide insight into emerging conditions, behavioural signals and decision readiness, not solely confirmation that controls are operating as intended.

Executives

Executives shape the conditions that determine how effectively the organization responds when uncertainty materializes.

1. **Strengthen the circle of influence**
   Focus attention on culture, communication, incentives and decision-making. These factors often determine whether organizations adapt effectively under pressure.
2. **Create space for adaptation**
   Operating models should preserve sufficient flexibility to absorb disruption and respond to changing conditions. Excessive optimization can remove the capacity needed to adjust.
3. **Surface weak signals early**
   Encourage the identification and discussion of emerging concerns before they become material issues. Delayed escalation increases the likelihood of surprise.

Chief risk officers and risk leaders

Risk leaders help organizations move beyond prediction towards preparedness and adaptation.

1. **Distinguish risk from uncertainty**
   Ensure that governance discussions recognize the difference between measurable risks and conditions where assumptions, probabilities or outcomes remain unclear.
2. **Challenge resilience blind spots**
   Regularly assess where known vulnerabilities, dependencies or emerging threats may be receiving insufficient attention despite being visible.
3. **Strengthen foresight capabilities**
   Integrate scenario analysis, horizon scanning and early warning indicators into decision-making processes so that uncertainty informs action rather than reporting alone.

Resilience is not built through a single initiative, framework or recovery plan. It emerges through thousands of decisions that determine how information is interpreted, how concerns are escalated and how effectively organizations adapt when conditions change.

KEY TAKEAWAYS

- **Resilience is not recovery.** Continuity and recovery remain important, yet resilience is ultimately the capacity to adapt when conditions change and assumptions no longer hold.
- **Deep uncertainty requires a different leadership approach.** When probabilities, outcomes and system boundaries are unclear, prediction becomes less valuable than adaptability, optionality and preparedness.
- **Most resilience failures are behavioural before they are technical.** Delayed escalation, weak challenge, information bottlenecks and misplaced incentives often create fragility long before operational failures become visible.
- **Resilience emerges from organizational design.** Governance, culture, trust, decision rights and leadership behaviour shape how effectively an organization responds under pressure.

- **Resilience is a leadership responsibility.** Boards, executives and CROs cannot eliminate uncertainty but they can create the conditions that enable the organization to recognize change, adapt early and remain viable as circumstances evolve.

Reframing forward

This chapter has argued that resilience is not the ability to preserve stability. It is the capacity to adapt when conditions change and assumptions no longer hold.

Resilience cannot be installed through policy, predicted through models or delegated to a single function. It emerges through the interaction of governance, culture, leadership and organizational design. When disruption occurs, these conditions determine whether an organization freezes, absorbs the shock or adapts.

Understanding resilience is only the starting point. The practical challenge is building the capabilities that allow organizations to operate effectively under uncertainty rather than simply recover from it. Resilience provides the capacity to endure disruption. Agility provides the means to respond within it.

The next chapter moves from understanding resilience to developing adaptive capacity. It explores how organizations create the structures, behaviours and decision-making conditions that allow them to adjust, co-ordinate and act as uncertainty unfolds.

Endnotes

1 Water Corporation (2024) Perth and Peel Long-Term Water Supply Strategy, Perth: Water Corporation

2 BioNTech S E (2023) BioNTainer: Scalable mRNA Manufacturing Solutions, Mainz: BioNTech S E, Mainz

3 Taleb, N N (2012) *Antifragile: Things that gain from disorder*, Random House, New York

4 Minsky, H P (1986) *Stabilizing an Unstable Economy*, Yale University Press, New Haven, CT

5 Kahneman, D (2011) *Thinking, Fast and Slow*, Farrar, Straus and Giroux, New York

6 Perrow, C (1999) *Normal Accidents: Living with high-risk technologies*, Princeton University Press, Princeton, NJ

7 OECD (2018) *Governance for Critical Risks: Boosting Resilience to Global Shocks*, OECD Publishing

8 Knight, F H (1921) *Risk, Uncertainty, and Profit*, Houghton Mifflin, Boston

9 Intergovernmental Panel on Climate Change (IPCC) (2023) Climate Change 2023: Synthesis Report, Contribution of Working Groups I, II and III to the Sixth Assessment Report of the Intergovernmental Panel on Climate Change, IPCC

10 Power, M (2004) *The Risk Management of Everything*, Demos, London

11 Holling, C S (1973) Resilience and stability of ecological systems, *Annual Review of Ecology and Systematics*

12 Maslach, C and Leiter, M P (1997) *The Truth About Burnout*, Jossey-Bass, San Francisco

13 Covey, S R (1989) *The 7 Habits of Highly Effective People*, Simon & Schuster, New York

02

The anatomy of organizational agility

Building foresight, adaptability and execution capability

> CHAPTER OBJECTIVES
>
> - Define organizational agility as the decision and execution capability that activates resilience in practice.
> - Examine how foresight, adaptability and execution capability enable organizations to respond effectively under uncertainty.
> - Demonstrate how agility transforms resilience into a source of strategic advantage by preserving alignment, learning and coordinated action.

Resilience is the discipline of endurance; it ensures you are still standing when the dust settles. Agility is the discipline of motion; it determines who shaped the outcome.

Resilience determines whether an organization survives disruption but it does not dictate how it behaves once that disruption is in motion. This distinction is the difference between surviving a storm and navigating it.

Many organizations invest heavily in resilience and still fail strategically. They absorb shocks, maintain continuity and remain operational, yet emerge diminished, constrained or displaced. Survival is achieved, but advantage is lost. The missing element is not strength. It is movement.

The contrast between Kodak and Fujifilm during the digital transition illustrates this clearly. Both organizations were resilient, with deep patent portfolios and substantial financial reserves. Kodak used that strength to defend its legacy film business, preserving value until it eroded. Fujifilm used resilience to fund rapid repositioning into healthcare and advanced materials. The difference was not resources but orientation. One protected the past. The other moved towards a new future.

Agility is the mechanism through which resilience becomes active rather than static.[1] It governs how organizations sense change, how they decide when certainty is unavailable, and how they act without fragmenting under pressure. Where agility is present, uncertainty preserves optionality. Where it is absent, uncertainty compresses choice and accelerates fragility.

Fragility, in this sense, is not the opposite of resilience. It is the consequence of systems that cannot adjust in time. Stability delays recognition. Familiar decision logic lingers beyond its relevance. Action arrives after assumptions have already failed. What appears as control often masks misalignment.

Agility vs fragility: Why stability no longer protects organizations

For decades, organizational resilience has been implicitly equated with stability. Leaders invested in scale, efficiency, standardization and control on the assumption that a well-optimized organization would absorb shocks more effectively than a loosely structured one. In relatively predictable environments, that assumption often held. Stability reinforced existing advantages and allowed organizations to scale proven models efficiently. The challenge is that resilience built around preservation assumes tomorrow will resemble yesterday. In volatile environments, that assumption becomes increasingly costly.

Highly stable organizations tend to lock in assumptions about demand, technology, talent and delivery models. These assumptions remain invisible while conditions remain familiar. When conditions shift, stability delays recognition of the change. Decisions are taken using outdated reference points and responses arrive late, fragmented or misdirected. The organization appears strong until it fails abruptly.

This is the anatomy of fragility. As we have seen in Chapter 1, fragility emerges from over-optimization.[2] As systems become more efficient, buffers are removed. Slack is treated as waste and variation is designed out. What remains is a tightly coupled organization that performs exceptionally well within narrow parameters and deteriorates rapidly outside them. Stress does not bend the system; it exposes its limits.

The dynamic is similar to a monoculture forest. A forest engineered for peak timber production might consist of identical, fast-growing trees, all the same age, planted in perfect rows. It is a model of efficiency and predictability until a single pest or disease arrives. In a natural, biodiverse forest, diversity provides resilience. Different species offer varied resistance to disease. Redundancy creates natural firebreaks. Genetic variation limits the spread of failure. The monoculture forest lacks these buffers. Optimized for one outcome, it becomes uniformly vulnerable. What should have been a localized disruption escalates rapidly into systemic collapse. Organizations designed for maximum efficiency behave in the same way under stress.

Where stability preserves existing advantage, agility preserves decision optionality. It allows organizations to adjust direction without waiting for certainty. It creates room to reconfigure resources, priorities and execution paths as conditions evolve. Agility does not reject efficiency; it prevents efficiency from becoming a trap. Resilience without agility only limits damage but it does not enable repositioning.

Many organizations invest in resilience as a defensive capability. They strengthen continuity plans and critical processes. They prepare for recovery. These investments reduce loss severity once disruption occurs. They do not change the organization's ability to respond while disruption is unfolding. The result is often a delayed response that preserves survival while forfeiting opportunity.

Agility changes the role resilience plays

When organizations sense change earlier, decide faster under uncertainty and act coherently across functions, resilience stops being a shield and becomes a lever. It enables leaders to move before competitors. It allows capital, talent and attention to be redeployed while options remain open. It supports strategic repositioning rather than reactive containment. This is the point at which resilience becomes a source of competitive and strategic advantage.

The difference is not speed alone. Fast action without alignment creates noise. Agility combines speed with coherence. Decisions travel through the organization without distortion. Execution adapts without fragmenting. Learning feeds back into subsequent choices. The organization remains oriented even as it moves.

The three pillars of systemic agility

The following framework shows how these pillars interact to transform agility from a defensive necessity into a strategic advantage. Figure 2.1 illustrates how organizational agility emerges from the interaction of foresight, adaptability and execution, enabled by leadership, governance and strategy.

Pillar 1: Agility is a leadership capability

It depends on how leaders frame uncertainty, allocate decision rights and treat escalation. Leaders who equate control with certainty slow the organization precisely when uncertainty increases. Conversely, leaders who treat

FIGURE 2.1 The agility-fragility framework

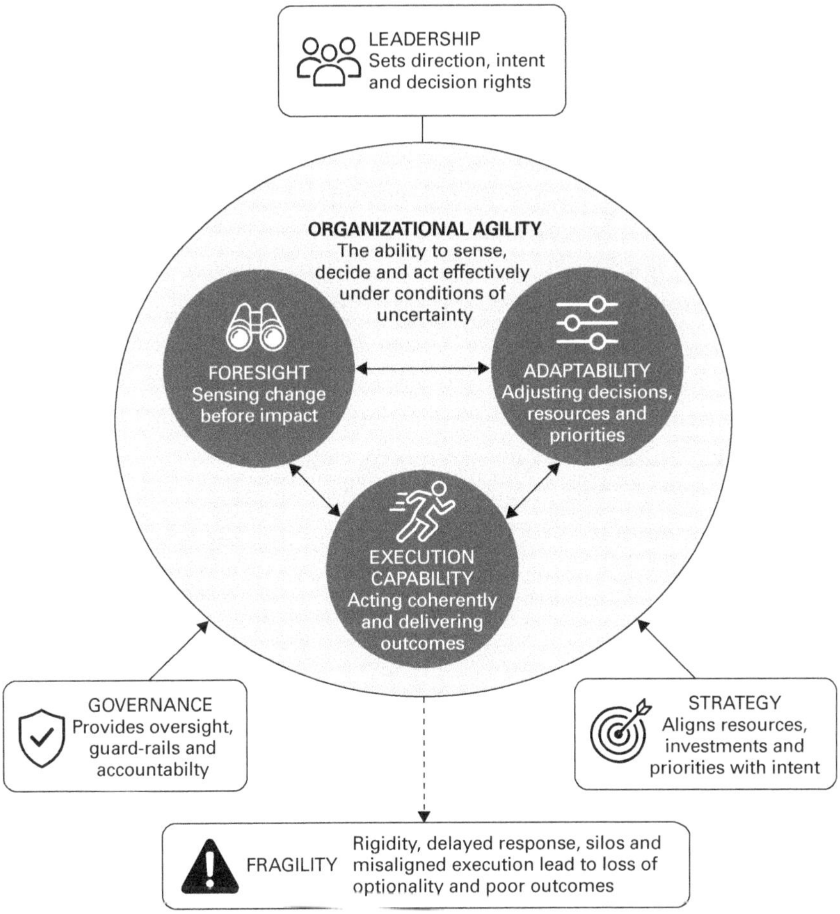

uncertainty as a design condition create space for adaptation while maintaining direction. This requires moving away from the 'command and control' model towards a facilitative approach[3] that empowers teams to act on local intelligence.

Pillar 2: Agility is a governance outcome

Decision architecture, escalation pathways and performance incentives determine whether agility emerges or collapses under pressure. Governance that prioritizes assurance over learning suppresses early signals. In contrast, governance that values transparency and optionality enables earlier intervention and better trade-offs. [4] This shift ensures that governance frameworks support rapid realignment rather than acting as a bureaucratic brake.[5]

Pillar 3: Agility is a strategic differentiator

In volatile environments, advantage does not come from predicting the future more accurately than others. It comes from adjusting faster as the future reveals itself. Organizations that preserve optionality outperform those optimized for a single expected outcome.[6] By treating agility as a core strategy, the firm moves from a posture of 'bracing for impact' to one of 'navigating the flow'.

Fragility hides inside efficiency. It rarely appears in performance metrics. It surfaces when conditions move outside design assumptions. By the time it becomes visible, strategic choice has already narrowed. Agility expands that window. It protects not only the organization's ability to withstand shocks but its ability to shape outcomes.

The remainder of this chapter examines how agility is built in practice. It breaks agility into three interlocking dimensions: foresight, adaptability and execution capability.

Foresight: Sensing before impact

If agility determines whether resilience creates advantage, foresight determines whether agility arrives in time.

Foresight is often misunderstood as prediction. In practice, resilient organizations rarely succeed because they forecast the future more accurately than others. They succeed because they detect change earlier and respond while there is still time to act.

FIGURE 2.2 The three dimensions of agility

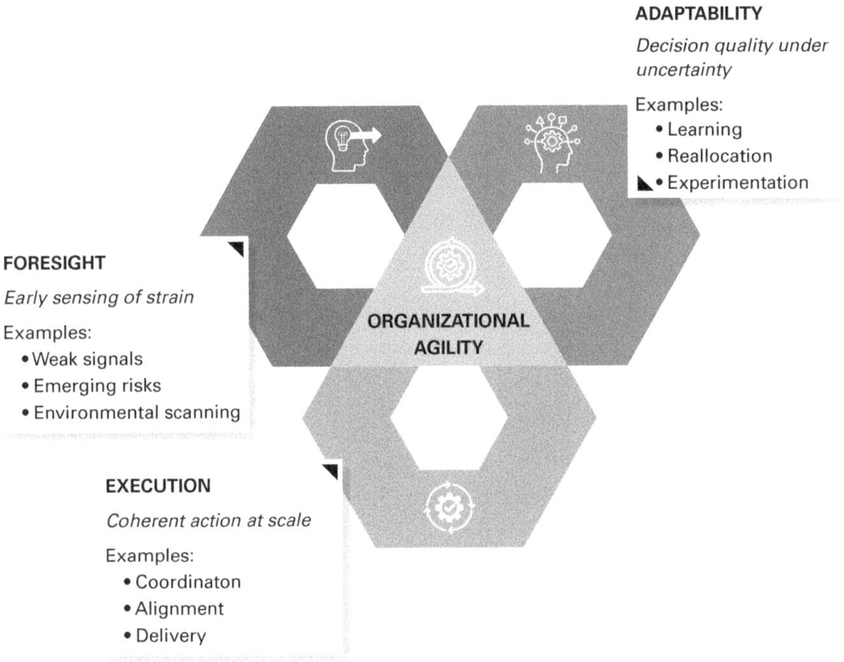

The challenge is that early signals rarely arrive as clear warnings. They appear as small anomalies, emerging tensions and subtle shifts in behaviour that are easy to dismiss because performance remains stable. By the time these signals become visible in financial results or operational failures, the opportunity to respond has often diminished.

Figure 2.2 illustrates the three mutually reinforcing capabilities that underpin organizational agility: foresight, adaptability and execution.

It is vital to note this difference. Most formal risk indicators are lagging by design. They confirm what has already happened. Performance metrics, incident counts, customer complaints and financial thresholds provide reassurance that the system is still functioning within expected bounds. By the time they change meaningfully, the underlying conditions that caused them have already shifted.

To compensate, organizations often introduce leading indicators, measures intended to track inputs and conditions before they crystallize into outcomes. These are useful but they remain proxies. Table 2.1 summarizes how these three dimensions contribute to organizational agility.

TABLE 2.1 Lagging and leading indicators of organizational strain

Lagging indicator (the 'what')	Leading indicator (the 'warning')
Incident counts	Number of 'near-miss' reports or bypassed safety checks
Financial thresholds	R&D spend vs technical debt backlog
Customer complaints	Employee turnover rates in customer-facing roles
System outages	Mean time to detect (MTTD) during routine drills

Early strain signals behave differently. They appear as small deviations in behaviour, informal workarounds, near-misses, quiet reprioritization or changes in escalation patterns at the frontline. They rarely trigger alarms and they often look anecdotal, subjective or inconvenient. Yet these signals reveal where the system is being stretched beyond its design assumptions. The tension between frontline insight and senior dashboards sits at the heart of foresight failure.

Frontline teams experience friction first. They see processes becoming harder to execute and they notice customers behaving differently. They adapt locally to keep delivery moving. Senior leaders, by contrast, see aggregated indicators designed to smooth variation. Dashboards reduce noise so patterns are easier to interpret. In doing so, they often suppress the very signals that matter most under uncertainty. With that, foresight breaks down when organizations privilege clean data over messy reality.

This is why foresight failures are usually cultural rather than analytical. Organizations do not lack signals. They lack permission to treat ambiguity as actionable. Weak signals challenge established narratives and they arrive without certainty. Acting on them can feel premature or disruptive. In cultures that reward confidence and penalize escalation, early sensing is quietly discouraged. As a result, organizations wait for confirmation. By the time certainty arrives, strategic choice has already narrowed.

REAL-WORLD EXAMPLE

Foresight as advantage in the technology sector (US/EN)

During the early stages of the Covid-19 disruption, technology organizations faced extreme volatility. Work patterns shifted abruptly, demand signals conflicted and formal data lagged reality. The differentiator was how early weak signals were taken seriously.

Organizations that demonstrated strong foresight paid attention to behavioural change before performance metrics moved. Collaboration patterns shifted and productivity rhythms altered, while support requests increased in unexpected areas. None of these signals, in isolation, justified decisive action. Together, they indicated structural change.

Crucially, these organizations did not wait for certainty. Incomplete information was treated as a design input rather than a reason to pause. Decision rights were pushed closer to where signals emerged. Teams were encouraged to surface friction without first proving impact and adjustments were made with the explicit expectation that they would be revised.

This enabled rapid repositioning. Delivery models adapted before stress became visible in outputs and investment priorities shifted while competitors were still debating reversibility. Workforce policies evolved while options remained open.

Others, facing the same early signals, waited. They sought validation through data that had not yet caught up. By the time confirmation arrived, flexibility had already been lost and responses became reactive.

The strategic advantage did not come from predicting the future more accurately. It came from acting earlier than competitors, while uncertainty was still high and optionality still available.

Foresight is not an analytical function. It is an organizational capability. It depends on how signals are surfaced, interpreted and legitimized. It relies on trust between frontline teams and leadership and it requires governance structures that tolerate ambiguity long enough for learning to occur.

Organizations with strong foresight do not eliminate uncertainty. They shorten the distance between sensing and deciding. They accept that early action will sometimes be imperfect and they recognize that the cost of acting too late is usually higher than the cost of adjusting course.

Foresight creates time. Time to explore options. Time to reposition resources. Time to respond before disruption hardens into constraint. Without foresight, agility arrives too late to matter.

Adaptability: Deciding under uncertainty

If foresight creates time, adaptability determines how that time is used.

Adaptability is often confused with flexibility or speed. In practice, it is neither. Adaptability is the capacity to make sound decisions under uncertainty, to adjust assumptions without losing direction, and to act without waiting for clarity that will only arrive too late. At its core, adaptability is a decision capability.

In stable environments, decision quality is often judged by accuracy. Leaders are rewarded for getting it right. Under uncertainty, accuracy becomes a misleading standard, as information is incomplete and signals conflict. Waiting for confirmation narrows options. Adaptable organizations therefore judge decision quality differently. They prioritize coherence, reversibility and alignment with intent over precision. This requires clarity of decision rights.

When uncertainty increases, many organizations instinctively recentralize authority. Decisions are escalated upward in the name of control. Approval layers multiply. The organization slows precisely when speed and judgement matter most. Centralization creates the illusion of control while increasing fragility.[7]

Adaptable organizations do the opposite. They clarify who decides what, under which conditions and within which boundaries. Decision rights are distributed deliberately, not by default. Strategic intent sets direction. Local teams are trusted to adapt execution within defined guard-rails. Escalation is reserved for moments when capacity, not competence, is the constraint. This reframes escalation in an important way.

In fragile systems, escalation is treated as failure. It signals loss of control or inadequate performance. In adaptable systems, escalation is treated as a capacity signal. It indicates that local decision space has been exhausted and that a broader trade-off is required. Rather than suppressing escalation, adaptable organizations design for it. The ability to adjust assumptions without losing direction is the distinguishing feature.

Adaptability does not mean abandoning strategy at the first sign of stress. It means recognizing which assumptions no longer hold and updating them while preserving purpose. Direction remains stable even as execution paths change. This balance allows organizations to move and adapt without fragmenting.

REAL-WORLD EXAMPLE

Disciplined adaptability in manufacturing (JP)

Manufacturing organizations operating under just-in-time principles are often cited as fragile under disruption. Tight coupling, minimal inventory and precise sequencing appear vulnerable when supply chains are stressed. In practice, the outcome depends less on the model itself and more on how adaptability is designed into decision-making.

In organizations that demonstrated disciplined adaptability, just-in-time was not treated as a rigid doctrine. It was treated as a conditional operating model. Leaders understood where flexibility existed and where it did not. Decision rights were clear before disruption occurred.

When supply chain stress emerged, these organizations did not abandon just-in-time. They adjusted the assumptions underpinning it. Sourcing rules were temporarily widened. Production sequencing was revised. Buffer policies were selectively relaxed where risk outweighed efficiency. Local teams were empowered to make trade-offs within defined parameters, rather than waiting for central approval.

Crucially, these adjustments were not improvised. Decision flexibility had been designed into the system. Escalation thresholds were known. Exception processes were rehearsed. Leaders expected assumptions to be challenged under stress and had mechanisms to review and reset them quickly.

Other organizations, operating under similar models, responded differently. Faced with disruption, they either froze execution while awaiting central direction or abandoned their operating model entirely. In both cases, coherence was lost. Decisions lagged events. Adaptation became reactive rather than purposeful.

Adaptability is not an individual trait. It is an organizational architecture. It emerges from how decision rights are allocated, how escalation is treated and how assumptions are reviewed under pressure.

Organizations that build adaptability do not eliminate uncertainty. They create decision structures that remain functional within it. They allow local variation without strategic drift. They treat adjustment as a normal response to change rather than an admission of error. Adaptability preserves direction while enabling movement.

Without it, foresight remains unused. Signals are seen but not acted upon and decisions are delayed until options narrow. Agility collapses under the weight of control.

With it, organizations convert early sensing into purposeful action. They remain aligned while adjusting course. They move through disruption without fragmenting.

Designing for adaptability requires more than empowering teams or encouraging flexibility. It requires deliberate decision architecture. Organizations need clarity over decision rights, escalation pathways, strategic guard-rails and the mechanisms used to review assumptions as conditions change.

Readers looking to apply these principles can access the accompanying Decision Architecture for Agility toolkit, which provides practical guidance for clarifying decision rights, designing escalation pathways, establishing governance guard-rails and reviewing decision effectiveness under uncertainty.

Execution capability: Acting coherently at scale

Execution capability determines whether foresight and adaptability translate into impact. It is the ability to turn intent into coordinated action, to maintain coherence under pressure, and to move at speed without losing trust.

Execution often breaks down not because people resist change but because ownership becomes unclear. Under stress, roles blur, decisions overlap and accountability fragments. Teams hesitate, duplicate effort or work around formal processes to keep delivery moving. From the centre, this looks like resistance.[8] In reality, it is a signal that execution has outpaced clarity. Effective execution relies on alignment rather than control.

In resilient organizations, ownership is explicit before disruption occurs. Decision authority, escalation points and interfaces between teams are understood and rehearsed. When pressure increases, these structures allow action to accelerate without confusion. Trust replaces supervision and feedback replaces command.

Control-heavy execution models behave differently. They rely on approvals, reporting and central oversight to maintain order. Under disruption, these mechanisms slow response and distort information. Feedback loops lengthen and local adaptation is suppressed. Execution becomes brittle.

The contrast between the earlier cases is instructive. In the technology context, execution speed came from alignment. Shared intent and clear ownership allowed teams to move quickly without constant coordination. In the manufacturing context, coherence came from structure. Disciplined interfaces and predefined flex points enabled adaptation without fragmentation.

In both cases, execution worked because trust and clarity were designed into the system before they were needed. Agility fails when decisions outrun trust.

Execution capability is therefore not an operational afterthought. It is the final test of organizational agility. Without it, foresight remains insight and adaptability remains intent. With it, organizations act decisively without coming apart.

Agility tools by degree of unpredictability

Agility depends not on speed or intent alone but on the ability to apply tools that match the nature of uncertainty being faced. When organizations use familiar tools in inappropriate conditions, the result is not simply under-performance, it is accelerated fragility.

Where risk is present and cause and effect are broadly understood, models, controls and thresholds provide discipline. Used within their proper domain, they stabilize execution and allow exposure to be optimized within defined boundaries. Used beyond it, they create false reassurance. Assumptions stiffen, relationships are treated as stable when they are not, and signals of change are suppressed rather than explored.

As uncertainty increases, the logic must change. When outcomes cannot be predicted reliably but plausible futures can be examined, precision becomes less useful than range. Scenarios, options and contingency pathways preserve choice without forcing commitment. They allow organizations to prepare for divergence and to adapt more quickly as conditions clarify. Applying control-heavy tools in this domain narrows vision. It anchors decisions to a single expected outcome and delays adjustment when reality moves elsewhere.

Under deep uncertainty, prediction gives way to discovery. When neither outcomes nor probabilities can be agreed, action becomes a source of information. Bounded experimentation, pilots and learning loops are not signs of immaturity. They are the only means of building understanding when analysis cannot precede action. The risk in this domain lies at both extremes. Modelling creates false confidence and postpones learning. Unbounded improvisation fragments effort and undermines coherence.

Agility therefore requires more than access to multiple tools. It requires the ability to shift decision logic as unpredictability increases and the discipline to avoid shifting too far. Organizations become fragile when they overextend familiar approaches into unfamiliar conditions, either by over-modelling what cannot be predicted or by over-improvizing what still requires structure.

Resilient organizations recognize that no single approach works across all conditions. They design their use of tools to evolve with uncertainty, combining discipline with exploration and structure with learning. The ability to match tools to unpredictability determines whether organizations adapt deliberately or stumble reactively as conditions change. Table 2.2 illustrates how decision tools should evolve as unpredictability increases.

TABLE 2.2 Agility tools by degree of unpredictability

Degree of unpredictability	What characterizes the situation	Tools (with concise definition)	Primary purpose	Failure mode if misapplied
Risk	Cause and effect broadly understood Outcomes can be estimated with reasonable confidence.	**Models** (quantify known exposure) **Controls** (constrain behaviour within limits) **Thresholds** (trigger escalation when limits are breached)	Optimise known exposure and maintain stability within defined boundaries	False confidence when models assume conditions that no longer hold
Uncertainty	Multiple plausible futures Outcomes unclear, but assumptions can be explored	**Scenarios** (explore plausible futures) **Options** (preserve choice without commitment) **Contingency pathways** (predefine alternative responses)	Preserve optionality and prepare for divergence	Lock-in to a single expected outcome and delayed adaptation
Deep uncertainty	Novel conditions Outcomes and probabilities unknowable or contested	**Experimentation** (learn through bounded action) **Pilots** (test viability at small scale) **Learning loops** (convert action into rapid insight)	Discover what works through action and feedback	False confidence from modelling or fragmentation from unbounded improvisation

Decision-making in context: Cynefin and organizational agility

Organizational agility often fails for a simple reason. Decisions are taken using the wrong logic for the context at hand. With that, agility fails not because organizations act too slowly, but because they *misinterpret* the context they are operating in.

The Cynefin framework[9] offers a useful way to understand this failure. It distinguishes between simple, complicated, complex and chaotic contexts, each requiring a different approach to sense-making and decision-making. Its value lies not in categorization for its own sake but in highlighting how often organizations apply familiar decision logic to unfamiliar conditions.

Many organizations are designed for environments that can be analysed, measured and controlled. Governance, reporting and performance systems assume that better information will lead to better decisions. This works when conditions are relatively stable. Problems emerge when uncertainty increases and certainty cannot be produced through additional analysis.

Under these conditions, organizations often respond in one of two ways. Some continue to demand more data, more forecasts and more evidence, delaying action while waiting for clarity that may never arrive. Others swing in the opposite direction, recentralizing authority and tightening control in an attempt to restore order. Both responses reduce agility because they apply inappropriate decision logic to the situation at hand.

The lesson is not that analysis or control are ineffective. Both remain essential in the right context. Agility depends on recognizing when conditions have changed and adjusting decision-making accordingly. Leaders need to know when established practices remain appropriate, when expertise should guide action, and when learning must occur through experimentation and adaptation.

Seen this way, agility is fundamentally a context-awareness capability. Organizations that recognize changing conditions early are better able to adapt their decision-making, governance and responses. Those that fail to recognize the shift often turn uncertainty into fragility through their own actions.

Becoming aware of context is less about analysis and more about attention. Leaders recognize context through the quality of signals they receive, the degree of disagreement between experts, the speed at which assumptions are invalidated, and the level of coordination required to move forward. When interpretation lags reality, context has likely shifted. When certainty is demanded but cannot be produced, the challenge is no longer technical.

Agile organizations cultivate a shared understanding of context, legitimize different responses under different conditions and design governance, escalation pathways and decision rights that adapt as environments evolve. Where this capability is absent, foresight is misused, adaptability is misdirected and execution becomes brittle. Where it is present, organizations respond proportionately, learn deliberately and avoid turning uncertainty into fragility of their own making.

Agility as feedback speed: The OODA loop in organizations

Agility is often mistaken for decisiveness. Organizations celebrate rapid action, compressed timelines and bold moves, assuming that speed alone creates advantage. In practice, speed without orientation amplifies error. What differentiates agile organizations is how quickly they learn, not how quickly they act.

This distinction is captured in the **OODA loop: observe, orient, decide, act.** Developed by military strategist and fighter pilot John Boyd[10] to explain decision-making in aerial combat, the loop offers a useful way to understand organizational agility when uncertainty is high. Its relevance lies not in the sequence itself but in what constrains it under the pressure of rapidly changing conditions.

Most organizations focus on decisions and actions, yet the real bottleneck often lies in orientation: how information is interpreted and given meaning. The same signal can lead to very different conclusions depending on assumptions, incentives, experience and perspective. The challenge is rarely access to information; it is how that information is understood.

This is where agility is won or lost. Organizations that cling to existing assumptions become slower to adapt even when signals are visible. By contrast, agile organizations treat feedback as a source of learning. They challenge interpretations, update understanding and adjust decisions as conditions evolve.

The three capabilities explored in this chapter strengthen different parts of this cycle. Foresight improves what is observed. Adaptability improves how information is interpreted and decisions are made. Execution ensures that action generates feedback quickly enough to inform the next cycle.

Seen this way, agility is not about acting faster than competitors. It is about learning faster than conditions change. Organizations that achieve this continuously update their understanding, adjust course deliberately and avoid becoming trapped by yesterday's assumptions.

INSTITUTIONALIZING AGILITY

Covid-19 demonstrated that many organizations already know how to operate with agility. Cross-functional teams formed quickly, information flowed more freely, decision cycles shortened and local judgement was empowered. The mistake was not the response itself. It was the failure to institutionalize what worked once the crisis passed. (Adapted from insights shared during interviews conducted for this book.)

Board and executive implications

Organizational agility is often viewed as an operational capability. In practice, it is a leadership and governance responsibility. The speed and quality of adaptation are shaped by how organizations interpret change, challenge assumptions and adjust decisions as conditions evolve.

For boards, this shifts the focus from resilience as protection towards resilience as adaptation. Oversight extends beyond continuity plans, recovery capabilities and performance outcomes. It includes understanding whether the organization can recognize changing conditions early enough to respond before options narrow. The critical question is not whether disruption can be managed. It is whether leadership can adapt while meaningful choices still exist.

For executive teams, agility becomes a design challenge. Decision rights, governance structures, reporting processes and incentives all influence how information is interpreted and acted upon. Organizations often struggle because existing ways of thinking persist after conditions have changed. When certainty is demanded before action can be taken, adaptation slows regardless of the quality of available information.

For CROs and risk leaders, agility requires a broader perspective on uncertainty. Traditional risk management focuses on identifying and assessing known exposures. Organizational agility requires understanding whether the decision-making approach remains appropriate for the conditions being faced. This means helping leadership distinguish between situations that can be analysed, those that require judgement and those that demand experimentation and learning. The objective is not simply to identify risk but to challenge assumptions when the environment begins to change.

Across all three groups, the common challenge is context awareness. Leaders must recognize when existing assumptions no longer hold, when interpretation is lagging reality and when decision-making approaches need to adapt. The organizations that respond most effectively are rarely those with the best forecasts or the fastest decision cycles. They are those that recognize changing conditions early, adjust decision logic accordingly and translate learning into coordinated action.

Agility therefore depends as much on how organizations think as on how they act. It emerges when foresight, adaptability and execution operate together, enabling leaders to respond to uncertainty without becoming constrained by it.

Practical playbook

Building organizational agility involves creating the conditions that allow organizations to recognize change, adapt decisions and execute coherently as uncertainty increases.

Boards

Boards shape the organization's capacity to adapt by ensuring that oversight extends beyond performance outcomes to the conditions that influence future performance.

1. **Challenge assumptions, not only results**
   Regularly examine the assumptions underpinning strategy, risk assessments and performance expectations. Stable outcomes do not necessarily indicate stable conditions.
2. **Seek visibility on emerging change**
   Require discussion of weak signals, emerging trends and areas of uncertainty alongside traditional performance reporting.
3. **Monitor adaptability as a governance capability**
   Assess whether decision-making structures remain effective when conditions change, rather than focusing solely on whether plans are delivered.

Executives

Executives create the operating environment within which agility either emerges or deteriorates.

1 **Clarify decision rights**
Ensure that authority is distributed appropriately and that teams understand when decisions can be made locally and when escalation is required.

2 **Create space for adaptation**
Encourage teams to challenge assumptions, surface concerns and adjust execution when circumstances change.

3 **Reduce decision friction**
Review governance forums, approval processes and reporting requirements to identify where unnecessary delays are limiting responsiveness.

Chief risk officers and risk leaders

Risk leaders help organizations understand uncertainty and adapt decision-making accordingly.

1 **Distinguish between risk, uncertainty and complexity**
Help leadership recognize when traditional risk management approaches remain appropriate and when experimentation, learning or adaptation may be required.

2 **Surface changing conditions early**
Focus on emerging patterns, weak signals and shifts in assumptions that may affect future decisions.

3 **Challenge outdated decision logic**
Support leadership in recognizing when existing controls, assumptions or governance approaches no longer match the operating environment.

KEY TAKEAWAYS

- **Agility activates resilience in practice**. Resilience limits the impact of disruption. Agility enables organizations to adapt, reposition and respond before uncertainty hardens into constraint.
- **Organizational agility rests on three mutually reinforcing capabilities**. Foresight enables early sensing of change. Adaptability converts signals into decisions under uncertainty. Execution capability translates intent into coordinated action at scale.

- **Decision-making must match the conditions being faced**. Approaches that work in stable and predictable environments become less effective as uncertainty increases. Agility depends on recognizing changing conditions and adjusting decision logic accordingly.
- **Agility is a learning capability**. Organizations become fragile when they rely on outdated assumptions or wait for certainty before acting. Agile organizations learn faster than conditions change and continuously update their understanding of the environment.
- **Agility is a leadership and governance responsibility**. Boards, executives and CROs create the conditions that determine how effectively organizations sense change, challenge assumptions, distribute decision-making and adapt under pressure.

Reframing forward

This chapter shifted the focus from resilience as endurance to resilience in motion. Resilience preserves the organization's ability to absorb disruption. Agility determines how the organization responds as conditions evolve.

Agility is not speed or flexibility alone. It is the capacity to sense, decide and act coherently while uncertainty is still unfolding. Where agility is present, uncertainty expands options. Where it is absent, uncertainty compresses them.

Seen this way, fragility is not simply the absence of resilience. It emerges when organizations cannot adjust quickly enough as assumptions change. Familiar decision logic lingers too long, signals are misinterpreted and action arrives after meaningful choices have narrowed.

Agility changes the organization's relationship with uncertainty. It does not eliminate volatility or restore predictability. It enables organizations to move within disruption rather than waiting for disruption to pass.

What remains unresolved is why these capabilities so often fail under pressure, even when they are formally designed. The next chapter turns to the human dynamics beneath agility: how leadership behaviour, culture and trust determine whether adaptive capacity strengthens or deteriorates as uncertainty intensifies.

Endnotes

1 Hollnagel, E, Woods, D D and Leveson, N (2006) *Resilience Engineering: Concepts and Precepts*, Ashgate, Aldershot

2 Reeves, M, Levin, S and Ueda, D (2016) The biology of corporate survival, *Harvard Business Review*, January–February

3 Novo Leadership Consulting (2025) Leadership Agility: The New Competitive Advantage, https://novoexec.com/insights/leadership-agility-the-new-competitive-advantage

4 Agile Management Officer (2025) Balancing Agility & Stability: How to Adapt Without Losing Control, https://agilemanagementoffice.com/balancing-agility-stability-how-to-adapt-without-losing-control

5 Alvarez, A and Bordel, A (2025) Understanding How Business Transformation Processes Are Driven: A Business Agility Model, www.mdpi.com/2076-3387/15/4/128

6 Hensellek, S, Kleine-Stegemann, L and Kollmann, T (2023) Entrepreneurial leadership, strategic flexibility, and venture performance: Does founders' span of control matter? www.sciencedirect.com/science/article/pii/S0148296322010098

7 Mintzberg, H (1979) *The Structuring of Organizations*, Pearson, Harlow

8 Schein, E H (2017) *Organizational Culture and Leadership* (5th edn), Wiley, Hoboken, NJ

9 Snowden, D J and Boone, M E (2007) A leader's framework for decision making, *Harvard Business Review*

10 Boyd, J R (1996) The Essence of Winning and Losing, briefing slides, US Air Force

03

The human core of resilience

Trust, connection and culture as performance assets

CHAPTER OBJECTIVES

- Demonstrate that resilience depends on both structural design and the quality of human relationships.
- Position trust and psychological safety as performance capabilities rather than cultural aspirations.
- Show how relational density influences coordination, escalation and adaptation under pressure.
- Explain why organizations adapt more effectively when concerns can be surfaced before disruption becomes irreversible.

Observation reveals where systems are under strain. Resilience ensures that strain travels before it breaks them.

Resilience is often described in structural terms. Organizations strengthen frameworks, refine controls and tighten governance arrangements. Yet, as useful these interventions may be, they do not explain why two organizations with similar systems behave differently under pressure.

The difference lies in how people interpret, transmit and act on what they see.

Resilience depends on both organizational structures and human relationships. It relies on whether uncomfortable information can travel without distortion, whether dissent is processed as intelligence rather than resistance, and whether coordination accelerates or fragments when uncertainty rises. Structures provide the scaffolding. Human dynamics determine how effectively that scaffolding performs under pressure.

Many organizations invest heavily in controls and still experience strategic failure. They possess dashboards, escalation pathways and documented responsibilities. Yet when disruption unfolds, leaders often discover that the critical signals were present long before impact. Information was available but it did not reach the right group to influence decisions.

This chapter examines the human core of resilience. It explores how trust operates as invisible infrastructure, how psychological safety governs escalation quality, how relational density determines coordination under strain, and how fear quietly reshapes language before decisions are made. These dynamics are often labelled 'culture'. In practice, they function as performance variables.

Understanding them is uncomfortable. It requires recognizing that resilience does not break when systems collapse. It breaks when signals stop travelling, when saying nothing becomes rational and when courage carries disproportionate cost. It breaks when small failures to communicate create disproportionately large consequences.

If resilience determines whether an organization survives disruption, the human system determines whether it adapts before disruption becomes irreversible.

This is where resilience becomes real.

Why resilience breaks down at the human level

Human fallibility is a core driver of resilience breakdown, yet organizational crises rarely begin with a single error. More often, they develop through delayed responses, missed opportunities to intervene and signals that fail to influence decisions while options still exist.

An issue is noticed, exceptions accumulate and process drift gradually becomes accepted as normal. At that point, escalation is no longer a technical process but a human judgement. Someone must decide whether the concern warrants interruption, whether the evidence is sufficient and whether speaking up is likely to lead to action. That judgement is shaped less by policy than by organizational experience, including incentives, hierarchy, time pressure and the memory of how previous concerns were received.

When that context discourages interruption, doing nothing becomes a rational response. Concerns are addressed locally to avoid creating noise, discussed informally rather than escalated and gradually absorbed into normal operations. Formal indicators may remain reassuring, yet the flow of information resilience depends on is already weakening.

People do not withhold concerns because they are careless or resistant. They learn, often through experience, how information is received and what consequences may follow. Over time, urgency is softened, uncertainty is filtered out, and emerging issues lose momentum before they reach decision makers.

This dynamic is particularly visible in environments with extensive controls, formal oversight and strong compliance expectations. The more mature the framework, the more effectively it manages known risks. Yet the same structures can also absorb, reframe or defer early concerns before they trigger meaningful intervention.

UK financial services provides a useful illustration of how this dynamic unfolds in practice.

REAL-WORLD EXAMPLE

UK financial services and the accumulation of silence

A recurring theme in UK financial services enforcement shows how resilience can erode through gradual human filtering rather than sudden breakdown. In many cases, post-incident reviews conclude that the relevant risks were visible within parts of the organization long before harm materialized. The issue was that warning signs failed to travel with sufficient clarity and urgency to influence senior decisions while options still existed.

The London Capital & Finance (LCF)[1] collapse is a perfect example. The firm entered administration in 2019 and subsequent reviews concluded that significant harm had built up over time rather than emerging overnight. For example, concerns about misleading marketing had been raised by some advisers as early as 2015, yet those signals did not translate into timely organizational action. Within the business, they were treated as isolated communications issues rather than symptoms of a model-level problem. The right information did not reach the right person or governance body at the right time to alter course.

The same dynamic appears in high-growth environments, where momentum and performance narratives increase the pressure to normalize emerging issues. In October 2024, the Financial Conduct Authority (FCA) fined Starling Bank £29 million for anti-money laundering control laxism.[2] The FCA's findings highlighted how rapid expansion, from around 43,000 to 3.6 million customers, outpaced aspects of the control environment. For six years (2017–2023), a system misconfiguration meant sanctions screening only covered a small fraction of the required list. It is difficult to see how such a fundamental flaw persisted for years without being identified, unless the signals of failure were being filtered out by a culture prioritizing growth over resilience.

These cases show why self-censorship scales risk faster than error. When controls are weakened by a culture that filters uncomfortable signals, the organization loses its most valuable asset: time. What appears to be a sudden regulatory collapse is almost always the end point of prolonged delay and accumulated institutional mutism.

This is where asymmetry takes hold. Early signals carry limited cost and high optionality. If repositioned as a capacity signal rather than an admission of failure, escalation becomes a tool for deliberate prioritization. When human signals fail to move, however, the organization forfeits the time advantage that resilience depends on.

The same dynamic applies to foresight. Analytical capability matters but it is secondary to whether early insight can interrupt decisions before certainty hardens. Weak signals are not ignored because they are invisible. They are ignored because acting on them requires judgement under ambiguity, and judgement exposes people to risk. When that risk is personal rather than shared, foresight collapses regardless of how sophisticated the tools appear.

This is why the human dimension cannot be treated as an overlay to resilience design. Escalation is not primarily a behavioural choice; it is an output of governance design. It is the condition that determines whether asymmetry works for or against the organization and whether foresight remains possible while choice still exists.

Trust as infrastructure: How resilience actually travels

If resilience fails when human signals do not move, trust determines whether they move at all.[3]

Trust governs three critical properties of decision-making under uncertainty: speed, fidelity and courage. Speed determines whether concerns reach decision makers while options still exist. Fidelity determines whether information arrives intact or reframed through interpretation. Courage determines whether people are willing to surface concerns that may be incomplete, uncomfortable or unwelcome.

Trust cannot be treated as a cultural backdrop. It functions as infrastructure. Like any form of infrastructure, its presence is most noticeable when it is missing. Low trust does not usually stop information from flowing entirely. It slows it, distorts it and increases the personal cost of transmitting it. Messages take longer to surface. Language becomes cautious. Ambiguity is resolved downward rather than escalated upward. Over time, the organization loses its ability to respond proportionately because what reaches the top no longer reflects what is happening on the ground.

A common source of confusion here is the distinction between trust and confidence. Confidence is often high in organizations with strong reporting, mature frameworks and positive performance indicators. Trust, by contrast, is situational and relational. It reflects whether individuals believe that raising an issue will lead to thoughtful engagement rather than dismissal, delay or reputational damage. An organization can display high confidence while operating with low trust. In such environments, resilience appears strong until it is tested. Table 3.1 illustrates how different combinations of trust and confidence shape resilience outcomes.

Under pressure, trust also becomes a coordination mechanism.[4] When time is limited and information is incomplete, people rely less on formal processes and more on their assessment of how others will respond. They choose whom to involve, how quickly to escalate and how directly to frame concerns. Where trust exists, coordination accelerates. Where it does not, people default to self-protection, duplication or delay. These behaviours are often misread as inefficiency or resistance, when they are in fact rational adaptations to a low-trust context.

TABLE 3.1 The trust vs confidence matrix

	Low confidence (weak reporting/frameworks)	High confidence (strong reporting/frameworks)
High trust (safe/relational)	**Emerging resilience:** The culture is strong, but the systems are 'noisy' and inefficient.	**Antifragile:** Information flows with speed and fidelity. The organization learns and adapts in real time.
Low trust (censored/ transactional)	**Chaos:** High risk and no visibility. Failure is frequent and unpredictable.	**The performance trap:** Everything looks green on the dashboard but critical risks are 'filtered' or 'contained'. **Resilience is an illusion until tested.**

REAL-WORLD EXAMPLE

Trust under extreme conditions at Médecins Sans Frontières

The role of trust as operational infrastructure is particularly visible in high-risk environments where formal oversight is limited by distance, urgency and uncertainty. Médecins Sans Frontières (MSF)[5] operates in contexts where central control is neither feasible nor desirable. Field teams routinely face rapidly changing conditions, incomplete information and ethical trade-offs that cannot be escalated for prior approval without compromising outcomes and individual security.

In this environment, decision rights are deliberately decentralized. Authority is pushed to the edge because responsiveness depends on local judgement. Trust is the mechanism that makes this model viable. Field teams must trust that headquarters will support difficult decisions made under significant pressure. Headquarters must trust that teams will escalate when local judgement reaches its limits. That trust is built through shared purpose, clear expectations and consistent responses over time, not through detailed procedures.

Formal authority exists but it is secondary to relational clarity. What matters most is not who has approval rights but who is expected to act, when and on what basis. Where that clarity is present, coordination under stress improves. Where it breaks down, teams either hesitate or act defensively, increasing risk to both staff and mission.

MSF's experience illustrates a broader principle. In environments of deep uncertainty, resilience depends less on tight control and more on trust that enables timely, proportionate action. The absence of trust would not simply slow decisions; it would make the operating model unworkable.

The following tool will help you to distinguish healthy reliance on trust from structural over-dependence on it. Resilient organizations design systems that acknowledge trust as infrastructure, while ensuring it is reinforced by clarity, accountability and shared expectations rather than left to chance.

Ultimately, a board's primary role in resilience is not to monitor the dashboard but to protect the flow of uncomfortable truths that the dashboard is designed to hide.

PRACTICAL TOOL: BOARD-LEVEL TRUST DIAGNOSTICS

For boards and senior leaders, the challenge is not to promote trust as a value but to understand where it already substitutes for process and where it should not. Useful diagnostic questions include:

- Where do we rely on informal escalation to compensate for rigid processes?
- Where do people bypass formal routes because they believe they will not lead to action?
- Where is trust enabling speed and judgement, and where is it masking gaps in accountability?
- How consistently do leaders respond when early concerns are raised without complete evidence?

Psychological safety as a performance capability, not a value statement

Trust determines whether signals move. Psychological safety determines what those signals look like when they arrive.

In many organizations, psychological safety is described in aspirational terms. It appears in culture surveys, leadership commitments and engagement programmes. Yet its operational significance is often misunderstood. Psychological safety is not primarily about comfort or harmony. It is about whether individuals can surface incomplete, ambiguous or uncomfortable information without anticipating disproportionate personal cost.

In escalation terms, that distinction matters. Early risk signals are rarely precise. They are often fragmentary, subjective or difficult to evidence. If people believe they must present a fully formed case before raising a concern, escalation will occur late by design. Psychological safety governs whether partial insight can enter decision-making while uncertainty is still manageable.

The goal is not a flood of raw data. When every minor friction is escalated, the organization experiences 'infobesity', where decision makers become immunized to urgency through sheer volume. True resilience depends on signal quality rather than quantity. It requires a system that filters out the routine while ensuring that 'material' truths travel with speed and fidelity.

This is why escalation quality depends on psychological safety. In low-safety environments, concerns are filtered until they appear defensible. Alternatively, issues are withheld entirely until evidence becomes overwhelming. By that stage, the organization is responding to symptoms rather than escalating based on trajectory.

The gap between stated encouragement and lived safety is often subtle. Leaders may repeatedly invite challenge and policies may emphasize openness. Yet individuals interpret safety through experience rather than instruction. They observe how prior dissent was received. They notice which issues triggered friction and which were welcomed. They watch how promotions and rewards align with behaviour. Over time, these observations shape a collective judgement about what is truly safe to raise.

Safety is also uneven. It varies by hierarchy, function and context. A senior executive may feel able to challenge in a boardroom while a frontline analyst does not feel able to challenge the same decision in a team meeting. A control function may experience support during steady performance but resistance when commercial pressure intensifies. Psychological safety is therefore situational rather than uniform. It rises and falls with context, leadership behaviour and incentive structures.

Timothy Clark's *The 4 Stages of Psychological Safety*[6] provide a practical diagnostic structure when treated as a maturity lens for risk governance. The stages describe a progressive path of participation: inclusion safety, learner safety, contributor safety and challenger safety. In resilience terms, the final stage is critical. Challenger safety determines whether the organization's 'human sensors' can question assumptions, flag emerging risks and interrupt momentum before a trajectory of failure becomes irreversible.[7]

This model should not be used as a moral label but as a way to identify behavioural blind spots in the risk life cycle. It helps leaders ask practical, structural questions:

- **Inclusion:** Who is missing from our risk conversations and why?
- **Learning:** Are post-incident reviews a source of systemic learning or a blame-oriented compliance exercise?
- **Contribution:** Do people feel true ownership of controls or do they merely defer responsibility upward?
- **Challenge:** Under what performance pressures does the willingness to dissent disappear?

The answers reveal where escalation capacity is a functional performance asset and where it is being quietly consumed by 'governance friction' and 'institutional mutism'.

REAL-WORLD EXAMPLE

Psychological safety after conduct failure in a UK retail bank

A UK retail bank[8] that faced significant conduct scrutiny illustrates how psychological safety shifts escalation patterns in practice. Following regulatory intervention, the institution introduced extensive rule enhancements, additional training and new reporting mechanisms. Yet internal reviews showed that escalation behaviours changed only marginally. The structural paradox remained: the more formal the controls became, the easier it was for early concerns to be absorbed or deferred.

What shifted patterns more meaningfully was a change in leadership response. Senior leaders began publicly acknowledging early stage concerns rather than waiting for fully evidenced cases. They separated the act of raising a concern from the outcome of the investigation, explicitly training managers to respond with inquiry rather than immediate evaluation. This shifted the focus from 'who is to blame' to systemic learning.

However, progress remained uneven. In high-revenue business units, challenger safety continued to lag until incentive structures were adjusted. As long as performance metrics implicitly rewarded uninterrupted growth, individuals remained cautious about raising issues that might slow momentum. The lesson was clear: psychological safety cannot be sustained by rhetoric or 'speak-up' posters alone. It is an output of governance design that must be reinforced by consistent behavioural responses and aligned incentives.

This example reinforces the operational framing of psychological safety. It is not an abstract cultural aspiration; it is a performance capability that determines whether early warnings travel with sufficient speed and fidelity to influence decisions while strategic options still exist.

Why resilience is relational, not individual

Resilience is often described as a personal quality. Leaders are encouraged to be resilient. Teams are trained to build resilience. Employees are expected to demonstrate it under pressure. While individual capacity matters, this framing is incomplete and in some cases, counterproductive.

In high-pressure environments, decisions rarely sit within a single role. They cross functions, hierarchies and disciplines. Risk does not escalate neatly through reporting lines. It moves across informal networks, shared

TABLE 3.2 Individual resilience vs system resilience

Individual narrative	Relational reality
Personal stamina	Coordination quality
Heroic intervention	Distributed judgement
Composure under pressure	Signal flow under pressure
Strong leader	Strong network

judgement and mutual expectations. When these relationships are strong, uncertainty can be absorbed and adapted to. When they are weak, even highly capable individuals struggle to compensate.

The narrative of the 'resilient individual' can therefore mask systemic fragility. A talented risk officer cannot compensate for a disengaged commercial team. A courageous manager cannot offset misaligned incentives. A highly experienced executive cannot stabilize a system where information is siloed and trust is uneven. Personal strength cannot repair relational weakness. Table 3.2 contrasts the individual and relational perspectives on resilience.

Coordination under pressure

Under stress, organizations default to relational patterns that already exist. If teams have a history of constructive challenge, coordination accelerates. If they have a history of defensiveness or competition, coordination slows. People either seek input early or retreat into their own functions.

This is why coordination under pressure is a more reliable indicator of resilience than individual composure. Calm leadership does not guarantee adaptive response if the surrounding system is fragmented. Conversely, visible tension does not necessarily signal fragility if the underlying relationships support rapid adjustment.

In reality, resilient coordination is characterized by three features that function as the connective tissue of the organization:

- **Clarity of roles:** not as isolated job descriptions but as a shared understanding of how information must travel across boundaries to become a decision input.

- **Mutual respect across functions:** the removal of the 'us vs them' dynamic between the front line and control functions, ensuring that warnings are treated as strategic intelligence rather than administrative friction.
- **Predictable responses to escalation:** a consistent, inquiry-led leadership response that eliminates the 'lottery' of speaking up.

These are not individual attributes; they are relational properties of the system design. They determine whether the organization's 'human sensors' function as a network or as a collection of disconnected silos.

Why resilient individuals fail in fragile systems

If organizations employ talented people, invest heavily in training and encourage resilience at the individual level, why do the same patterns of failure continue to appear?

The answer lies less in the capability of individuals than in the quality of the connections between them. When relational density is low, individuals expend energy navigating politics, negotiating authority or seeking validation rather than solving the underlying issue. Effort is redirected from adaptation to survival within the system.

The expectation that individuals should 'be more resilient' in such environments only compounds fragility. It shifts responsibility downward while leaving coordination mechanisms unchecked. Over time, this erodes trust and reduces willingness to surface concerns, further weakening collective capacity.

Relational density as a hidden resilience indicator

Relational density refers to the strength and reliability of connections across roles and functions. It is rarely measured directly, yet it strongly predicts how an organization behaves under strain.

High relational density means that information can move quickly across boundaries without formal escalation. It means that challenge is not interpreted as attack. It means that roles are understood beyond job descriptions. In such environments, adaptation occurs through dialogue rather than delay.

Low relational density, by contrast, creates dependence on formal hierarchy. Decisions queue. Issues wait for validation. Informal networks are narrow and functionally confined. Under pressure, this structure becomes brittle. Figure 3.1 illustrates how relational density influences the way information and decisions move through an organization under pressure.

FIGURE 3.1 Relational density vs hierarchical fragility

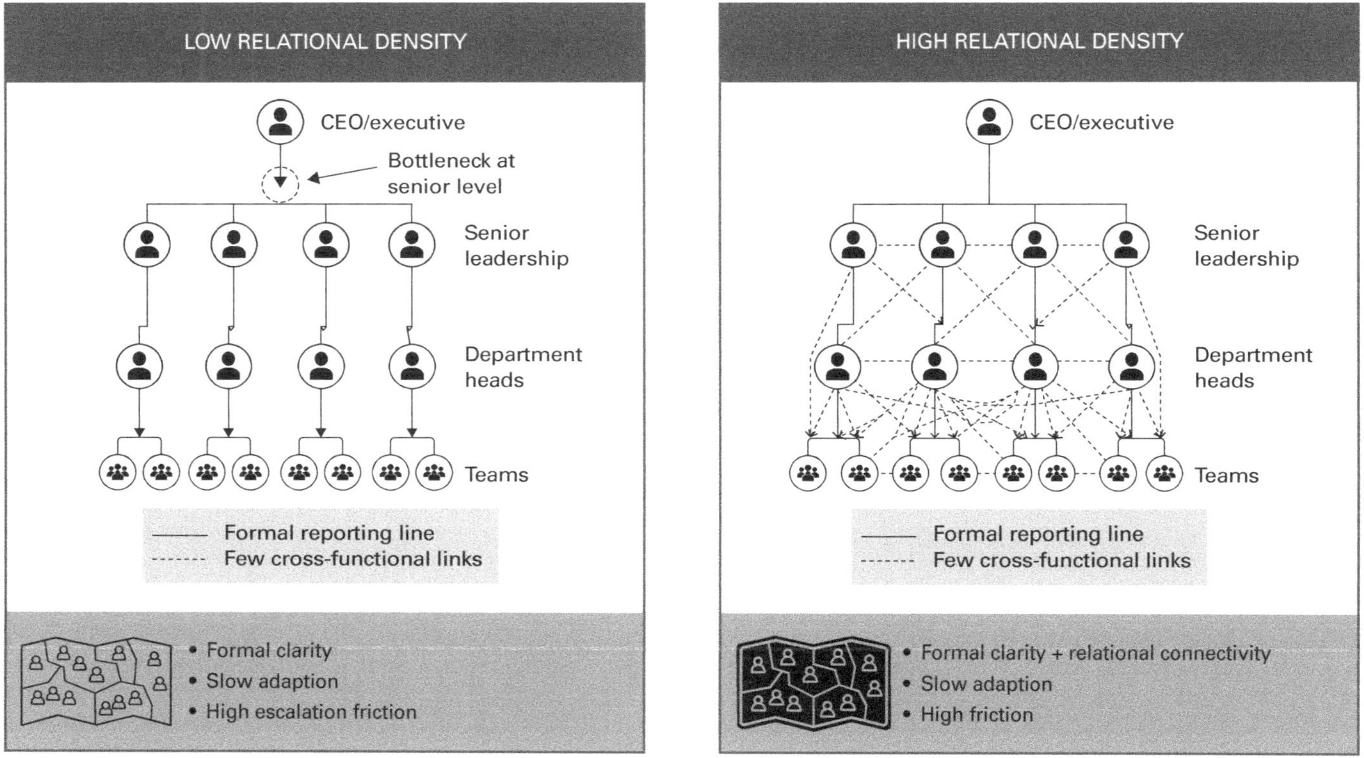

REAL-WORLD EXAMPLE

When relationships outperform playbooks

A large UK financial institution experienced a major technology outage that temporarily prevented customers from accessing online accounts and payment services. The organization had a detailed incident management framework, with predefined escalation pathways, role allocations and communication protocols.

In the first hours of the disruption, teams initiated the formal playbook. However, progress stalled as responsibility for certain decisions moved sequentially through hierarchical channels. Critical dependencies between technology, operations and customer communications created bottlenecks that the documented structure had not anticipated.

A parallel coordination dynamic then emerged. Senior managers who had previously collaborated across risk, technology and operations bypassed the formal sequence and convened directly. Because they understood each other's constraints and decision thresholds, they were able to clarify priorities quickly, reallocate resources and align external messaging without waiting for formal approval cycles to complete. Post-incident review showed that customer impact was significantly reduced during the period when this informal coordination took place. Other business areas that adhered strictly to hierarchical escalation experienced slower decision-making and greater internal friction. The difference did not lie in technical competence or procedural clarity; it lay in relational familiarity and trust built through routine collaboration.

The playbook was not flawed; it functioned as intended. What determined the quality of response was the density of relationships supporting it. Where those relationships were strong, adaptation accelerated. Where they were thin, formal structure became a constraint rather than a support.

Fear, silence and the economics of delayed truth

Fear is often discussed in cultural terms, yet its impact on resilience is operational. It changes what is said, when it is said and how it is framed. In doing so, it alters the timing and quality of decision-making.

Fear does not typically prevent people from noticing risk. But it dictates what they do with that observation.

In organizational settings, fear takes several forms. Reputational fear arises when individuals believe that raising concerns may associate them with failure rather than foresight. Social fear emerges when dissent risks exclusion or friction within a team. Career fear appears when escalation may slow momentum in high-performing units or create tension with senior stakeholders. Cognitive fear is subtler: it reflects discomfort with uncertainty and the risk of being wrong in public.

Each of these forms shapes behaviour in predictable ways. Concerns are softened to avoid appearing alarmist. Probabilities are overstated or understated to fit expectations. Ambiguity is resolved prematurely so that reporting feels defensible. Issues are framed as 'monitoring items' rather than as signals requiring interruption. None of these adjustments appear unreasonable in isolation. Collectively, they delay clarity. Figure 3.2 illustrates how fear progressively alters the quality of escalation before information reaches decision makers.

This is where the economics of delayed truth become visible. Raising a concern early often carries an immediate cost. It may slow delivery, challenge assumptions or attract scrutiny. Delaying escalation appears cheaper. Projects continue, performance narratives remain intact and difficult conversations are postponed. Yet the cost of delay compounds silently. Options narrow, dependencies deepen and corrective action becomes more expensive.

Many strategic failures start with a series of reasonable decisions made under local incentives. Each choice to wait, gather more evidence or soften a message can be justified in isolation. What disappears is not logic but time.

Fear influences not only whether concerns are escalated but how they are communicated. Signals lose strength as they move through the organization. A failing control becomes an area for enhancement. A material concentration risk becomes an exposure requiring continued monitoring. The information remains technically accurate, yet its urgency is diluted.

Leadership behaviour often determines the price of honesty. When emerging concerns are met with frustration, defensiveness or demands for immediate solutions, employees learn to contain problems before escalating them. Incentives can reinforce the pattern. Organizations frequently celebrate those who solve problems more visibly than those who identify them, making optimism feel safer than accuracy. None of this requires deliberate concealment. It is a natural response to performance pressure, reputational concerns and the desire to maintain credibility. The result is that critical information reaches decision makers later and with less clarity than the situation requires. By the time a risk can no longer be softened, the organization is responding to consequences rather than influencing outcomes.

FIGURE 3.2 How fear alters escalation quality

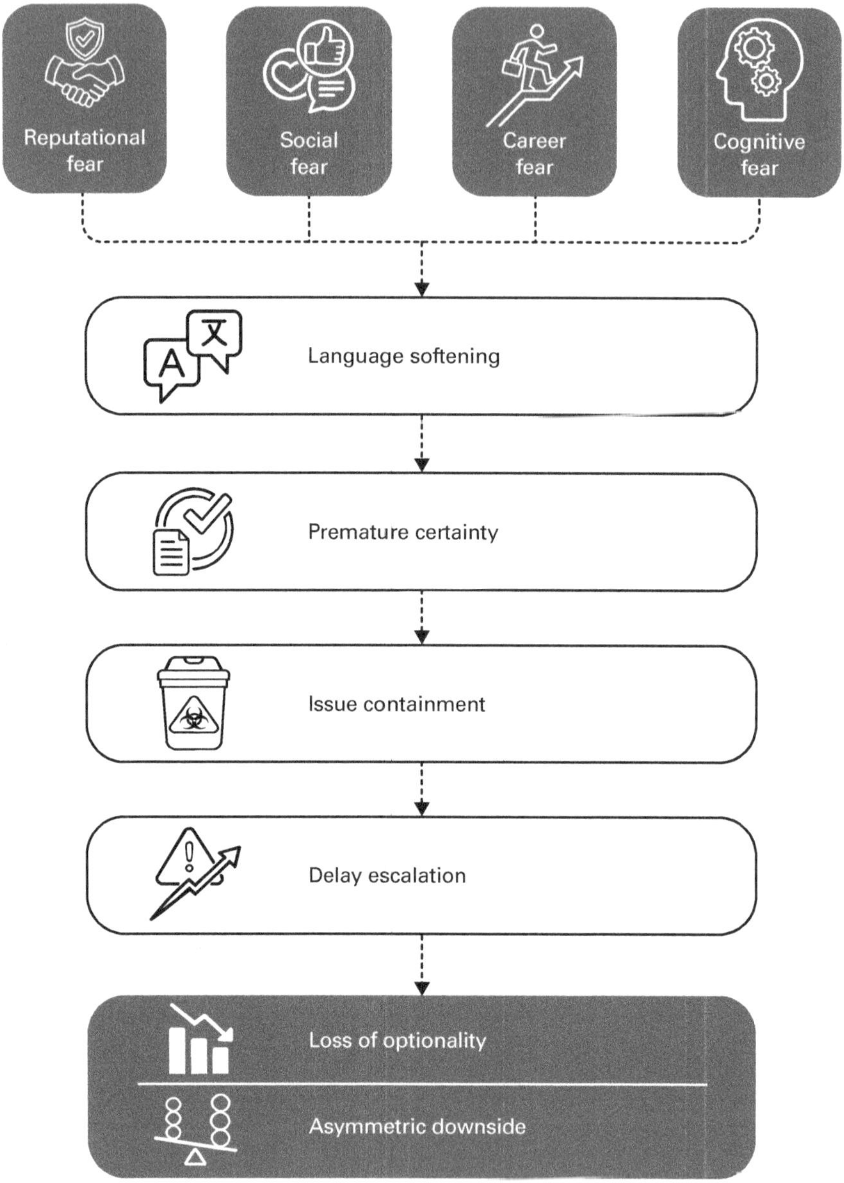

In that context, fear acts as a structural variable that shapes information flow, decision quality and organizational adaptability. Where leaders reduce the cost of candour, signals travel early enough to influence outcomes. Where they do not, silence becomes a rational strategy.

Board and executive implications

Trust, psychological safety and relational resilience are often discussed as cultural attributes. In practice, they are governance concerns. They determine whether information reaches decision makers early enough to influence outcomes.

For boards, this shifts the focus from reviewing resilience indicators to understanding the quality of information flowing into those indicators. A board may receive comprehensive reporting and still remain unaware of emerging vulnerabilities if uncomfortable information cannot travel through the organization without distortion.

For executive teams, resilience depends on the environment they create. Leadership behaviour influences whether concerns are raised early, whether teams coordinate effectively under pressure and whether uncertainty can be discussed openly. Ultimately, resilience depends on whether honesty is easier than silence.

For CROs and risk leaders, resilience depends on the quality of escalation as much as the quality of controls. Risk frameworks can create visibility but they cannot guarantee that concerns will be raised when uncertainty is highest. Understanding how incentives, leadership behaviour and organizational relationships influence information flow is therefore just as important as designing the framework itself.

Across all three groups, the common challenge is signal integrity. Resilient organizations protect the movement of information from observation to decision. They recognize that trust, psychological safety and relational connectivity are not soft cultural considerations. They are performance assets that influence how quickly the organization can recognize change, coordinate action and adapt under pressure.

Practical playbook

Building resilience at the human level requires establishing the conditions in which information can move quickly, concerns can be raised openly and teams can coordinate effectively under pressure.

Boards

Boards influence resilience through the questions they ask and the behaviours they reward.

1 **Test the quality of escalation**
Look beyond reporting volumes and challenge whether important concerns are reaching decision makers early enough to influence outcomes.

2 **Monitor trust as a performance asset**
Seek evidence that employees are willing to challenge assumptions, surface concerns and escalate emerging risks without fear of disproportionate consequences.

3 **Challenge information quality**
Ask how concerns were identified, debated and escalated, not simply what conclusions have been reached.

Executives

Executive teams create the environment in which trust and psychological safety either strengthen or deteriorate.

1 **Reduce the cost of speaking up**
Respond to emerging concerns with curiosity and challenge rather than frustration or blame.

2 **Reward early identification**
Recognize those who surface issues early, not only those who resolve them after they have become visible.

3 **Strengthen cross-functional relationships**
Create opportunities for teams to build trust and coordination before pressure arises.

Chief risk officers and risk leaders

Risk leaders help ensure that important information reaches decision makers with sufficient clarity and urgency.

1 **Assess escalation quality**
Review how concerns move through the organization, where delays occur and how information changes as it is escalated.

2 **Examine behavioural incentives**
Identify where performance measures, governance processes or leadership responses may discourage transparency.

3 **Monitor signal integrity**
Focus not only on whether risks are reported but whether they retain sufficient clarity to support timely action.

TRUST AND INCOMPLETE INFORMATION

Many organizations assume that concerns should only be raised once the facts are fully understood. In practice, resilience depends on the opposite capability. The organizations that adapt most effectively are those where individuals can surface concerns before evidence is complete and while uncertainty still exists. Trust determines whether weak signals travel early enough to influence decisions. Adapted from insights shared during interviews conducted for this book.

KEY TAKEAWAYS

- **Resilience is experienced before it is measured**. By the time formal indicators deteriorate, the underlying conditions that sustain resilience have often already shifted. The critical question is whether concerns reach decision makers while meaningful options still exist.
- **Trust and psychological safety are performance assets**. They determine whether concerns are raised early, whether challenge is welcomed and whether important information reaches decision makers with sufficient clarity to influence outcomes.
- **Fear alters escalation quality**. Concerns are softened, delayed or contained long before they are formally reported. The result is not an absence of information but a gradual loss of signal strength as risks move through the organization.
- **Resilience is relational rather than individual**. Personal capability remains important, yet organizations adapt through the quality of their relationships, coordination and information flows. Strong individuals cannot compensate indefinitely for weak connections between teams and functions.
- **Leadership behaviour shapes resilience**. Boards, executives and risk leaders influence the cost of honesty, the quality of escalation and the conditions under which people coordinate under pressure. Resilience strengthens when organizations make honesty easier than silence.

Reframing forward

This chapter examined the human conditions that allow resilience to function in practice. Trust influences whether concerns are raised. Psychological safety influences how they are expressed. Relationships determine how effectively information, judgement and action move across the organization.

With that, resilience depends less on individual capability than on the quality of coordination between people, teams and functions. Organizations adapt more effectively when challenge is welcomed, information travels without distortion and concerns can be surfaced before consequences become visible.

This creates an important leadership tension. If resilience depends on collective capability, why do organizations continue to place so much emphasis on individual intervention?

The next chapter examines this enduring assumption through one of the most persistent myths in organizational life: the hero leader.

Endnotes

1 Gloster, E (2020) Report of the Independent Investigation into the Financial Conduct Authority's Regulation of London Capital & Finance plc, www.fca.org.uk/transparency/independent-investigation-london-capital-finance

2 Financial Conduct Authority (2024) FCA fines Starling Bank £29m for failings in their financial crime systems and controls, www.fca.org.uk/news/press-releases/fca-fines-starling-bank-failings-financial-crime-systems-and-controls#:~:text=The%20FCA%20has%20fined%20Starling,to%203.6%20million%20in%202023

3 Fukuyama, F (1995) *Trust: The Social Virtues and the Creation of Prosperity*, Free Press, New York

4 McEvily, B, Perrone, V and Zaheer, A (2003) Trust as an organizing principle, *Organization Science*, 14 (1), 91–103

5 Médecins Sans Frontières (2016) Operational Decision-Making in High-Risk Environments, MSF Operational Centre briefing paper

6 Clark, T R (2020) *The 4 Stages of Psychological Safety: Defining the path to inclusion and innovation*, Berrett-Koehler Publishers, Oakland, CA

7 Haye, J (2025) Building Psychological Safety in Risk Management: A practical guide to the four stages, Aevitium Ltd, www.aevitium.com/post/four-stages-of-psychological-safety-risk-management

8 Financial Conduct Authority (2020) *DP20/1: Transforming culture in financial services – driving purposeful cultures*, FCA, London

PART TWO

Risk culture, leadership and hidden frictions

04

The myth of the hero leader

Effective leadership through shared accountability

CHAPTER OBJECTIVES

- Define what effective leadership looks like in resilient organizations.
- Demonstrate how shared leadership and distributed decision-making create structural strength.
- Show how over-centralized hero leadership models create fragility under pressure.

Relying on individual strength is a fragile substitute for systemic design. While charisma can ignite an organization, it cannot sustain it. Resilience is found in the transition from ego-centric command to architectural authority, ensuring the mission survives the man.

The prevailing assumption is that strong organizations require strong leaders. Strength, however, is often equated with visibility, decisiveness or personal authority. These qualities can stabilize organizations in moments of uncertainty. They do not, on their own, secure resilience. Resilient enterprises require strong leadership systems.

Effective leadership in complex organizations is not defined by dominance, public profile or crisis intervention. It is defined by clarity of design: decision rights are proportionate to exposure, escalation mechanisms operate independently and accountability is distributed rather than absorbed.

Charisma may accelerate momentum; it might also impede it. Architecture sustains performance.

Resilience should not be seen as a personal attribute but as the outcome of deliberate leadership configuration.

Leadership architecture under increasing complexity

Organizations today operate at a level of scale and interconnectedness that was far less common even a decade ago. Digital platforms enable rapid expansion across markets and strategic decisions can affect thousands of customers or transactions simultaneously. Regulatory regimes increasingly assign personal accountability to senior executives. At the same time, executive visibility has intensified through investor communications, traditional media and digital platforms, where many leaders now cultivate public profiles.

In this environment, authority concentration carries greater consequences than it once did. When decision rights remain narrowly held while organizational complexity expands, errors can spread further and faster before detection and corrective action becomes more difficult to coordinate. Governance structures that appeared proportionate at smaller scale may prove insufficient as interdependencies multiply.

Resilience should not be viewed as an innate personal attribute. It is the deliberate outcome of leadership architecture. In resilient organizations, effective leadership is expressed through shared authority and distributed decision-making rather than personal concentration of power.

COMPLEXITY REQUIRES DIFFERENT LEADERSHIP DESIGN

Futurist Roger Spitz argues that many firms respond to increasing complexity by adding additional controls, approvals and layers of oversight. Yet complexity often requires the opposite response. Simplifying control structures and distributing decision authority can increase responsiveness, allowing expertise, information and challenge to flow more effectively across interconnected systems. (Adapted from insights shared by Roger Spitz during an interview conducted on *RiskMasters*.)

As performance becomes increasingly associated with a single identifiable individual, a halo effect can take hold. Success is attributed to that leader's personal qualities and stakeholders may become more tolerant of lapses or less inclined to question judgement. Over time, visibility and recognition begin to reinforce authority.

This heightened visibility introduces structural risk. External narratives that frame performance around a 'hero' figure can subtly reshape internal dynamics. Decision influence gravitates toward the visible leader and challenge becomes more cautious. The system's stability becomes more closely tied to one individual rather than to institutional design. When authority and resilience are conflated with personality, the organization becomes more exposed under strain.

Authority concentration itself is not new. What has changed is the scale and speed at which its limitations become apparent. As complexity increases, narrowly configured decision structures become more exposed. Leadership architecture must evolve in proportion to organizational interdependence.

Scale and technological leverage

Digital infrastructure, automation and capital mobility allow organizations to expand rapidly across products, jurisdictions and customer segments. Strategic decisions are increasingly embedded into systems and deployed at scale. Product parameters, risk thresholds and customer interactions can be configured centrally and applied across large populations almost instantaneously. The nature of exposure changes accordingly.

Technology magnifies the consequences of leadership design. When decision authority remains concentrated while operational reach expands, a single flawed assumption can affect thousands of customers, transactions or processes before corrective action is taken. As technological leverage increases, authority, challenge and oversight must evolve accordingly.

In founder-led or technically driven businesses, authority often consolidates around early vision and expertise. During initial growth phases, this concentration can provide coherence and speed. As expansion continues, authority distribution must evolve alongside organizational reach. Where it does not, dependency on a small number of individuals increases and resilience weakens. The hero leader model becomes particularly fragile under these conditions because the reach of decisions expands faster than any individual's capacity to oversee their consequences.

As technology increases the distance between decision makers and operational outcomes, leadership becomes less about direct oversight and more about designing systems of accountability, challenge and review. The governance implications of increasingly automated decision environments are significant and will become a defining leadership consideration in the years ahead.

Under these conditions, distributed decision rights, independent review mechanisms and documented rationale help maintain alignment between authority, challenge and accountability as operational reach expands.

Accelerated decision cycles

Market expectations increasingly reward decisiveness. Boards look for clarity of direction; investors often interpret hesitation as uncertainty and competitive environments place a premium on rapid execution.

Behavioural research has long demonstrated that confidence tends to increase with authority and prior success. In *Thinking, Fast and Slow*, Daniel Kahneman describes the 'illusion of validity',[1] in which coherent narratives reinforce conviction beyond the evidence available. Studies on group decision-making by Irving Janis[2] similarly illustrate how cohesive leadership groups can suppress dissent and overestimate collective judgement.

As Socrates argued, individuals do not err on purpose but out of a mistaken belief in the correctness of their path. These tendencies are predictable features of human cognition and leadership architecture must assume their presence. When authority is concentrated and review mechanisms are limited, the opportunity to correct this 'intellectual ignorance' reduces. Distributed leadership introduces a structural counterbalance, ensuring that alternative interpretations are considered before a leader's miscalculations are finalized as commitments.

With increased decision velocity, the importance of leadership architecture becomes more pronounced. Speed does not eliminate uncertainty; it reduces the time available for structured interrogation of assumptions. Organizations must differentiate clearly between categories of decisions, aligning governance intensity with impact and risk exposure.

Some decisions define enterprise direction and require structured challenge before commitment. Others concern operational execution and benefit from proximity to expertise. Still others involve immediate adjustments that depend primarily on clarity of delegated authority rather than collective review. This differentiation can be formalized as shown in Table 4.1.

TABLE 4.1 Decision type and governance intensity

Decision category	Typical scope	Governance requirement	Authority allocation
Strategic	Enterprise-wide commitments, capital allocation, risk posture	Structured challenge, documented alternatives, cross-functional review	Shared authority with formal oversight
Operational	Business-line execution, policy implementation	Domain expertise review and performance monitoring	Distributed to accountable executives
Tactical	Immediate adjustments, situational response	Clear accountability and defined thresholds	Delegated to designated authority holders

Where this differentiation is unclear, decisions tend to migrate upward. Escalation becomes permission-seeking rather than structured review, gradually shifting leadership from a distributed capability to a concentrated function. The result is a decision environment increasingly dependent on a small number of individuals precisely when speed requires broader participation.

Distributed leadership does not imply equal involvement in all decisions. It requires proportional governance aligned to the nature of the decision. Strategic commitments benefit from challenge, operational matters from expertise, and tactical actions from clarity and speed.

Architecture clarifies where review is essential and where delegation strengthens responsiveness.

Visibility and the personalization of performance

Executive visibility has intensified significantly. Media narratives, investor communications and digital platforms frequently frame organizational outcomes through individual leadership stories. Research on executive 'celebrity' by Hayward, Rindova and Pollock[3] highlights that heightened media attention not only increases public attribution of success to individual leaders but can also influence strategic behaviour and risk tolerance within firms.

This personalization reflects a broader mental model. Attribution theory, first articulated by Fritz Heider,[4] shows that observers tend to assign outcomes to individuals rather than to systems or structures. In organizational settings, this bias concentrates recognition around visible leaders even when performance results from distributed effort.

When performance becomes closely associated with specific individuals, credit accumulates accordingly. Decision influence often follows visibility. Over time, disagreement may be experienced as personal opposition rather than procedural challenge. Research in high-reliability sectors such as aviation has demonstrated that steep authority gradients significantly reduce the likelihood that junior crew members will challenge captains, even when safety risks are perceived. Helmreich and Merritt's work on crew resource management shows that dissent suppression is not a cultural accident but a structural function of hierarchy when challenge is not formally protected.[5]

In environments where leaders are publicly associated with strategic direction, escalation can become mediated by informal influence rather than protected by structure.

To address this situation, resilient organizations separate recognition from authority design. Visibility need not translate into centralization. Governance architecture must ensure that accountability remains institutional even when leadership presence is prominent.

Regulatory accountability and defensive centralization

Across sectors, regulatory and governance regimes increasingly emphasize individual accountability. In financial services, senior manager frameworks, like the Senior Managers and Certification Regime (SMCR) in the UK, assign named responsibility for defined functions. In healthcare, clinical directors carry explicit accountability for patient safety outcomes. In energy and infrastructure, executive officers may be personally liable for environmental breaches. In technology firms, data protection and algorithmic governance frameworks assign identifiable ownership of compliance.

These developments seek to prevent diffusion of responsibility. In complex organizations, collective decision-making can blur ownership, allowing material failures to be attributed to 'the system' rather than to identifiable role holders. When accountability is explicit, ambiguity narrows. Decisions are traceable. Responsibility cannot dissipate across committees or hierarchies.

Clarity of accountability strengthens governance. However, when accountability design is not matched by corresponding authority architecture, unintended effects can emerge.

When personal exposure increases, executives often respond defensively. Authority over decisions is drawn closer to the individual who carries regulatory or reputational liability. As approval thresholds rise and delegated decision space shrinks, fewer matters can be resolved at distributed levels. Executives retain sign-off authority more frequently, broader decision forums are convened less often and escalation becomes increasingly vertical. Yet, this situation is not limited to regulated banking environments.

In a healthcare context, a medical director who is personally accountable for patient outcomes may begin to centralize clinical decision approval, reducing autonomy of experienced practitioners. In a technology company, a chief data officer facing regulatory scrutiny over algorithmic bias may restrict decision rights to a small compliance team, limiting cross-functional input. In manufacturing, an executive accountable for safety metrics may consolidate sign-off authority, slowing operational escalation rather than strengthening distributed oversight. The intention is self-protection. The structural consequence is concentration.

Decision tempo intensifies this tendency. When decisions must be taken quickly and liability is visibly attached to named individuals, retaining control can appear rational. Authority gradually shifts from a shared governance resource to a mechanism for managing personal exposure.

Temporary authority concentration can support decisive action under pressure. Long-term resilience depends on authority distribution evolving as conditions stabilize.

When accountability is personalized but authority distribution remains ambiguous, delegation begins to feel like exposure. Escalation shifts from independent challenge to hierarchical clearance. Over time, challenge narrows and resilience weakens.

Effective leadership architecture therefore requires explicit separation between accountability, authority and escalation, as outlined in Table 4.2.

Personal accountability does not require centralized authority. Effective leadership architecture separates accountability, authority and escalation, ensuring that named responsibility coexists with distributed expertise and independent challenge. When these elements remain aligned, regulatory clarity strengthens governance while preserving organizational responsiveness. When they become conflated, authority concentrates, challenge narrows and resilience weakens. Figure 4.1 illustrates how effective authority design

FIGURE 4.1 Proportionate authority calibration model

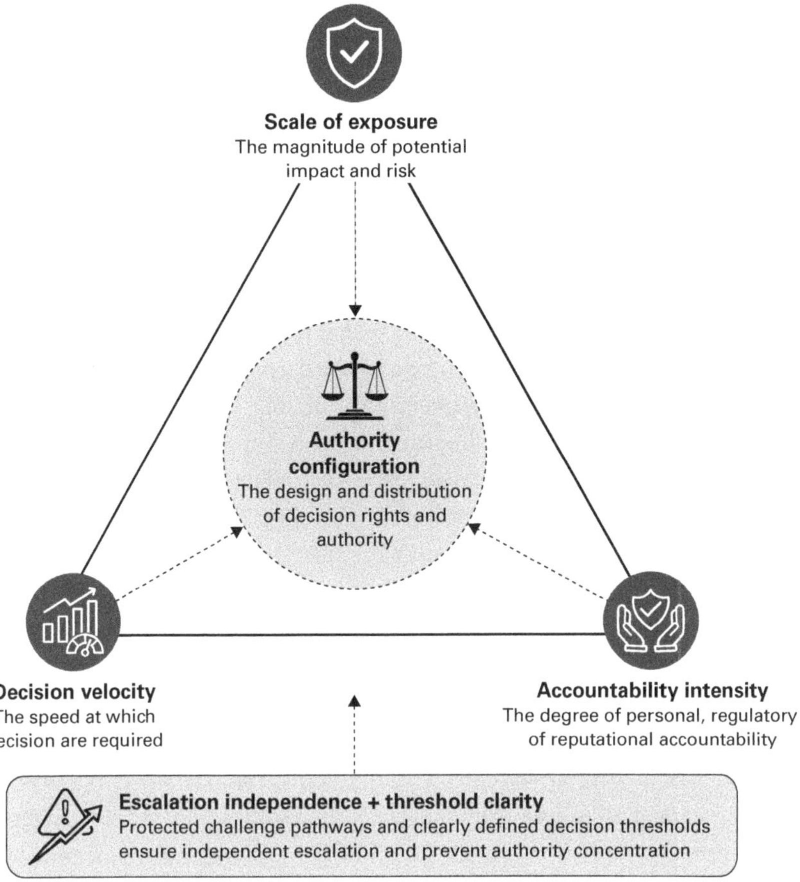

TABLE 4.2 Separation of accountability, authority and escalation

Dimension	What it governs	Structural characteristics
Personal accountability	Who is answerable for outcomes	Named role ownership, performance responsibility, regulatory or reputational exposure
Decision rights allocation	Who has authority to decide	Defined decision thresholds, delegated authority levels, role-based discretion
Escalation independence	Who can challenge decisions and how	Protected challenge channels, independent review forums, documented dissent

sits at the intersection of exposure, decision velocity and accountability intensity, supported by independent escalation and clear decision thresholds.

Organizational symptoms of structural imbalance

Under conditions of scale, speed, visibility and regulatory pressure, authority concentration often becomes visible retrospectively through inquiry findings and empirical research.

Post-incident investigations across sectors have identified similar structural features. The collapse of Enron revealed that critical financial decisions were shaped within a limited executive group despite formal oversight structures. The BP Deepwater Horizon inquiry highlighted constrained escalation of safety concerns within hierarchical decision environments. Reviews of the Boeing 737 MAX certification process similarly identified commercial pressure impacting review forums before commitments were finalized.

Academic research identified similar themes. Malmendier and Tate[6] demonstrate that overconfident CEOs are more likely to pursue aggressive investment strategies. Hayward, Rindova and Pollock show that executive visibility can increase strategic boldness and performance variance. Upper echelons theory[7] provides a broader framework linking executive characteristics and organizational outcomes.

Across sectors and governance environments, the pattern is remarkably consistent: influence concentrates, challenge diminishes and formal structures provide limited protection when escalation is not structurally safeguarded.

These observations do not suggest that strong leadership is inherently destabilizing. They indicate that concentrated authority requires deliberate counterbalance. Where escalation independence and decision transparency remain structurally embedded, visibility and accountability strengthen governance. Where they erode, concentration increases systemic exposure.

With that, resilience depends less on the presence of decisive leaders and more on whether leadership architecture remains proportionate to organizational scale and tempo.

The distributed leadership architecture model

As organizations grow in scale and complexity, resilience depends less on individual capability and more on how decision authority and challenge mechanisms are structured.

The distributed leadership architecture model provides a structural lens for evaluating how authority, challenge and accountability operate within an organization. It does not describe leadership style. It describes configuration.

The model rests on four interdependent pillars (Figure 4.2). Together, they determine whether resilience is embedded within the institution or remains dependent on individual leaders.

Pillar one: Authority distribution

Authority distribution concerns the deliberate allocation of decision rights. In resilient organizations, authority aligns with role clarity, domain expertise and defined accountability boundaries. Decisions sit where competence and responsibility intersect.

Distribution does not imply consensus governance. Strategic oversight remains distinct from operational execution. The objective is proportional allocation, not dispersion for its own sake, to expand decision bandwidth while reducing structural dependency on individuals.

Pillar two: Escalation independence

Escalation independence concerns the structural reliability of challenge mechanisms. Individuals must be able to raise material concerns without requiring approval from those whose decisions are under review.

Effective systems define escalation routes clearly and give challenge forums formal standing. The authority to question a decision is embedded in governance design rather than dependent on personal confidence or informal influence. Dissent is documented and visible within institutional processes.

Escalation independence determines whether alternative interpretations are examined before commitments are formalized. Without structural protection, challenge can soften as it moves through hierarchy.

PRACTITIONER PULSE: PSYCHOLOGICAL SAFETY BEGINS WITH LEADERSHIP

In a LinkedIn poll[8] of risk and governance professionals, 75 per cent identified leadership tone as the primary enabler of psychological safety. Safe escalation routes received 13 per cent of responses, while peer support and training each received 6 per cent.

FIGURE 4.2 The distributed leadership architecture model

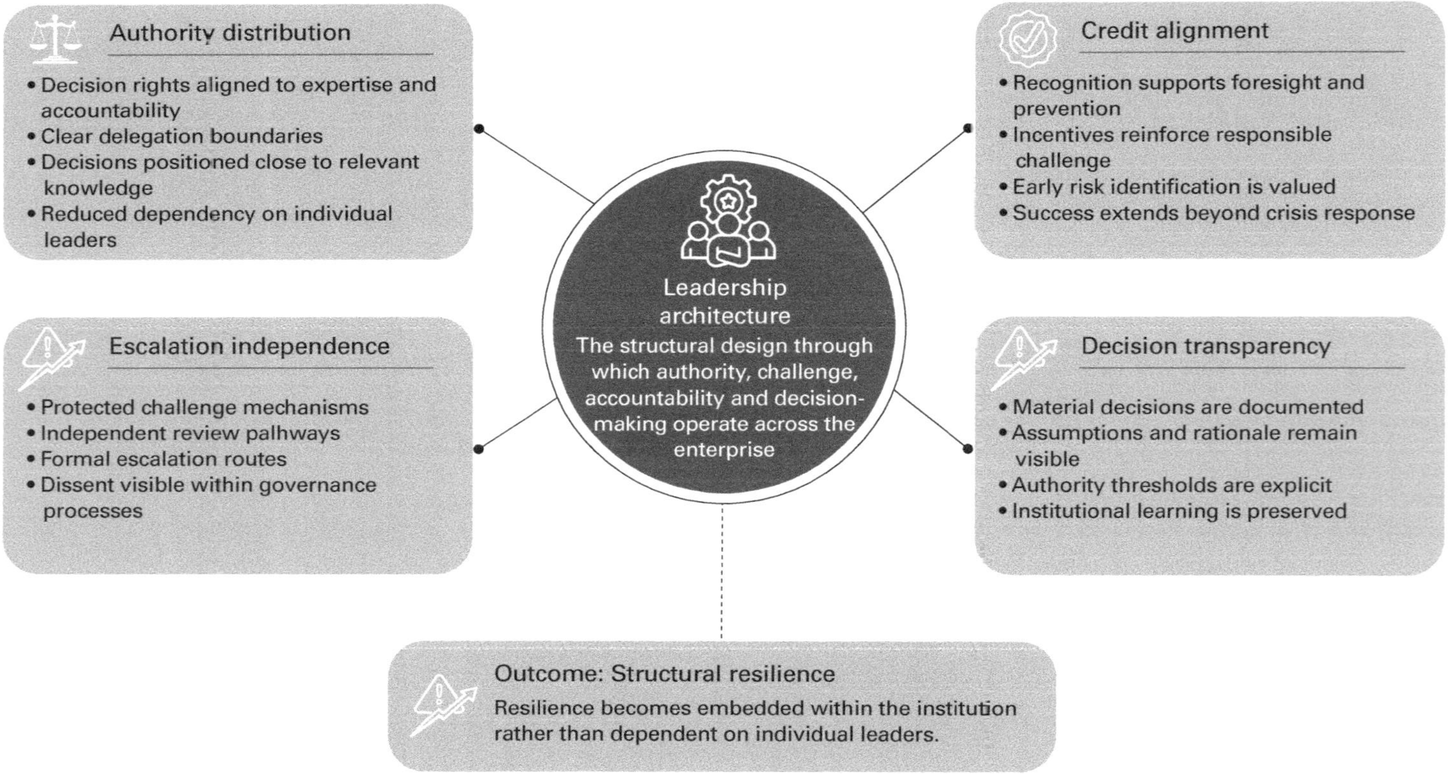

Respondents viewed psychological safety primarily as a leadership capability rather than a training or process issue. The finding aligns with the chapter's argument that escalation behaviour is shaped as much by leadership response as by formal governance design.

Pillar three: Credit alignment

Credit alignment concerns how incentives and recognition shape behaviour. Resilient organizations signal that preventive discipline and early risk identification contribute to performance. When recognition concentrates primarily around visible crisis response, escalation behaviour adjusts accordingly.

For example, remuneration frameworks often reward successful delivery of objectives while giving limited visibility to leaders who identify vulnerabilities before losses occur. Alignment ensures that foresight, not only correction, is reinforced. Boards influence this pillar directly through remuneration frameworks and narrative framing of success.

Pillar four: Decision transparency

Decision transparency refers to the visibility and traceability of material choices. Significant commitments are documented with rationale, assumptions and authority thresholds.

Transparency creates institutional memory. It allows organizations to evaluate not only outcomes but reasoning quality. Where reasoning remains informal and personalized, governance continuity weakens during leadership transition.

Interaction of the pillars

The pillars operate interdependently. Authority without independent challenge risks untested conviction. Escalation without aligned incentives weakens participation. Transparency without defined authority produces documentation without accountability. Resilience emerges when all four pillars operate together.

Why the hero myth disrupts effective leadership

The distributed leadership architecture model assumes that authority, challenge and accountability are deliberately configured. The hero narrative operates differently. It gradually reorganizes leadership around individuals rather than roles and over time, alters how the four pillars function on the ground. Many organizations operate this way.

In practice, organizations frequently adapt structure around exceptional performers. Authority expands incrementally, the scope of decision forums informally shrinks to make space for them and governance processes begin to orbit around individuals rather than roles. Over time, functional boundaries blur and structural independence weakens.

This is not about people's capabilities however exceptional these leaders might be. The difficulty arises when organizational effectiveness becomes closely associated with a particular person rather than with the system enabling them. As decision authority accumulates around one figure, structural guard-rails begin to erode.

Decisions that were previously distributed and benefited from context and diverse viewpoints migrate toward visible leaders. Strategic debates increasingly anchor around a centralized and individual judgement. Even where formal decision rights remain unchanged, influence consolidates and authority becomes personalized.

At a certain threshold, concentration produces a structural constraint. No individual can process the full complexity of a growing organization across domains, geographies and risk categories. Context and capacity matter in decision-making.

In practical terms, decision latency increases because issues queue for senior attention. Cross-domain trade-offs are resolved sequentially rather than collectively. Information is filtered upward through summarized reports rather than debated across functions. Risk signals compete for limited executive bandwidth. Matters that require specialist scrutiny are reduced to brief discussions.

As dependence on a single individual increases, so does key person risk. The absence or departure of that leader can expose how much organizational capability has become concentrated in one person rather than embedded within the system.

REAL-WORLD EXAMPLE

Authority without counterweight – the collapse of FTX

The rise and collapse of FTX[9] illustrates how authority concentration, when not matched by institutional counterweights, can create systemic governance failure. Founded in 2019, FTX grew rapidly to a valuation of approximately $32 billion. Growth was extraordinary but governance maturity was not.

Strategic direction, capital allocation and operational control were concentrated within a narrow executive circle. As we have seen, founder influence is common in early stage firms and FTX reached global scale while retaining decision structures more typical of a small startup.

Board independence was limited relative to organizational scale and financial controls were rudimentary. The company operated without sustained senior financial oversight and bankruptcy proceedings later described a 'complete failure of corporate controls'. Material decisions were communicated through informal digital channels, with limited documentation commensurate with the scale of assets under management.

These weaknesses corresponded directly to failures across the four pillars.

1. Authority remained highly concentrated.
2. Escalation mechanisms lacked independence.
3. Visibility reinforced personal influence.
4. Decision transparency was insufficient for institutional accountability.

By 2022, internal mechanisms enabled the transfer of approximately $8 billion in customer funds to an affiliated entity, Alameda Research. When liquidity pressures emerged, there were no independent institutional counterweights capable of containing the exposure.

Subsequent criminal proceedings resulted in the conviction and imprisonment of founder Sam Bankman-Fried. Asset recovery efforts continue through bankruptcy administration. These legal outcomes address restitution.

FTX failed because authority concentration outpaced governance design. Independent challenge, transparent documentation and distributed oversight were insufficiently embedded. This is the trade-off between necessary founder momentum in early start-up stages versus the need to institutionalize decision process away from individuals as the organization matures.

By contrast, resilient leadership architecture recognizes this limit. It assumes cognitive and bandwidth constraints and distributes authority before concentration becomes structural dependency.

This shift affects more than decision flow. It reshapes incentives. When success is attributed primarily to visible leadership, recognition follows visibility. Crisis intervention becomes highly rewarded. Preventive discipline remains comparatively unseen. Over time, individuals who identify emerging risks may receive less recognition than those who resolve visible disruptions.

This imbalance alters behaviour and escalation becomes more selective. Risk identification may be framed cautiously. The organization's learning cycle shifts from anticipatory design to corrective response.

In that context, the hero narrative does not simply centralize authority. It modifies the incentive structure within which authority operates. Escalation integrity becomes also affected. When leadership identity becomes strongly personalized, challenge acquires a relational dimension. Disagreement can be interpreted as opposition rather than contribution. Individuals may weigh the reputational implications of raising concerns, particularly if decisions are closely associated with specific leaders.

Formal governance processes may remain intact. Yet the functioning of those processes becomes subtly mediated by influence and perception. Over time, the independence of escalation weakens. The result is not immediate failure. It is gradual narrowing of institutional challenge.

REAL-WORLD EXAMPLE

Escalation without independence – the crisis at Petrobras

The corruption crisis at Petrobras[10] illustrates how authority concentration, when embedded within hierarchical and politically sensitive environments, can weaken institutional counterweights even where formal governance structures exist.

Petrobras, Brazil's state-controlled oil company, operated within a complex nexus of political oversight, executive influence and commercial ambition. While formal board structures and compliance mechanisms were in place, decision authority and strategic influence were heavily shaped by senior executives operating within a politically charged environment.

Investigations under 'Operation Car Wash' revealed a systemic bribery and procurement scheme in which contracts were inflated and funds diverted through intermediaries. The scheme persisted for years despite the presence of formal governance committees and internal controls.

Authority over major procurement and capital projects was concentrated within a small leadership circle influenced by political dynamics. Escalation pathways existed formally but were rendered ineffective by loyalty pressures and hierarchical norms. Independent challenge mechanisms lacked sufficient protection from executive and political influence.

Viewed through the four pillars of distributed leadership architecture:

1 **Authority distribution**: decision-making influence over major contracts and projects was highly concentrated.

2 **Escalation independence**: formal compliance structures existed but lacked independence in practice.

3 **Credit alignment**: strategic expansion and visible growth were rewarded, while procurement discipline received less attention.

4 **Decision transparency**: documentation mechanisms were insufficient to prevent systematic manipulation of contracting processes.

Structural permissiveness enabled individual misconduct. When authority consolidates within politically exposed leadership structures, challenge mechanisms can become 'politically correct' and compliance functions effectively become checkbox functions without teeth.

Petrobras demonstrates that formal governance frameworks do not guarantee distributed accountability. Where escalation independence and authority separation are not protected on the ground, structural vulnerabilities can persist beneath visible compliance architecture. This is especially true for any organization operating under political, reputational or strategic pressure, where authority concentration can weaken oversight unless institutional counterweights are deliberately maintained.

Resilient leadership design requires that independence of challenge survives power asymmetry. Formal committees and documented processes are insufficient if authority in practice is personalized or politically mediated.

Risk perception bias as a structural consideration

Leadership architecture must also account for predictable human tendencies. Research in behavioural decision-making has demonstrated that confidence often increases with authority and prior success. Overconfidence bias can strengthen conviction beyond the available evidence. Illusion of control can lead individuals to overestimate their ability to manage uncertain environments. Authority bias may discourage dissent as hierarchical distance grows. Availability bias can cause recent or vivid events to shape risk perception disproportionately.

Governance systems cannot rely on the accuracy of individual judgement alone. They must create conditions in which assumptions are interrogated before commitments are made. This requires structured dissent (e.g. premortem or red teaming), independent review forums and documentation of reasoning that allows retrospective evaluation.

High reliability organization research reinforces this principle. Weick and Sutcliffe identify 'reluctance to simplify interpretations' and 'preoccupation with failure' as core characteristics of resilient systems.[11] These are not personality traits; they are organizational disciplines embedded in routines and reporting structures. Where dissent is institutionalized and anomaly detection is encouraged, error signals surface earlier and decision quality improves.

The purpose of distributed leadership is not simply to dilute authority. It is to introduce cognitive diversity into decision-making processes. Multiple interpretive lenses increase the probability that hidden assumptions surface before exposure materializes.

Resilient organizations therefore design governance as a corrective mechanism for predictable bias. They do not assume that experience eliminates distortion. They embed review and challenge so that risk perception improves through structure rather than relying solely on personal insight.

Board and executive implications

If leadership effectiveness is architectural rather than personal, governance oversight must extend beyond the evaluation of individuals. It must also examine how authority is distributed, how challenge is protected, and how accountability operates across the organization.

For boards, this means looking beyond formal structures to understand where material decisions are made in practice. Authority concentration should be treated as a governance consideration in its own right, particularly when organizational complexity increases without a corresponding distribution of decision-making responsibility. Boards should also consider whether strategic continuity could be maintained if key executives were unexpectedly absent.

For executive teams, resilience depends on balancing decision speed with distributed accountability. Rapid execution does not require authority to converge around a single individual or small leadership group. As organizations grow, decision-making capability, expertise and challenge must remain embedded across functions rather than becoming concentrated around visible leaders.

For CROs and risk leaders, leadership concentration should be viewed as a potential source of organizational risk. Structural conditions that weaken challenge, constrain escalation or increase dependency on key individuals can create vulnerabilities long before they appear in traditional risk indicators.

Across all three groups, the common challenge is maintaining institutional capability as organizations scale. Resilient organizations ensure that authority, challenge and accountability remain embedded within the system rather than becoming dependent on individual leaders.

Practical playbook

Building resilient leadership architecture requires deliberate attention to how authority is distributed, how challenge is protected and how accountability operates in practice.

Boards

Boards strengthen resilience by ensuring that governance remains anchored in institutional design rather than individual influence.

1. **Review authority concentration**
   Look beyond formal delegations and examine where material decisions are made in practice. Pay particular attention to recurring concentration of authority or informal routing of decisions through a small group.
2. **Examine the quality of challenge**
   For significant decisions, ask what alternative assumptions were considered, what objections were raised and how those issues were resolved before approval.
3. **Monitor leadership dependency**
   Consider whether strategic continuity could be maintained if key executives were unexpectedly absent and whether critical authority has become concentrated around particular individuals.

Executives

Executive teams shape how authority, challenge and accountability function across the organization.

1. **Maintain clear decision rights**
   Periodically review authority thresholds across strategic, operational and tactical decisions to ensure they remain aligned with organizational complexity.
2. **Protect independent challenge**
   Separate decision and challenge roles in high-risk initiatives and establish clear escalation routes for unresolved disagreement.
3. **Broaden leadership exposure**
   Avoid concentrating major initiatives around the same individuals. Expanding leadership responsibility strengthens institutional capability and reduces key person dependency.

Chief risk officers and risk leaders

Risk leaders help identify structural conditions that may weaken governance resilience over time.

1. **Monitor authority concentration**
   Assess whether material decisions consistently converge on a small number of individuals or executive groups.
2. **Review escalation effectiveness**
   Examine how concerns move through the organization, where delays occur and whether challenge remains independent of hierarchy.
3. **Assess governance resilience**
   Extend reporting beyond risk exposures to consider authority distribution, escalation independence and leadership dependency as potential sources of organizational risk.

KEY TAKEAWAYS

- **Leadership is a structural capability.** Resilience depends less on individual leaders and more on how authority, challenge and accountability are distributed across the organization.

- **Authority concentration creates hidden vulnerabilities.** As decisions, expertise and influence accumulate around a small number of individuals, organizations become increasingly exposed to bottlenecks, reduced challenge and key person risk.
- **Effective challenge requires structural protection.** Escalation pathways, independent review and documented dissent help ensure that important concerns can influence decisions before commitments become difficult to reverse.
- **Leadership dependency weakens organizational resilience.** Organizations become more resilient when knowledge, decision-making capability and accountability are embedded within systems rather than concentrated in individuals.
- **Resilient leadership architecture balances authority and accountability.** Authority distribution, escalation independence, credit alignment and decision transparency work together to create organizations that can adapt, coordinate and perform beyond the contribution of any single leader.

Reframing forward

This chapter examined leadership through the lens of structural design. Resilience depends not only on leadership capability but also on how authority, challenge and accountability are configured across the organization.

Organizations can perform strongly under concentrated leadership, particularly in stable conditions. The durability of governance becomes visible as complexity increases, dissent tests alignment and leadership transitions occur. In those moments, institutional design determines whether performance is sustained.

This creates an important question. If resilient leadership depends on distributed authority and protected challenge, what enables people to exercise that authority and challenge effectively in practice?

The next chapter examines the cultural conditions that allow leadership architecture to function. Formal governance defines how authority flows. Culture influences how that authority is exercised.

Endnotes

1 Kahneman, D (2011) *Thinking, Fast and Slow*, Allen Lane, London

2 Janis, I L (1972) *Victims of Groupthink: A Psychological Study of Foreign-Policy Decisions and Fiascoes*, Houghton Mifflin, Boston, MA

3 Hayward, M L A, Rindova, V P and Pollock, T G (2004) Believing one's own press: The causes and consequences of CEO celebrity, *Strategic Management Journal*, 25 (7), 637–53, https://doi.org/10.1002/smj.405

4 Heider, F (1958) *The Psychology of Interpersonal Relations*, Wiley, New York

5 Helmreich, R L and Merritt, A C (1998) *Culture at Work in Aviation and Medicine: National, Organizational and Professional Influences*, Ashgate, Aldershot

6 Malmendier, U and Tate, G (2005) CEO overconfidence and corporate investment, *Journal of Finance*, 60 (6), 2661–700

7 Hambrick, D C and Mason, P A (1984) Upper echelons: The organization as a reflection of its top managers, *Academy of Management Review*, 9 (2), 193–206

8 Source: Haye, J (2026) What most enables psychological safety in risk governance? LinkedIn poll, 18 December, www.linkedin.com/feed/update/urn:li:activity:7407295529375735808

9 Source: Adapted from findings reported in John J Ray III, 'First Day Declaration', In re FTX Trading Ltd et al, United States Bankruptcy Court for the District of Delaware, 2022; United States Department of Justice, United States v. Samuel Bankman-Fried, 2023–2024

10 Source: Adapted from findings reported by the Brazilian Federal Public Prosecutor's Office (Ministério Público Federal) under Operation Car Wash (Lava Jato), Petrobras investigations and related corporate disclosures, 2014–2021

11 Weick, K E and Sutcliffe, K M (2007) *Managing the Unexpected: Resilient Performance in an Age of Uncertainty* (2nd edn), Jossey-Bass, San Francisco, CA

05

Culture, energy and hidden risk

How fear, blame and suppression corrode resilience across the resilience cycle

> CHAPTER OBJECTIVES
>
> - Examine how organizational culture influences risk sensing, decision quality, crisis response and organizational learning.
> - Strengthen resilience through signal integrity and effective information flow.
> - Develop middle-layer capability and cultural maturity to sustain resilience over time.

Resilience depends on what people know. Culture determines what they do with that knowledge.

Stability is a poor stress test. In calm conditions, organizational systems often appear stronger than they are. Governance structures function smoothly, friction seems limited and management reports do not flag any immediate concerns. Under those conditions, it is difficult to distinguish genuine resilience from the absence of pressure.

At that point, resilience becomes less a question of information and more a question of energy. People must challenge decisions, accept accountability, support colleagues and adapt their behaviour as conditions change. Some organizations mobilize quickly. Others slow down, fragment or retreat into silos.

The difference is culture

This argument extends the analysis developed in the previous chapter. Chapter 4 examined how resilient organizations distribute authority so that leadership capability is embedded in institutional design rather than concentrated in individuals. Authority distribution creates the architecture of resilience. Culture determines whether that architecture functions when pressure rises.

Throughout this chapter, resilience is examined as a cycle. Risks must first be detected, then debated, managed during disruption and ultimately translated into learning. Culture influences every stage of this cycle by shaping how information moves, how decisions are challenged and how organizations respond under pressure.

Fear, blame and the erosion of signal integrity

Culture determines how organizations behave when pressure rises. Fear, blame and performance expectations influence what people challenge, what they ignore and what they choose to escalate. Failure is behavioural before being technical.

The behavioural logic of silence

As we have seen in Chapter 3, psychological safety creates the conditions for challenge. When those conditions weaken, concerns are raised less frequently, difficult conversations are postponed, and silence gradually becomes normal.

Over time, silence becomes rational behaviour. If speaking up carries a personal downside while remaining quiet carries none, employees optimize for safety. They do not withhold information because they are negligent. They withhold it because the incentive structure makes suppression sensible.

When individuals feel exposed professionally or politically, they shift from long-term judgement to short-term self-protection and begin to prioritize alignment over accuracy. In meetings, the question subtly moves from 'What are we missing?' to 'Can we defend this?' Material weaknesses become 'operational challenges', emerging patterns are described as 'isolated incidents' and uncomfortable data is softened to become a non-issue rather than examined.

The impact starts small. A difficult conversation is postponed. A report is 'repositioned' before it reaches the board. A challenge is left unspoken in the meeting. Each choice appears minor in isolation, yet together they reshape how the organization understands and ultimately responds to its own risk.

When this behaviour becomes widespread, the cumulative impact is systemic. Blind spots widen because the same risks are repeatedly softened, deferred or diluted at multiple levels. Resilience erodes not through a single dramatic failur, but through accumulated hesitation that gradually distorts how the organization sees itself until impact makes the problem impossible to ignore.

Target cultures and the cost of doubt

High-performance cultures often pride themselves on speed, decisiveness and ambition. These qualities drive growth. They can also create conformity risk.

When performance pressure dominates, three distortions commonly take hold:

1. Agreement is read as competence because it accelerates execution, while dissent is treated as friction because it slows momentum and introduces uncertainty.
2. Strategic overconfidence increases. Success reinforces the belief that existing judgement is sufficient, causing early anomalies to be treated as noise rather than signal.
3. Attention shifts towards the immediate. Short-term performance priorities dominate leadership focus, while investments that strengthen long-term resilience are acknowledged but repeatedly deferred.

In this environment, no one needs to be told to stay quiet. People watch what happens to those who challenge and draw their own conclusions. The colleague who pushes too hard is labelled difficult. The manager who slows a decision is seen as obstructive. Over time, employees adjust. They raise fewer objections, soften their language and choose their battles carefully because alignment carries less personal risk than challenge.

This dynamic does not spare oversight functions. Risk, compliance and internal audit are designed to introduce friction where necessary. Their role is to question assumptions, test downside exposure and slow decisions when risk is rising. In a culture that equates speed with strength, that role can be reframed as obstruction. Challenge softens in tone. Objections are raised later in the process. Language becomes advisory rather than assertive. The organization still has oversight structures but the behavioural authority to challenge gradually shifts from being consequential to being performative. The organization does not ignore risk; it simply gives it less weight than it needs.

> SILENCE AND OVERCONFIDENCE COEXIST
>
> Resilience often weakens when silence and overconfidence develop simultaneously. As information moves through organizational layers, uncertainty is frequently filtered, softened or delayed. Leaders become increasingly confident in the information they receive while frontline concerns become progressively less visible. The result is a dangerous illusion of control at precisely the moment organizations most need challenge, escalation and debate. Adapted from insights shared during interviews conducted for this book.

Information asymmetry across layers

Even in organizations with formal reporting channels, information asymmetry can persist. Frontline teams experience operational pressures directly, while executives and boards rely primarily on reporting, summaries and management interpretation.

Middle managers often sit at the point of greatest distortion. They face:

- high accountability for performance
- limited tolerance for disruption
- ambiguous authority to escalate issues that challenge senior direction.

The consequence is not simply incomplete information. Different organizational layers begin operating from different assumptions about the same situation. Frontline teams may experience growing operational strain while senior leaders believe risks remain contained. Executives may believe remediation is progressing while those responsible for delivery see persistent barriers and resource constraints.

Under these conditions, decisions are made against different versions of reality. The challenge is not whether information exists. It is whether the organization shares a common understanding of what that information means.

Disproportionate consequences of suppressed signals

The most damaging organizational crises often begin with issues that appear too small to matter. A minor operational anomaly, left unexamined, can evolve into a systemic outage. A cultural complaint that appears isolated may later surface as a conduct scandal. A strategic assumption, insufficiently challenged, can culminate in material capital misallocation.

Risks that appear marginal in isolation can produce disproportionate consequences when they accumulate. What is later described as 'unexpected' frequently reflects a pattern of predictable neglect.

This dynamic can be understood through a cultural reframing of the Swiss Cheese Model[1]. Traditionally, the model illustrates how defensive layers, each containing minor weaknesses, may align to permit failure. In organizational terms, those weaknesses are not only technical control gaps but behavioural ones. Reluctance to challenge, incentives that discourage transparency, confidence reinforced by past success and hesitation to escalate concerns all create openings within the system. The model shows how behavioural weaknesses across risk sensing, decision-making and crisis response can align, allowing small problems to develop into systemic events.

REAL-WORLD EXAMPLE

Lufthansa and the normalization of strain

When a major organization faces repeated strikes, the outside world often sees a sudden crisis. Internally, however, such events are frequently the culmination of a longer period in which emerging tensions were visible but not treated as strategically material. In the period leading up to its 2024 operational disruptions, Lufthansa navigated mounting workload and pay pressures that were initially framed as manageable complexity. Over time, those pressures contributed to an estimated €350 million impact on strategic targets.

For 2024, the group reported net profit of €1.38 billion, down 18 per cent from 2023, despite revenues rising 6 per cent to €37.6 billion and passenger numbers increasing to 131 million.[2] Growth and deterioration coexisted.

The year was marked by repeated strikes, rising cost pressures and aircraft delivery delays. Industrial action, particularly in the first half of the year, weighed on the passenger airlines. While such disputes are not uncommon in unionized sectors, their persistence reflected tensions that had been accumulating over time rather than emerging abruptly.

In high-performance environments facing cost discipline and competitive intensity, emerging strain is often interpreted as negotiable friction rather than structural vulnerability. Middle managers must balance operational continuity with workforce dissatisfaction and financial targets. Under these conditions, signals of fatigue and misalignment may be reported upward in moderated form, framed as industrial relations challenges rather than indicators of systemic exposure.

When disruption intensifies, leadership attention shifts to containment. Outlooks are revised, turnaround programmes are launched and communication emphasizes external headwinds. Yet the visible crisis is often the result of earlier signals that did not trigger strategic recalibration while flexibility remained.

Lufthansa's results demonstrate that resilience erosion does not always manifest as collapse. It may appear instead as margin compression, reputational strain and reactive restructuring within an organization that continues to grow. The critical question is not whether tension exists but whether persistent strain is treated as background condition or as early warning.

Overcoming the frozen middle: Decision quality under pressure

If signal integrity erodes at the edges of the organization, decision quality is most vulnerable in the middle. Between frontline experience and executive authority sits a layer of management that translates operational reality into strategic narrative. This middle layer carries disproportionate influence over how risk is framed, prioritized and debated. When it functions well, it acts as a stabilizing force, ensuring that emerging issues are contextualized accurately and transmitted without distortion. When it freezes, risk dialogue degrades long before leaders recognize the scale of the problem.

The structural tension of the middle layer

Middle managers are responsible for delivering strategy, managing cost discipline and meeting operational targets, yet they rarely control the strategic parameters within which those targets are defined. Accountability for performance rests with them; authority to reshape constraints typically does not.

From this position, they function as translators of risk. Frontline signals pass through their judgement before reaching senior forums, and the framing applied at this stage often determines whether emerging strain is treated as structural vulnerability or absorbed as manageable complexity. Table 5.1 illustrates how accountability, authority and risk experience differ across organizational layers, creating unique pressures at the middle-management level.

When psychological safety is weak, this translation tends to become risk-averse. Middle managers are primarily assessed on delivery, cost control and stability. Few performance systems explicitly reward the early surfacing of uncertainty or the challenge of underlying assumptions. In that context, the personal exposure associated with raising uncomfortable questions can feel more immediate than the institutional exposure associated with containing them.

Emerging risks are often described in ways that allow initiatives to proceed. Structural strain is reframed as execution difficulty. Resource constraints become prioritization challenges. Foundational assumptions

TABLE 5.1 The structural asymmetry of the middle layer

Dimension	Frontline/operational layer	Middle management layer	Executive/board layer
Primary focus	Immediate delivery and service continuity	Target attainment and cost discipline	Strategic direction and capital allocation
Accountability	Task execution and compliance	Performance outcomes and operational stability	Long-term value and risk appetite
Authority	Limited discretion	Operational discretion, limited strategic authority	Strategic design and constraint setting
Risk experience	Direct exposure to strain	Interpretation and translation of strain	Review of aggregated risk information
Typical framing of strain	'This is not working'	'We can manage this'	'Performance remains within tolerance'
Escalation threshold	Experience-based	Judgement-based	Formalized through governance

are treated as operational hurdles rather than as points for strategic review.

Table 5.2 illustrates how the same management layer can produce very different resilience outcomes depending on whether challenge is encouraged or constrained.

This behaviour reflects rational adaptation rather than poor intent. Middle managers are held responsible for outcomes without having authority to redefine the assumptions that shape them. When operational strain emerges, judgement often defaults to containment rather than strategic challenge. Over time, organizations become more capable of managing symptoms while delaying examination of underlying causes.

TABLE 5.2 Middle-layer decision behaviour and system impact

Dimension of control	Strong psychological safety	Weak psychological safety	Resilience consequence
Framing of risk	Structural issues elevated early	Structural issues reframed as execution challenges	Strategic misalignment detected earlier or allowed to persist
Escalation behaviour	Ambiguity surfaced for debate	Ambiguity resolved locally	Signal delay increases exposure accumulation
Interpretation of constraints	Resource gaps flagged as strategic risk	Resource gaps treated as efficiency issues	Structural underinvestment remains uncorrected
Treatment of assumptions	Assumptions openly tested	Assumptions treated as fixed	Foundational risks remain unchallenged
Dialogue with executives	Early, direct challenge	Moderated or delayed challenge	Decision quality strengthened or degraded
Decision latency	Slower initial approval, reduced downstream correction	Faster initial approval, increased rework	Exposure accumulates before recalibration
Personal risk perception	Raising concern signals professionalism	Raising concern signals disruption	Silence scales faster than error
Organizational outcome	Adaptive recalibration	Accumulated strain	Resilience strengthened or eroded

Decision quality and the discipline of constructive dissent

Strategic resilience depends on the quality of debate preceding material decisions. Risk appetite, capital allocation frameworks and governance structures all assume that challenge occurs before strategic commitments and associated exposures are taken. When the middle layer freezes, that assumption no longer holds true.

Two distortions follow.

1. First, risk appetite shifts from boundary-setting discipline to justificatory language. Instead of defining the limits within which exposure is acceptable, it becomes a tool for framing decisions as compliant. The question subtly changes from whether exposure is appropriate to whether it can be presented as consistent with stated tolerance.
2. Second, judgement becomes increasingly centralized. As upward challenge becomes less frequent, executive confidence may strengthen by default. Leaders need not suppress dissent for scrutiny to weaken; the absence of sustained counterargument reduces the range of scenarios explored before deciding.

Constructive dissent is not a brake on execution. It is the process through which exposure is examined before it is accepted. Absent dissent, decisions may appear decisive while resting on insufficiently tested assumptions.

In that context, strengthening the middle layer requires more than empowerment. Authority boundaries must be explicit. Managers need defined criteria for when operational friction warrants strategic review rather than local resolution. Decision forums should institutionalize challenge so that questioning assumptions becomes part of the process rather than an act of individual courage.

Many organizations lack clear criteria for when operational friction should trigger strategic reconsideration. Figure 5.1 illustrates the decision boundary between operational management and strategic reassessment.

Visible acknowledgement of dissent, even when decisions proceed unchanged, signals that challenge is institutional rather than personal. Early challenge may lengthen deliberation. Over time, it reduces rework, corrective intervention and crisis-driven reversal. The objective is not friction but calibrated scrutiny that surfaces exposure before commitments are made.

Assessing whether this discipline is present requires mechanisms that reveal how risk is debated before decisions are taken. Three diagnostic tools are particularly useful.

FIGURE 5.1 From operational friction to strategic review

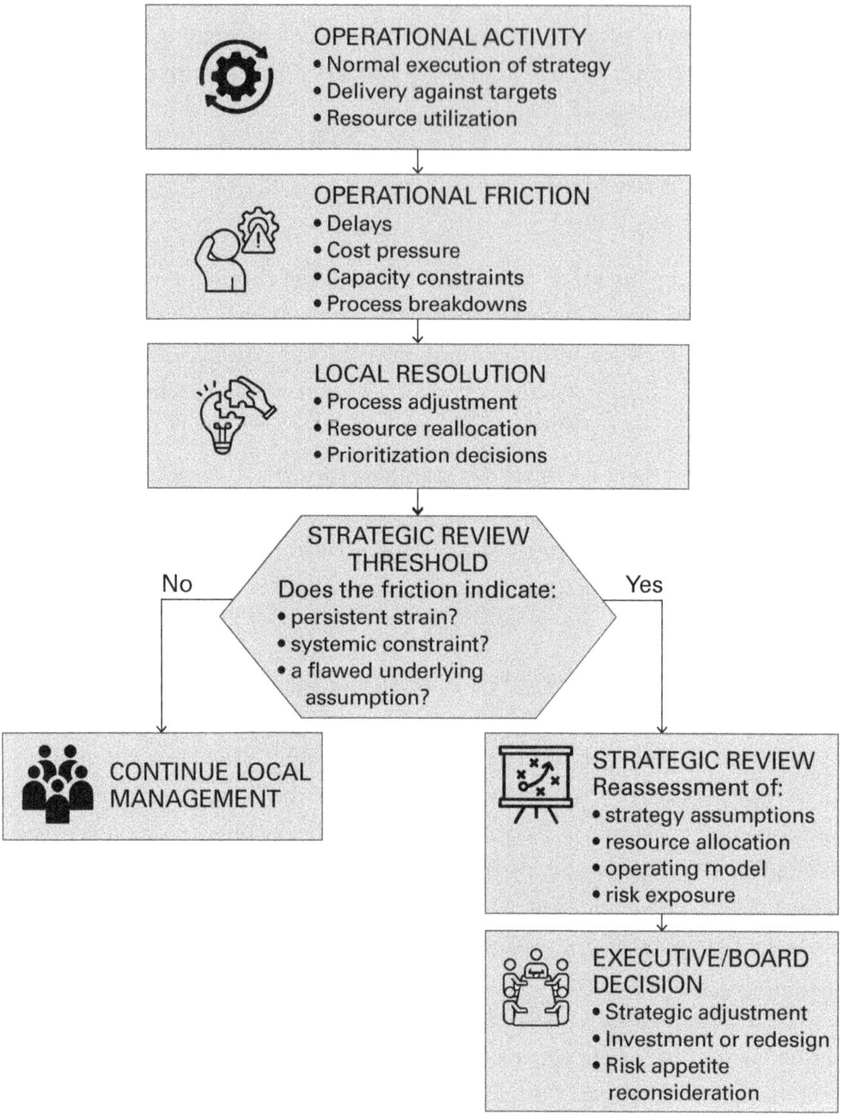

Operational friction is a normal feature of execution. The critical governance question is when persistent friction should trigger review of underlying assumptions rather than continued local management.

- **Decision challenge audits** examine whether material decisions were preceded by documented alternative views, explicit downside scenarios and recorded dissent.

- **Signal lag measurement** assesses the time between first identification of a material risk and its formal recognition in senior governance discussions.
- **Cultural stress testing** evaluates how decision forums respond when confronted with uncertainty, incomplete information or dissenting perspectives.

While these diagnostic tools can strengthen the quality of organizational scrutiny, they are most valuable when applied deliberately rather than routinely. Boards rarely observe the moment when challenge begins to stall; signals often appear as operational friction rather than governance concern. Recognizing when to deploy deeper diagnostic review is therefore as important as the tools themselves.

PRACTICAL TOOL

When boards should deploy decision scrutiny diagnostics

Decision challenge audits, signal lag measurement and cultural stress testing are not tools that need to be used constantly. They become most valuable when boards suspect that performance tension may be masking deeper strategic tension.

Boards may consider deploying these diagnostics when:

- operational pressures are repeatedly presented as execution challenges rather than prompts for strategic review
- performance targets continue to be met while teams report persistent capacity strain or delivery friction
- strategic initiatives appear to progress smoothly despite recurring operational workarounds
- early concerns raised by management rarely reach board discussion unless accompanied by visible impact
- decision papers emphasize mitigation plans but provide limited examination of assumptions or downside scenarios.

These signals do not necessarily indicate governance failure. They suggest that operational friction may be absorbed within the system rather than examined as a potential indicator of strategic misalignment. In such circumstances, diagnostic tools can help determine whether challenge is occurring at the right level of the organization.

The objective is not to increase escalation volume but to ensure that emerging strain is examined at the level where underlying assumptions can still be challenged.

Energy, engagement and resilience capacity

Resilience is often described through systems, controls and escalation mechanisms. Yet the endurance of those systems during disruption ultimately depends on the human relationships that sustain them. When trust, cooperation and discretionary effort weaken, the organization's ability to absorb shock and recover from disruption declines long before a crisis becomes visible.

This collective capacity is often described as social capital: the network of trust, mutual support and shared responsibility that allows people to coordinate effectively under pressure (Putnam, 2000).[3] Social capital determines whether individuals remain willing to invest effort beyond formal responsibilities, support colleagues under strain and sustain performance during prolonged disruption.

Where the previous sections examined how information travels through the organization and how decisions are scrutinized, this section focuses on the conditions that determine whether this social capital remains strong. Engagement is therefore more than a cultural aspiration; it represents a structural component of resilience.

Organizations with strong social capital maintain coordination, initiative and shared problem-solving even when conditions deteriorate. Organizations experiencing disengagement may continue to operate normally under stable conditions, yet their capacity to endure prolonged stress declines rapidly. The difference lies not only in the design of systems but in the strength of the human networks that sustain them.

The hidden cost of disengagement

Disengagement changes how people participate in the organization's work. Formal responsibilities continue to be met, at least on paper, yet the effort invested beyond minimum requirements becomes more limited. Initiative declines, collaboration becomes more selective and fewer individuals intervene when problems fall outside their immediate remit. These shifts carry important implications for resilience.

Burn-out is often framed as a human resources issue. In resilience terms, it reduces the organization's ability to sustain coordinated effort during disruption. Teams operating under prolonged strain find it harder to maintain attention, support one another across functions or adapt procedures when established routines no longer hold.

Discretionary effort becomes particularly important during disruption. Many stabilizing actions fall outside formal job descriptions: reallocating resources informally, supporting overstretched colleagues or adapting procedures when established routines no longer fit the situation. These actions depend on collective commitment rather than formal obligation.

When engagement weakens, behaviour often becomes more self-preserving. Individuals concentrate on protecting their own responsibilities and performance metrics rather than intervening beyond their immediate remit. Informal cooperation declines and fewer people step forward to resolve problems that fall between teams. The organization continues to function, yet the collective initiative that stabilizes systems under strain becomes less reliable.

Under sustained operational pressure, these behavioural shifts tend to follow a recognizable pattern. Attention progressively narrows from collective coordination towards the protection of individual responsibilities. Teams focus first on maintaining delivery, then on containing strain within their own boundaries. Over time, initiative beyond defined roles becomes less frequent.

Cultural fatigue as a leading indicator

When these behavioural patterns persist, they gradually reshape the organization's operating culture. What begins as temporary adaptation to pressure becomes normal practice. Teams concentrate on maintaining delivery within their own boundaries, while cross-organizational initiative becomes less frequent. Over time, this condition produces what can be described as cultural fatigue.

Cultural fatigue describes a state in which the organization continues to perform, yet the collective energy required to sustain cooperation, initiative and learning becomes increasingly strained. It is not simply exhaustion. It reflects a shift in how individuals relate to the organization and its mission.

Cultural fatigue reduces recovery capacity before performance visibly deteriorates. People continue to fulfil formal responsibilities, yet fewer invest effort in improving systems, supporting colleagues or addressing issues beyond their immediate remit. Trust weakens, initiative declines and learning becomes procedural rather than developmental. The organization continues to operate, although its ability to recover from future disruption is gradually diminished.

Reversing cultural fatigue requires more than engagement initiatives. Resilient organizations create ownership by aligning accountability with discretion. Individuals are expected to exercise judgement, raise concerns and respond to emerging problems without waiting for constant direction. Responsibility therefore becomes an active contributor to resilience rather than a passive assignment of tasks.

Building a culture of contribution

Ownership becomes most visible through contribution. In resilient organizations, individuals participate actively in identifying problems, sharing information and supporting solutions beyond formal role boundaries. Contribution becomes a distributed source of resilience, reducing reliance on central coordination. Table 5.3 summarizes the characteristics commonly observed in cultures where contribution is actively encouraged.

TABLE 5.3 Characteristics of a culture of contribution

Cultural characteristic	Observable behaviour	Resilience effect
Shared problem-solving	Teams collaborate across functions to address emerging issues	Problems are addressed before they escalate
Open information flow	Information moves horizontally and vertically without delay	Situational awareness improves
Adaptive participation	Individuals act beyond formal roles when circumstances require it	Response capacity expands
Distributed responsibility	Employees feel accountable for organizational outcomes	Initiative is sustained during disruption

Crisis response and the engagement foundation

Crisis response rarely creates new behaviours. More often, it reveals behaviours that already existed. Teams characterized by trust, ownership and shared accountability before disruption typically respond with greater co-ordination and adaptability during it. Where disengagement has taken hold, response becomes more dependent on hierarchy, formal process and instruction.

Crisis reveals the underlying strength of an organization's social capital. Plans provide the structure of response. Trust, contribution and collective energy determine its effectiveness.

From fragility to antifragile adaptation

The difference between fragile, resilient and antifragile organizations often becomes visible after the immediate crisis has passed. Some focus primarily on restoring stability. Others seek to understand what the disruption revealed about their systems, assumptions and operating practices. The most adaptive organizations go further, using those insights to strengthen future capability. This distinction becomes particularly visible when crises expose cultural weaknesses that remained hidden under normal conditions.

Turning cultural weakness into strategic strength

Crisis situations frequently expose cultural weaknesses that remain hidden during normal operations. Communication breakdowns, hesitation in decision-making or gaps in coordination become visible when organizations operate under pressure. The question is not whether such weaknesses exist. Every organization carries structural and cultural limitations. The decisive factor is how leaders interpret what a crisis reveals.

Fragile organizations tend to interpret disruption through the lens of individual performance. Post-crisis reviews focus on identifying personal mistakes or procedural breaches. Attention concentrates on who acted incorrectly rather than on how the system shaped behaviour. While this approach may satisfy accountability expectations, it rarely strengthens the organization's underlying capability.

Research in safety science and organizational learning consistently shows that resilient organizations treat failure as a property of system behaviour rather than individual performance (Dekker, 2016[4]; Hollnagel, 2014[5]).

Instead of asking who failed, they examine how the system responded under stress. Investigations focus on how information moved through the organization, how decisions were framed and how teams coordinated when conditions changed. Problems uncovered during disruption become opportunities to redesign processes, strengthen coordination mechanisms and clarify decision authority.

Antifragile adaptation begins when these insights are embedded into the organization rather than documented and archived. Lessons learnt influence future decisions, governance arrangements and operating practices. Stress therefore becomes more than a test of resilience. It becomes a source of information that helps the organization evolve.

Jugaad: Improvisation as adaptive capacity

Jugaad represents both a resilience mechanism and a diagnostic signal. It demonstrates the organization's capacity to adapt while simultaneously highlighting where structural improvement may be required.

Learning-oriented cultures do more than analyse crises after they occur. They create conditions in which individuals feel able to respond constructively while disruption is unfolding.

When responsibility for outcomes is shared and individuals feel trusted to act within clear boundaries, teams are more willing to intervene when systems begin to strain. Instead of waiting for central direction, they adjust operations locally to stabilize the situation. During crises, organizations frequently rely on this form of improvisation to maintain continuity. Teams adjust procedures, repurpose resources and develop temporary solutions to address conditions that formal systems were not designed to handle.

In some contexts, this form of resourceful adaptation is described as jugaad, a term originating in India that refers to practical, low-cost solutions developed under constraint (Radjou et al, 2012).[6]

Improvisation should not be confused with disorder. In resilient organizations, it reflects adaptive capacity. Individuals understand the objectives they are protecting, the boundaries within which they can act and the circumstances that require escalation. When these parameters are clear, teams can adapt locally without creating governance confusion.

At the same time, improvisation reveals something important about the organization itself. When teams repeatedly rely on workarounds to maintain performance, it signals that formal processes, structures or tools may no longer match operational reality.

Cultures that convert disruption into innovation

Improvisation stabilizes organizations during disruption, yet the signal it produces is equally important. When repeated workarounds reveal that formal systems no longer match operational reality, resilient organizations treat these signals as input for structural improvement.

The most advanced stage of resilience maturity occurs when organizations systematically convert crisis experience into organizational learning. In such environments, disruption initiates learning cycles that strengthen future capacity.

Three mechanisms typically characterize cultures capable of this transformation.

1. First, learning processes are institutionalized. Post-event reviews move beyond compliance reporting to examine how systems functioned under real conditions. Insights are integrated into process redesign, governance adjustments and capability development.
2. Second, adaptive loops are embedded in organizational practice. Feedback from frontline teams, operational units and crisis response efforts is captured and analysed systematically. This information informs strategic and operational improvements.
3. Third, leaders signal that learning carries equal importance to accountability. Errors are examined to understand system behaviour rather than simply assigning responsibility. This approach encourages transparency and supports continuous improvement.

When these mechanisms are present, disruption becomes a source of organizational innovation. Stress reveals capability rather than triggering collapse.

Few organizations achieve full antifragility. However, they can cultivate elements of it by capturing lessons from improvisation, examining the structural causes of workarounds and embedding those insights into governance, processes and operating models. In this way, resilience evolves from endurance into adaptive capability. Stress no longer functions only as a test of the organization's strength; it becomes a source of information that reveals where the system can improve.

REAL-WORLD EXAMPLE

Spanish Red Cross: Adaptive supply networks during the Covid-19 crisis

The response of the Spanish Red Cross[7] during the Covid-19 pandemic illustrates how resilient organizations transform disruption into adaptive capacity. As the pandemic spread across Europe in early 2020, the organization faced a sudden surge in demand for personal protective equipment (PPE) required to support volunteers and humanitarian operations.

Global supply chains were under severe strain. PPE production was concentrated in a limited number of countries, international transport capacity had collapsed as commercial aviation shut down, and competition between governments and organizations intensified. Traditional procurement channels proved insufficient to meet the rapidly growing demand.

Rather than relying on a single procurement strategy, the Spanish Red Cross adopted a diversified supply approach. Six complementary channels were mobilized simultaneously, including domestic suppliers, government donations, the international Red Cross network, private sector partnerships, micro-donations from citizens and diaspora communities, and factories in Spain that converted production lines to manufacture protective equipment.

Partnerships with private companies played a particularly important role. Organizations with existing commercial networks in China provided market intelligence, supplier verification and logistics support, helping the Red Cross secure reliable PPE sources during a period characterized by fraud risks and unstable supply markets.

At the same time, grassroots initiatives contributed to operational continuity. Numerous small shipments of protective equipment sent by individuals and community networks created a steady flow of supplies during the early weeks of the crisis, when global markets were largely inaccessible.

These adaptations allowed the Spanish Red Cross to sustain operations at scale, supporting more than 48,000 volunteers and managing approximately one million pieces of protective equipment per month during the peak response period.

Cultural maturity and governance depth

Chapter 3 examined how trust and psychological safety influence signal flow, escalation and challenge. Psychological safety is not a single condition. Timothy Clark describes four progressive stages: inclusion safety, learner safety, contributor safety and challenger safety.

For resilience governance, challenger safety carries particular significance. It determines whether individuals feel able to question assumptions, raise concerns and challenge decisions before risks become consequences. Without challenger safety, organizations may appear collaborative and supportive while still suppressing the dissent that enables sound judgement.

From inclusion to challenger safety

Many organizations invest considerable effort in building inclusive environments. Inclusion expands participation and ensures that a wider range of individuals are present in organizational conversations. This depth of participation strengthens the sensing network through which early signals of disruption travel.

However, inclusion alone does not guarantee that these signals will surface. In many organizations, information stalls within what earlier sections described as the middle frozen layer of management. At this level, individuals often balance the professional risks of escalation against the perceived expectations of alignment and stability.

Resilient organizations move beyond inclusion towards challenger safety. Individuals must feel authorized not only to participate in discussion but also to question assumptions, raise concerns and challenge decisions when evidence suggests risk may be emerging. Without this permission, signals detected at the operational level frequently dissipate before reaching decision forums.

Operational resilience therefore depends on two cultural conditions working together.

1. First, the organization must possess network depth, created through inclusion. Diverse teams broaden the range of experiences, perspectives and information sources available to decision makers.
2. Second, the organization must enable signal permission, created through psychological safety. Individuals must believe that raising uncomfortable information will not create personal or professional risk.

When these two conditions align, organizations gain several important capabilities.

FRONT-LOADING FRICTION

Challenger safety moves disagreement earlier in the decision cycle. Plans are tested before execution begins and potential weaknesses surface during design rather than during crisis response. This early friction improves execution speed because decisions move forward with greater clarity and shared understanding.

CONVERTING COPING INTO ADAPTATION

During disruption, organizations initially mobilize coping capacity: people work harder, redeploy resources and stabilize operations. Challenger safety allows organizations to move beyond coping towards adaptive capacity. Teams feel able to question whether existing processes remain fit for purpose and propose structural improvements rather than temporary fixes.

PRESERVING HUMAN RESILIENCE CAPITAL

Crisis environments place intense psychological pressure on individuals. When people believe they have permission to speak openly and act within defined boundaries, the personal risk associated with raising concerns declines. This protects engagement, motivation and collective energy, sustaining the human resources required for prolonged response and recovery.

Without challenger safety, organizations may still function during disruption. Individuals continue working, systems remain operational and decisions are implemented. Yet important signals often remain unspoken, reducing the organization's ability to detect emerging risks or adjust strategy in time.

Resilient organizations therefore treat psychological safety not as a cultural aspiration but as risk infrastructure. It determines whether the information necessary for resilience can travel through the organization when it matters most.

Psychological safety as risk infrastructure

Psychological safety supports resilience across the entire resilience cycle. It influences whether risks are surfaced, whether challenge occurs during decision-making, whether information flows during disruption and whether organizations learn effectively after recovery. These capabilities can be observed through practical governance indicators. Table 5.4 provides a simple way to assess whether psychological safety is effectively supporting resilience.

TABLE 5.4 Psychological safety as resilience infrastructure

Resilience capability	What it enables	Observable governance signals	Example metrics
Risk sensing	Early identification of emerging concerns and operational vulnerabilities	Frontline escalation occurs regularly; weak signals appear early in risk reports or incident logs	• Number of frontline escalations per quarter • Average time from issue identification to formal escalation • % of risk reports originating from operational teams
Debate quality	Decisions are tested before commitment through challenge and alternative views	Board and committee discussions include scenario analysis, dissenting perspectives or documented challenge	• % of major decisions supported by alternative scenario analysis • Number of documented challenge points in committee minutes • resence of red-team/ challenge sessions for strategic initiatives
Crisis transparency	Operational difficulties are communicated quickly during disruption	Incident reporting occurs early and information flows rapidly across teams and leadership	• Time between incident occurrence and first escalation • % of incidents self-reported vs externally detected • Number of cross-functional incident updates during crisis
Recovery learning	Organizations learn from disruption and improve systems rather than assign blame	Post-event reviews analyse system conditions, coordination and decision context rather than focusing solely on individual accountability	• % of incidents followed by formal lessons-learned review • Number of systemic recommendations vs individual corrective actions • Implementation rate of post-incident improvements

Board and executive implications

Culture is often treated as a secondary layer that sits above governance structures, risk frameworks and operational resilience planning. This chapter has shown that culture determines whether these structures function as intended. The quality of challenge, the movement of information, the willingness to escalate concerns and the level of engagement across the organization all influence whether resilience mechanisms operate effectively. For boards and senior leaders, this requires reframing culture as an operational capability rather than a soft organizational attribute.

For boards, this shifts attention from the existence of governance frameworks to the conditions that determine whether those frameworks operate effectively. Escalation processes, challenge mechanisms and risk reporting may appear robust, yet information asymmetry, cultural fatigue or a frozen middle can prevent critical signals from reaching decision makers with sufficient clarity and urgency. Oversight therefore extends beyond reviewing risk exposure. It requires understanding whether concerns are surfaced early, whether strategic decisions are genuinely challenged and whether lessons from disruption are translated into lasting organizational improvement.

For executive teams, resilience depends on creating an environment where challenge is expected, contribution is valued and operational strain is examined before it becomes a strategic constraint. Leadership behaviour influences whether emerging tensions are surfaced early, whether difficult trade-offs are discussed openly and whether engagement remains strong during periods of sustained pressure. This requires aligning incentives with transparency, protecting constructive challenge before crises occur and responding to mistakes in ways that encourage learning rather than defensiveness. Executive behaviour ultimately determines whether cultural expectations remain rhetorical or become embedded in operational practice.

For CROs and risk leaders, resilience depends on understanding how culture influences the reliability of the risk management system. Risk frameworks create visibility but they cannot ensure that concerns are raised, assumptions are challenged or lessons are adopted. This extends beyond monitoring control effectiveness. It includes assessing decision quality, patterns of escalation and the behavioural factors that influence how risk information is interpreted and acted upon. Monitoring signal lag, cultural fatigue and the adoption of lessons learnt can provide important indicators of resilience long before disruption becomes visible through traditional metrics.

Across all three groups, the common challenge is cultural activation. Resilient organizations create environments in which information can travel, challenge can occur and learning can be translated into action. They recognize that engagement, accountability and psychological safety are not cultural aspirations. They are operational capabilities that influence how effectively the organization can anticipate, absorb and adapt to disruption.

Practical playbook

Building cultural resilience requires more than establishing values and expectations. It requires creating the conditions in which information can move, challenge can occur and learning can be translated into action.

Boards

Boards influence resilience through the behaviours they scrutinize and the conditions they reinforce.

1 **Assess signal flow across the organization**
Look beyond risk reports and examine how concerns travel from operational teams to executive and board forums.

2 **Monitor challenge in strategic decisions**
Seek evidence that major decisions have been tested through alternative scenarios, documented challenge and critical debate.

3 **Review learning adoption**
Assess how quickly lessons from incidents, disruptions and near misses are translated into governance, process and operating model improvements.

Executives

Executive teams shape the cultural conditions that determine whether resilience mechanisms function effectively.

1 **Protect challenger safety**
Create decision environments where assumptions can be questioned and concerns raised before consequences become visible.

2 **Align incentives with transparency**
Reward the early identification of problems and avoid creating pressures that encourage suppression, delay or excessive optimism.

3 **Monitor cultural fatigue**
Pay attention to signs of declining initiative, reduced collaboration and increasing reliance on workarounds following periods of sustained pressure.

Chief risk officers and risk leaders

Risk leaders help ensure that culture strengthens rather than weakens the resilience system.

1 **Monitor information asymmetry**
Assess where operational realities differ materially from the picture presented through governance reporting.

2 **Diagnose the frozen middle**
Review how concerns are translated as they move through management layers and identify where challenge or escalation may be constrained.

3 **Integrate behavioural indicators into resilience oversight**
Monitor signal lag, escalation quality, learning adoption and psychological safety alongside traditional risk and control measures.

KEY TAKEAWAYS

- **Culture determines whether resilience mechanisms function as intended**. Governance frameworks, escalation pathways and crisis procedures provide the formal architecture of resilience. Their effectiveness depends on how individuals interpret risk, communicate uncertainty and respond under pressure.
- **The quality of resilience is shaped by behavioural dynamics throughout the resilience cycle**. Early risk sensing depends on whether individuals feel authorized to surface weak signals. Decision quality depends on whether dissent and alternative perspectives are encouraged. Crisis response depends on whether operational difficulties are communicated transparently. Learning depends on whether organizations examine systemic conditions rather than assigning individual blame.
- **The organizational middle layer is a critical transmission point**. Risk signals rarely move directly from operational teams to senior leadership. They pass through layers of management where incentives, career considerations and perceived expectations influence how information is

interpreted, translated and prioritized. Resilience weakens when challenge narrows and important signals lose significance before reaching decision makers.

- **Engagement is a resilience asset**. Resilience is not only a question of structural preparedness but also of human endurance. Teams that remain engaged and connected sustain the capacity to coordinate, improvise and adapt during prolonged periods of uncertainty. Cultural fatigue erodes this capacity long before performance visibly deteriorates.
- **Mature cultures convert disruption into institutional learning**. Organizations that treat stress as information rather than failure strengthen their adaptive capacity over time. Crises do not simply test resilience. They reveal weaknesses, generate insight and stimulate organizational improvement.
- **Resilience crystallizes at the intersection of governance design, leadership behaviour and cultural conditions**. Systems provide structure, yet culture determines whether those systems function when uncertainty and pressure intensify.

Reframing forward

This chapter examined resilience through the lens of culture and human behaviour. Organizational systems may define escalation pathways, governance forums and crisis procedures, yet the effectiveness of these mechanisms depends on the behavioural environment in which they operate.

Resilience weakens when cultural conditions discourage early signalling, stifle debate or filter information as it travels through the organization. In such environments, risks rarely remain invisible. They become progressively sanitized as they pass through layers of interpretation, incentives and perceived expectations.

The analysis highlighted how psychological safety and engagement shape the resilience cycle. These conditions influence whether emerging risks are detected early, whether decisions incorporate genuine challenge, whether crises are managed transparently and whether organizations convert disruption into learning. In that context, culture acts not as an overlay to governance design but as the medium through which governance functions.

Culture determines how resilience functions across an institution. Sustaining that resilience across a complex organization requires systems, controls and governance structures that reinforce those behaviours consistently over time.

The next chapter examines how these cultural and behavioural conditions interact with the broader organizational system. If culture determines how resilience functions in practice, the design of systems, controls and governance structures determines how that resilience is sustained at scale.

Together, culture and system design transform resilience from a reactive capability into an enduring organizational property.

Endnotes

1 Reason, J (1990) *Human Error*, Cambridge University Press, Cambridge
2 The Business Times (2025) Lufthansa 2024 profits dive amid strikes, rising costs, *The Business Times*, 6 March, www.businesstimes.com.sg/companies-markets/transport-logistics/lufthansa-2024-profits-dive-amid-strikes-rising-costs
3 Putnam, R D (2000) *Bowling Alone: The Collapse and Revival of American Community*, Simon & Schuster, New York
4 Dekker, S (2016) *Just Culture: Restoring Trust and Accountability in Your Organization* (3rd edn), CRC Press, Boca Raton, FL
5 Hollnagel, E (2014) *Safety-I and Safety-II: The Past and Future of Safety Management*, Ashgate, Farnham
6 Radjou, N, Prabhu, J and Ahuja, S (2012) *Jugaad Innovation: Think Frugal, Be Flexible, Generate Breakthrough Growth*, Jossey-Bass, San Francisco, CA
7 International Federation of Red Cross and Red Crescent Societies (IFRC) (2020) *Increasing the supply chain agility for personal protective equipment (PPE) during the COVID-19 pandemic response: A real-time case study*, IFRC, Geneva

PART THREE

Resilience by design

06

Defining strategic risk boundaries

How leaders balance growth, resilience and capital

CHAPTER OBJECTIVES

- Explain how strategic risk boundaries shape growth, capital allocation and organizational resilience.
- Clarify the relationship between risk capacity, risk appetite and risk tolerance.
- Align strategic ambition with organizational resilience under conditions of uncertainty.
- Equip leaders with practical tools to embed risk boundaries into governance and decision-making.
- Strengthen the connection between strategy, capital discipline and long-term sustainability.

There is a deceptive comfort in a strategic plan that moves without friction. When capital is plentiful and governance indicators remain green, momentum can be easily mistaken for resilience. Investment accelerates, initiatives multiply and performance metrics reinforce the sense that the organization is operating within safe limits. Until it does not.

In many organizations, strategic ambition expands faster than the organization's capacity to absorb disruption. Many organizations maintain detailed risk appetite statements and clearly defined escalation thresholds. These mechanisms, however, often sit at a distance from the strategic decisions that determine how much risk the organization actually takes. Yet the relationship between strategy, capital capacity and aggregate exposure often remains indistinct. Individual decisions appear rational from that distance but their combined effect gradually increases vulnerability.

The problem rarely lies in the absence of risk frameworks. It lies in the gap between formal risk frameworks and the organizational layers where strategic decisions are translated into operational commitments.

Resilient organizations close this gap. They ensure that strategic boundaries remain visible where strategy is translated into operational commitments, preventing organizational layers from absorbing risk in the background, to preserve the appearance of alignment.

This chapter builds on the leadership and cultural foundations developed in the previous section. Chapters 4 and 5 examined how authority distribution and organizational culture influence the movement of information and the quality of decision-making. Authority determines where decisions are taken. Culture determines whether signals reach those decisions in time. Strategic boundaries determine whether those decisions remain sustainable.

In practice, risk strategy shapes resilience across several dimensions of organizational activity. It influences:

- which risks are deliberately accepted in pursuit of strategic objectives
- how capital capacity constrains expansion and investment
- when escalating exposure requires leadership intervention
- how resilience investments balance efficiency with long-term stability.

Risk appetite is strategic architecture, not compliance

Risk appetite is widely referenced in governance frameworks yet rarely understood with precision. In many organizations, it is treated as a regulatory artefact rather than a strategic discipline. Boards approve appetite statements, metrics are monitored and reporting cycles confirm adherence to defined thresholds. The framework exists but its influence on strategic decision-making is often limited.

This disconnect is particularly visible in the treatment of non-financial risk. Financial risks are typically embedded directly in decision processes because they affect capital, liquidity and earnings. Non-financial risks are often managed differently. They are framed primarily through regulatory compliance and control frameworks, which can leave them detached from the strategic and operational decisions that actually generate exposure.

Part of the difficulty lies in a persistent confusion of terms. In many boardrooms, risk appetite, risk tolerance and risk capacity are used interchangeably even though they represent different concepts. Risk appetite reflects the level of risk leaders are willing to accept in pursuit of strategic objectives. Risk tolerance defines the limits within which operations must remain. Risk capacity represents the maximum loss or disruption the organization can absorb without threatening its viability.

When these distinctions blur, risk frameworks lose their strategic purpose. Resilient organizations treat risk appetite not as documentation but as architecture, defining the boundaries within which strategy can be pursued without compromising long-term stability.

A combination of institutional habits and misaligned incentives keeps this perception in place. For one, regulatory expectations require institutions to define and document risk appetite frameworks. In practice, this often positions the exercise as a governance obligation rather than a strategic design question. Organizations demonstrate that appetite has been defined, monitored and reported, yet the framework may remain distant from the decisions that determine how risk is actually taken.

The contrast between financial and non-financial risk illustrates this dynamic clearly. Financial risk is typically embedded in strategic and capital decisions because its consequences are immediate and measurable. Credit, market and liquidity exposures influence pricing, balance sheet management and investment strategy. Strategic choices therefore translate naturally into measurable exposures that can be calibrated through limits, capital buffers and risk appetite metrics.

Non-financial risks rarely benefit from the same translation. Organizational objectives and strategic choices are often not converted into the operational and governance constructs that generate exposure. For example, many organizations do not define an explicit outsourcing strategy in the first place. Outsourcing decisions are instead taken within procurement programmes, technology transformations or cost reduction initiatives, often without a shared view of the long-term operational dependencies being created. As a result, operational dependencies and concentration risks grow over time without being translated into calibrated exposure limits or meaningful risk tolerance thresholds.

In this context, non-financial risk frameworks often focus on managing regulatory exposure through control standards rather than managing the underlying risk exposure itself. Organizations prioritize compliance with frameworks such as DORA, yet the strategic choices that shape operational concentration, technology dependencies or third-party reliance may remain insufficiently articulated. Appetite and tolerance exist conceptually, but they remain difficult to operationalize because the underlying drivers of exposure are not explicitly connected to strategy.

Under these conditions, risk appetite remains visible in governance documentation but largely absent from strategic debate. Organizations continue to pursue opportunity while the limits that should guide those decisions remain indistinct.

This dynamic also reveals the limits of the improvisational behaviours discussed in the previous chapter. Improvisation can strengthen resilience in the face of disruption, yet it cannot substitute for deliberate organizational design. When strategic intent is not translated into clear operational guardrails, these local adjustments begin to shape the system itself. Procurement choices, technology decisions and supplier relationships evolve through practical necessity rather than through a coherent design. Each decision addresses an immediate constraint, yet the broader exposure created by those choices often remains only partially visible.

At this point, resilience begins to rely on adaptation rather than architecture. The problem is one of design: where is the organizational blueprint that translates strategic ambition into the operational reality of the enterprise?

Without that translation, strategy remains an expression of intent while the operational landscape evolves through incremental adjustments. Risk appetite then struggles to function as a meaningful boundary because the drivers of exposure have never been clearly articulated.

Reframing

Risk appetite is best understood as a mechanism of organizational design. It translates strategic ambition into practical boundaries that guide how decisions are taken across the organization. In this sense, risk appetite performs a governing role in strategy execution, influencing how opportunities are pursued, how capital is deployed and how exposure is managed as the organization grows.

Effective risk appetite frameworks do more than define acceptable levels of risk. They help leadership determine how quickly exposure may expand, how widely it may spread across the organization and when intervention becomes necessary.

In practice, risk appetite clarifies three critical questions:

1. Which risks are essential to achieving strategic objectives?
2. Which exposures must remain constrained in order to preserve resilience?
3. When does increasing exposure require leadership intervention?

Strategic risk boundaries therefore do more than define acceptable risk levels. They shape how organizations pursue growth while maintaining the capacity to withstand disruption. In resilient organizations, risk appetite does not sit alongside strategy; it defines the conditions under which strategy can succeed. This perspective aligns with the view that risk appetite functions as a strategic governance tool rather than a compliance artefact.[1]

PRACTITIONER PULSE

Risk appetite remains underused in strategic decisions

In a LinkedIn poll of risk and governance professionals,[2] 59 per cent indicated that risk appetite is used only in a limited way during strategic decision-making. A further 24 per cent reported consistent use, while 11 per cent stated selective use and 6 per cent indicated that risk appetite is not used at all.

The findings suggest that many organizations continue to view risk appetite primarily as a governance requirement rather than a practical decision-making tool. This aligns with the chapter's argument that risk appetite creates value when it shapes strategic choices, investment decisions and growth priorities rather than remaining confined to board papers and policy documents.

The rising cost of strategic misalignment

The external environment in which organizations operate has become significantly more volatile and interconnected. Strategic decisions now unfold within systems characterized by technological acceleration, geopolitical tension and increasingly complex regulatory expectations. These forces do not simply increase uncertainty. They also increase the consequences of strategic misalignment.

When organizations expand into new markets, adopt new technologies or restructure operating models, strategic decisions increasingly reshape the organization at speed. Competitive pressure encourages rapid expansion, transformation programmes accelerate change and leadership teams must often act with incomplete information. Each decision may appear justified when assessed individually. Yet without clearly defined risk boundaries, the combined effect of these choices can gradually shift the organization's overall exposure in ways that remain only partially visible.

In such environments, the absence of clearly defined risk boundaries creates a coordination problem for leadership. Strategic initiatives emerge simultaneously across multiple parts of the organization, each competing for capital, management attention and operational capacity. Without a shared understanding of acceptable exposure, decisions are evaluated primarily through local priorities rather than their combined impact on the organization's resilience.

The result is a governance model that reacts to disruption rather than guiding strategy before vulnerabilities emerge. In some cases, it goes further. By allowing strategic initiatives to expand without clearly defined boundaries, the governance system itself can unintentionally manufacture vulnerabilities that only become visible once disruption occurs.

In these conditions, governance can become reactive rather than anticipatory. Vulnerabilities remain embedded within the system until disruption reveals them. Resilience therefore becomes inseparable from strategic design. Organizations that navigate uncertainty successfully do so not by eliminating risk but by defining the boundaries within which risk taking can occur without compromising long-term stability.

Risk appetite provides the mechanism through which ambition, capacity and resilience remain aligned. It enables organizations to pursue growth while maintaining visibility over the exposure created by strategic decisions.

REAL-WORLD EXAMPLE

HSBC and the strategic calibration of climate exposure

As climate transition risks have moved from long-term policy debate to near-term financial reality, major financial institutions have faced increasing pressure to align lending strategies with evolving environmental constraints. For global banks, the challenge is not only reputational or regulatory – it is strategic. Decisions taken today about sector exposure may shape balance sheet resilience for decades.

HSBC provides an illustration of how climate considerations can be incorporated into risk appetite frameworks rather than treated solely as compliance commitments. In recent years, the bank has integrated climate transition factors into its strategic risk management, establishing parameters for exposure to carbon-intensive sectors while expanding financing for transition activities.

The scale of the challenge reflects HSBC's position in the global economy. In 2023, the group reported profit before tax of approximately $30.3 billion and total assets exceeding $3 trillion,[3] with lending relationships spanning energy, infrastructure and manufacturing sectors across Asia, Europe and the Americas. Many of these sectors are central to the global transition towards lower-carbon systems yet remain economically essential in the near term.

In response, HSBC committed to mobilizing up to $1 trillion in sustainable finance and investment by 2030,[4] alongside policies intended to gradually reduce exposure to certain high-emission activities such as thermal coal financing. These commitments required translating broad climate ambitions into operational risk boundaries that could guide lending decisions across a large and geographically diverse institution.

The leadership challenge involved balancing several competing priorities. Banks must support clients navigating complex industrial transitions while maintaining profitability in sectors that continue to generate significant demand for capital. At the same time, they must manage the possibility that certain assets may lose value as regulatory frameworks, technologies and market expectations evolve.

Under these conditions, climate risk appetite becomes a strategic calibration exercise rather than a static policy statement. Lending decisions increasingly incorporate assumptions about long-term asset viability, transition trajectories and sectoral exposure limits. The objective is not simply to satisfy supervisory expectations but to align the bank's long-term portfolio with structural shifts in the global economy.

HSBC's approach illustrates a broader shift in risk governance. When risk appetite frameworks incorporate emerging systemic risks, they begin to shape strategic positioning rather than merely constrain operational behaviour. Decisions about which sectors to finance, how quickly to adjust exposure and where to support transition investment become expressions of strategic risk boundaries.

The lesson is not that climate risk can be predicted with precision. Rather, it demonstrates how risk appetite can serve as a mechanism through which organizations translate uncertain long-term risks into present-day strategic discipline.

For financial institutions navigating structural change, the question is therefore not only how to measure emerging risks, it is how to decide, in advance, which exposures remain compatible with the future they expect to finance.

Aligning strategy with risk boundaries

Strategic resilience depends on the relationship between three concepts: risk capacity, risk appetite and risk tolerance. Together, they define the boundaries

FIGURE 6.1 Relationship between risk capacity, risk tolerance and risk appetite

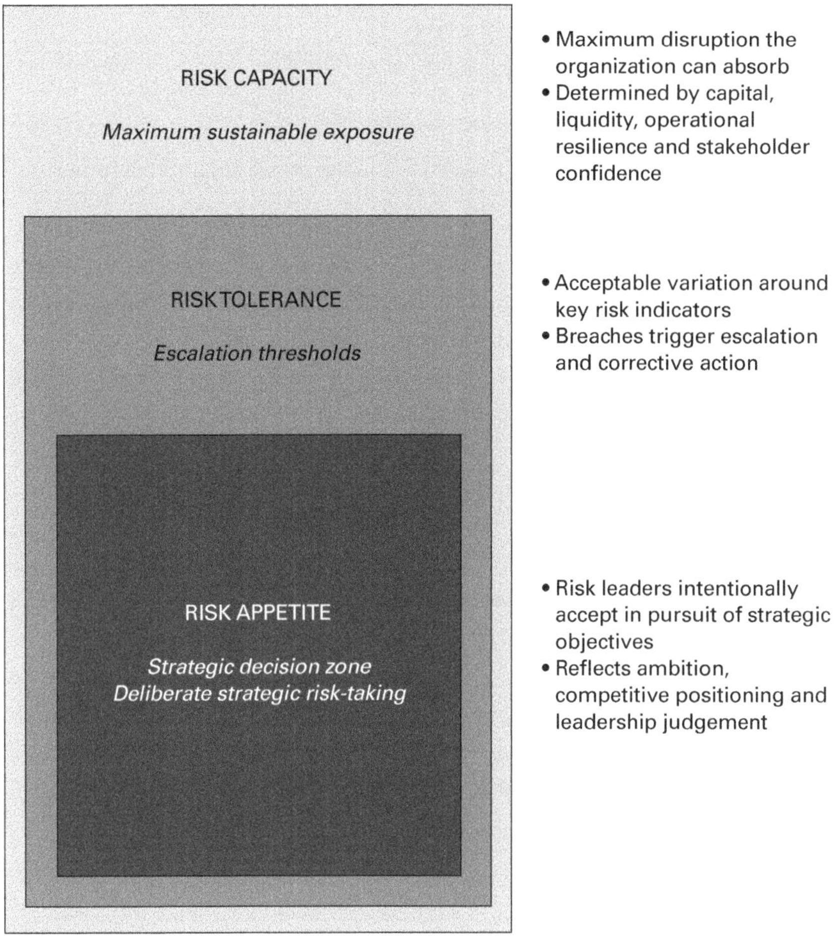

within which organizations pursue opportunity while maintaining the ability to withstand disruption. Figure 6.1 illustrates how these boundaries interact.

Risk capacity

Risk capacity represents the maximum level of loss or disruption an organization can absorb without threatening its viability. Unlike risk appetite, capacity is not a matter of leadership preference. It is determined by the structural characteristics of the organization and the constraints imposed by its operating environment.

Several dimensions of organizational resilience determine this boundary:

- capital strength and financial reserves
- liquidity and funding resilience
- operational resilience and system reliability
- stakeholder confidence, including regulators, investors and customers.

In regulated industries, risk capacity is also shaped by statutory or supervisory thresholds such as minimum capital or liquidity requirements. Breaching these limits may trigger regulatory intervention even before the organization reaches its true point of financial distress.

Risk capacity defines the outer limits of risk-taking beyond which financial stability, operational continuity or institutional legitimacy may be compromised.

In practice, organizations rarely fail because they misjudge a single risk. Failure occurs when cumulative exposure gradually exceeds the organization's underlying resilience. This threshold is often breached not by a single event but when multiple stresses occur simultaneously, placing pressure on financial resources, operational systems and stakeholder confidence at the same time.

For this reason, organizations frequently assess risk capacity through stress testing and scenario analysis designed to identify the point at which financial, operational or reputational resilience would begin to fail.

Risk appetite

Risk appetite reflects the level and types of risk leaders deliberately choose to accept in pursuit of strategic objectives. Unlike risk capacity, appetite is not determined by structural constraints. It is a matter of leadership judgement. It reflects how aggressively the organization intends to pursue opportunity and how much volatility it is prepared to tolerate along the way.

Risk appetite operates within the limits defined by capacity. While capacity defines the outer boundary of organizational resilience, appetite determines how much of that resilience leaders are willing to deploy in pursuit of strategic goals.

This choice has direct implications for resilience. Organizations with a conservative appetite preserve larger buffers to absorb unexpected shocks. Organizations with a more aggressive appetite deploy a greater portion of their risk capacity in pursuit of growth, innovation or market share. Neither approach is inherently superior. The critical question is whether leadership understands the resilience margin it is consuming when strategic risk-taking increases.

Risk appetite is shaped by several strategic considerations:

- the ambition embedded in the organization's strategy
- competitive positioning within the market
- leadership confidence in the organization's capabilities
- tolerance for earnings volatility, reputational exposure and operational complexity.

For executives, defining risk appetite involves confronting several practical questions:

- How much volatility can the organization sustain without undermining long-term strategy?
- How much of the organization's underlying resilience should be preserved for unexpected disruption?
- Which risks are essential to achieving strategic objectives and which should remain constrained?

In this sense, risk appetite expresses the organization's strategic posture towards uncertainty. It determines whether leaders pursue growth cautiously, opportunistically or aggressively while remaining within the resilience limits the organization can safely sustain.

When clearly articulated and consistently applied, risk appetite allows organizations to pursue opportunity deliberately rather than drifting into exposure through incremental decisions that gradually erode resilience.

Risk appetite is not static. As strategy evolves, market conditions shift or organizational capabilities mature, leadership may recalibrate the level of risk the organization is prepared to accept.

While risk appetite expresses strategic intent, it becomes operational only when translated into measurable tolerance thresholds that guide day-to-day decision-making.

Risk tolerance

Risk tolerance defines the operational thresholds that trigger escalation or corrective action. Table 6.1 shows how the position of middle managers differs across organizational layers.

TABLE 6.1 Strategic questions for calibrating risk-taking

Dimension	Strategic question
Risk capacity	What losses can the organization absorb without threatening viability?
Risk appetite	What risks are worth taking in order to achieve the strategy?
Risk tolerance	When must leaders intervene to prevent exposure from exceeding acceptable limits?

While appetite operates at the strategic level, tolerance translates that intent into practical decision discipline. It establishes measurable boundaries within which day-to-day activities must remain.

Tolerance thresholds therefore serve two important governance functions. They provide early warning when exposure begins to approach strategic limits and they define the point at which leadership intervention becomes necessary.

In this sense, risk tolerance plays a critical role in preserving organizational resilience. By triggering corrective action before exposures approach the organization's capacity limits, tolerance thresholds protect the resilience buffers that allow the organization to absorb unexpected shocks.

Without clearly defined tolerance thresholds, risk appetite remains conceptual rather than operational. Strategic ambition may encourage risk-taking, yet the mechanisms required to prevent exposure from gradually eroding resilience remain unclear.

Strategic alignment model

Resilient organizations maintain continuous alignment between capacity, appetite and tolerance. These three elements taken together define the boundaries within which strategy can be executed safely (see Table 6.1).

When these elements remain aligned, organizations can pursue strategic opportunity while maintaining resilience. Misalignment between them creates systemic vulnerability.

An organization may pursue strategic initiatives that exceed its underlying capacity. Appetite statements may encourage growth that tolerance thresholds fail to constrain. Or operational indicators may signal rising exposure long before governance mechanisms respond. In each case, the result is the same. The organization continues to pursue strategy while gradually drifting beyond the limits it can safely sustain.

Strategic resilience therefore depends not only on defining these concepts but on maintaining alignment between them as strategy evolves and external conditions change.

Balancing growth, resilience and capital

Every strategic decision involves trade-offs. Leaders continuously balance three competing forces: growth ambition, resilience buffers and capital efficiency.

Expanding resilience buffers often requires investments that reduce short-term financial efficiency. Additional redundancy, diversified supply chains, stronger liquidity reserves or more robust technology infrastructure all impose costs that may appear difficult to justify during stable periods.

Conversely, strategies that prioritize rapid growth or capital optimization may reduce the margin available to absorb disruption. Organizations that operate with minimal redundancy, concentrated suppliers or highly leveraged balance sheets can achieve impressive short-term performance while gradually eroding their risk capacity and resilience buffers.

The tension between growth, resilience and efficiency is not a technical problem but a leadership challenge. Effective executives recognize that these forces cannot be optimized simultaneously. Increasing resilience may reduce short-term returns. Pursuing aggressive growth may increase exposure to shocks. Maximizing capital efficiency may reduce the organization's ability to absorb unexpected disruption.

Strategic resilience emerges when these trade-offs are managed deliberately rather than implicitly. Leaders must decide how much organizational resilience to preserve, how aggressively to deploy resources in pursuit of opportunity and when additional investment in resilience becomes a strategic advantage rather than a cost. The governance mechanisms through which organizations manage these trade-offs are explored later in the book.

REAL-WORLD EXAMPLE

Microsoft: The return on resilience investment

In the years preceding the Covid-19 pandemic, Microsoft invested heavily in cloud infrastructure, cybersecurity capabilities and global data centre capacity. These investments required substantial capital expenditure and initially appeared expensive relative to short-term revenue growth.

Between 2016 and 2019, Microsoft significantly expanded its global cloud infrastructure, building one of the largest hyperscale data centre networks in the world. Capital expenditure increased steadily as the company prioritized long-term platform resilience, redundancy and scalability.

At the time, these investments were primarily justified by the anticipated growth of cloud computing. Their full strategic value became evident only when the Covid-19 pandemic accelerated remote work and digital collaboration across the global economy.

During 2020, the use of Microsoft Teams alone grew from approximately 20 million daily active users in late 2019 to more than 75 million by April 2020. Demand for cloud infrastructure and digital collaboration tools surged as organizations worldwide transitioned rapidly to remote operations.

This surge translated directly into financial performance. Microsoft's Azure cloud revenue grew by approximately 50 per cent year-on-year in fiscal 2020, reflecting the rapid expansion of enterprise cloud adoption during the pandemic.[5]

Microsoft's existing infrastructure allowed platforms such as Azure, Teams and Office 365 to scale rapidly in response to this sudden increase in demand. While many organizations struggled to adapt their systems and processes to the new environment, Microsoft's prior investments in resilient digital infrastructure enabled it not only to maintain service continuity but also to capture significant market opportunity.

The investments that had previously appeared conservative or costly suddenly became a decisive strategic advantage.

In the years preceding the pandemic, these investments were not universally viewed as obvious strategic priorities. Large-scale infrastructure expansion and cybersecurity capabilities required sustained capital expenditure at a time when technology companies faced continuing pressure to deliver short-term financial performance and shareholder returns. In stable conditions, investments that strengthen resilience can appear costly relative to more immediately profitable uses of capital.

Three conclusions can be drawn:

1. Resilience investments often appear inefficient during stable periods.
2. Their benefits become visible primarily during disruption.
3. Organizations with resilient infrastructure can capture opportunity while others struggle to adapt.

When resilience functions effectively, it often remains invisible. Systems continue operating, disruptions are absorbed and stakeholders experience continuity rather than crisis. As a result, the value created by resilience investments can be difficult to perceive.

This asymmetry of perception mirrors a familiar theme in risk management. Effective controls and safeguards prevent failures that never materialize, making their contribution easy to underestimate. Only when resilience mechanisms are absent or insufficient does their importance become fully visible.

Resilience produces asymmetric returns. It protects organizations against downside risk while simultaneously enabling disproportionate upside when disruption reshapes competitive conditions.

Human and cultural dynamics

Even well-designed governance frameworks can fail if behavioural dynamics undermine them. Risk capacity, appetite and tolerance may be clearly defined on paper, yet their effectiveness ultimately depends on how individuals interpret, communicate and respond to emerging signals within the organization.

With that in mind, resilience depends not only on the design of risk frameworks but also on the organizational behaviours that sustain them under stress. In practice, three recurring distortions frequently weaken the alignment between strategy and risk boundaries.

Growth bias

Strategic success can gradually distort organizational judgement. As revenue expands and market opportunities multiply, leadership attention often shifts towards capturing growth rather than preserving resilience buffers.

In such environments, risk appetite may expand incrementally without deliberate reassessment. Strategic initiatives accumulate, operational complexity increases and exposure rises across multiple dimensions of the organization. Because performance indicators remain positive, these shifts may appear justified in the short term.

Over time, however, the organization may find that its strategic ambitions have outpaced the underlying resilience required to support them.

Silence around limits

Even when risk boundaries are clearly defined, employees may hesitate to challenge initiatives that appear successful or strategically important. Teams responsible for delivering ambitious programmes often face strong incentives to demonstrate progress and avoid signalling difficulty. Raising concerns about capacity constraints, operational strain or emerging vulnerabilities can therefore feel personally risky.

As a result, early warning signals may remain unspoken or may be communicated in moderated form. Indicators that should trigger strategic reconsideration are interpreted as temporary operational challenges rather than as signs that the organization is approaching its limits.

When this occurs, the organization loses the informational feedback required to maintain alignment between strategy and resilience. Signals that should inform leadership decisions never fully reach the governance system.

Escalation distortion

In other cases, the problem does not lie in silence but in escalation. Early warning signals may be recognized locally, yet formal risk thresholds and escalation procedures prove difficult to activate. Managers responsible for major initiatives may hesitate to escalate breaches that could delay projects or attract senior scrutiny.

Tolerance thresholds are treated as flexible guidelines rather than meaningful boundaries. Breaches may be explained, deferred or temporarily managed until their cumulative impact becomes impossible to ignore.

By the time escalation occurs, the organization may already be operating beyond the limits it intended to respect. Governance mechanisms that were designed to prevent excessive exposure shift instead into reactive containment.

Board and executive implications

Risk appetite, tolerance and capacity are often presented as technical components of a risk framework. In practice, they are decision-making mechanisms. They determine how organizations balance ambition against resilience and how leaders recognize when strategic exposure is approaching unsafe levels.

For boards, the challenge is ensuring that risk boundaries influence strategic decisions rather than simply documenting them. Approval of a risk appetite statement is only the starting point. Effective oversight requires understanding whether strategic initiatives, capital allocation decisions and major investments remain consistent with the organization's capacity to absorb disruption. The key question is not whether risk boundaries exist but whether they are shaping the decisions that matter most.

For executive teams, the focus is calibration. Growth, innovation and transformation inevitably consume organizational resilience. Leaders must therefore make conscious choices about which risks are necessary to achieve strategic objectives and which exposures should remain constrained. Resilience weakens when appetite expands incrementally without a corresponding reassessment of capacity and operational limits.

For CROs and risk leaders, the challenge is maintaining the integrity of the relationship between capacity, appetite and tolerance. Risk frameworks create visibility, yet visibility alone does not influence outcomes. Appetite must be translated into meaningful thresholds, escalation mechanisms and governance discussions that influence day-to-day decisions. When tolerance breaches become normalized or escalation processes lose credibility, risk boundaries gradually lose authority.

Across all three groups, the common challenge is alignment. Resilient organizations ensure that strategic ambition, organizational resilience and operational decision-making remain connected. They recognize that risk appetite is not a compliance requirement or a reporting framework. It is a strategic discipline that guides how resilience is allocated in pursuit of long-term objectives.

Practical playbook

Embedding risk capacity, appetite and tolerance requires more than documenting risk boundaries. Leaders must ensure these concepts influence strategic choices, capital allocation and day-to-day decision-making.

Boards

Boards establish the boundaries within which strategic risk-taking occurs.

1 **Align risk appetite explicitly with strategic objectives**
Ensure risk appetite clearly reflects the organization's strategic priorities and identifies which risks are necessary to achieve them.

2 **Define unacceptable exposures alongside acceptable risks**
Clarify which exposures are incompatible with long-term resilience, even when they appear commercially attractive.

3 **Require regular reporting on proximity to risk capacity**
Seek visibility over how strategic initiatives, major investments and operational dependencies collectively consume organizational resilience.

Executives

Executive teams are responsible for translating strategic intent into operational decisions.

1 **Translate risk appetite into measurable exposure indicators**
Define indicators that demonstrate how strategic initiatives affect financial, operational and organizational exposure.

2 **Integrate risk appetite into capital allocation decisions**
Evaluate major investments, acquisitions and transformation programmes in terms of both expected value and resilience consumption.

3 **Monitor cumulative exposure across strategic initiatives**
Assess how multiple initiatives interact and whether combined exposure is approaching organizational limits.

Chief risk officers and risk leaders

Risk leaders help maintain alignment between strategic ambition and organizational resilience.

1 **Convert risk appetite frameworks into decision-support tools**
Ensure appetite frameworks inform strategic reviews, investment discussions and transformation governance.

2 **Identify emerging breaches before thresholds are crossed**
Use leading indicators and trend analysis to detect emerging exposure before formal tolerance limits are exceeded.

3 **Maintain independence in escalation processes**
Maintain the independence and credibility required to escalate concerns when strategic momentum begins to outpace resilience.

KEY TAKEAWAYS

- **Risk appetite is a strategic discipline**. Its purpose is not to satisfy governance requirements but to guide how organizations pursue opportunity while preserving resilience.
- **Capacity, appetite and tolerance perform different functions**. Capacity defines what the organization can absorb. Appetite defines what leaders choose to accept. Tolerance defines when intervention becomes necessary.
- **Strategic growth consumes resilience**. Expansion, transformation and innovation all draw upon organizational capacity. Effective leadership requires conscious decisions about how much resilience is allocated in pursuit of strategic objectives.
- **Risk boundaries fail through behaviour as much as design**. Growth bias, silence around limits and distorted escalation processes can gradually weaken the authority of risk frameworks even when governance structures appear robust.
- **Resilience depends on maintaining alignment**. Strategic ambition, organizational capacity and operational thresholds must remain connected as conditions evolve. Misalignment often develops gradually before becoming visible through disruption.
- **Risk appetite becomes meaningful only when it influences decisions**. Organizations strengthen resilience when risk boundaries shape strategy, capital allocation and operational choices before exposure becomes visible.

Reframing forward

This chapter examined resilience through the lens of strategic boundaries. Risk capacity defines what the organization can absorb. Risk appetite reflects the level of uncertainty leaders deliberately choose to accept. Risk tolerance translates that choice into operational discipline.

Together, these mechanisms help organizations balance ambition and resilience. Yet their effectiveness depends less on how clearly they are defined than on how consistently they influence decisions. Risk boundaries rarely fail because they are absent. They fail when they lose visibility, authority or relevance within the governance process.

This creates an important question. If strategic resilience depends on maintaining alignment between capacity, appetite and tolerance, how can organizations ensure that alignment survives changing priorities, competing interests and increasing complexity?

The next chapter examines governance as the mechanism through which strategic boundaries remain visible, debated and actionable. Because resilience depends not only on where limits are set but on how organizations ensure those limits continue to influence decision-making as conditions evolve.

Endnotes

1 Haye, J (2025) From Approval to Impact: Repositioning risk appetite as a board tool, *Aevitium Insights*, www.aevitium.com
2 Haye, J (2026) Using Risk Appetite in Decisions, LinkedIn poll, 12 March, www.linkedin.com/feed/update/urn:li:activity:7437750764053151744
3 HSBC Holdings plc (2024) *Annual Report and Accounts 2023*, HSBC Holdings plc, London, www.hsbc.com/investors/results-and-announcements
4 HSBC (2024) *HSBC Sustainability Report 2023*, HSBC Holdings plc, London, www.hsbc.com/who-we-are/sustainability
5 Microsoft Corporation (2020) *Microsoft Annual Report 2020*, Microsoft Corporation, Redmond, WA, www.microsoft.com/investor

07

Governance that adapts

Embedding foresight and alignment across the enterprise

> CHAPTER OBJECTIVES
>
> - Explain how governance systems translate strategic risk boundaries into everyday organizational decisions.
> - Align boards, executives and operational leaders around shared visibility of organizational exposure.
> - Strengthen escalation pathways so emerging pressures reach decision makers before exposure accumulates.
> - Integrate governance, planning and capital allocation to maintain alignment between strategic ambition and organizational capacity.

Boards do not approve strategies intended to create fragility. Yet organizations routinely accumulate exposures that leadership never consciously intended to accept.

Most organizations possess extensive governance structures. The critical issue is whether those structures maintain alignment between strategic decisions, operational realities and emerging exposure as conditions evolve. Signals about emerging stressors may exist across multiple functions. Risk reports circulate through committees, operational teams raise concerns and performance indicators highlight developing constraints. Yet these signals do not always reach the forums where strategic decisions are made.

When this occurs, governance continues to operate procedurally while the connection between strategy, risk and execution gradually erodes.

Strategic initiatives expand, operational complexity increases and the organization's risk profile evolves in ways that remain difficult to interpret at leadership level. Data is abundant, yet its decision relevance often dissipates as it moves upward through organizational layers.

This chapter examines governance from a different perspective. Rather than treating governance as a system designed primarily to monitor management behaviour, it reframes governance as the infrastructure through which organizations maintain alignment between three critical realities: strategic ambition, enterprise exposure and operational execution. As they grow, their strategies evolve and their operating environments become more volatile.

If risk appetite defines the strategic boundaries within which organizations pursue opportunity, governance determines whether those limits remain visible because resilience depends not only on defining boundaries; it depends on ensuring that decisions continue to respect them.

Governance is alignment infrastructure

Governance is commonly understood as a system designed to monitor management and ensure compliance with defined policies[1], standards and regulatory expectations. Boards establish committees, reporting cycles are defined and assurance functions review whether activities remain within the said approved boundaries. From this perspective, governance fulfils a supervisory role. It observes organizational activity, verifies that controls operate as intended and escalates concerns when not.

This interpretation reflects the way governance frameworks have historically evolved. In many sectors, governance structures expanded in response to corporate failures, financial reporting scandals and regulatory reforms. Oversight mechanisms were strengthened to ensure transparency, accountability and formal compliance with external obligations. The resulting structures emphasized monitoring functions such as audit, risk reporting and internal control reviews.

These mechanisms remain essential. They provide the discipline that allows organizations to demonstrate accountability and maintain the confidence of regulators, investors and stakeholders. Oversight and assurance therefore represent a necessary foundation of governance. However, they do not by themselves ensure that organizational decisions remain aligned with strategic intent.

Why this assumption persists

The persistence of the oversight model reflects both regulatory influence and institutional habit. Regulatory frameworks often require evidence that organizations maintain clear reporting lines, documented controls and independent assurance functions. Boards therefore devote considerable attention to demonstrating that these mechanisms operate effectively.

Over time, governance discussions become anchored around familiar artefacts: committee structures, dashboards, risk registers and compliance attestations. These instruments provide visibility into whether policies are followed and whether defined limits are respected. They allow leadership to confirm that governance processes are functioning as designed.

Yet this emphasis can gradually shift the centre of gravity of governance activity. Attention concentrates on verifying that the organization complies with established procedures rather than on examining whether strategic decisions remain coherent when considered across the enterprise. Reporting cycles multiply, committees expand and governance documentation grows increasingly detailed. The organization appears thoroughly governed, even as the relationship between strategy, risk exposure and operational activity becomes less visible.

Reframing governance

Effective governance performs a broader function than supervision alone. Beyond observation, its purpose is to ensure that decision-making remains aligned with strategic boundaries established by leadership. As we have seen in Chapter 6, risk appetite defines those boundaries by clarifying the level of exposure an organization is willing and able to accept in pursuit of its objectives.

In practice, governance connects three organizational realities that continuously evolve as the organization operates, as shown in Figure 7.1.

Each of these dimensions develops through different organizational channels. Strategy is set at the board level, risk accumulates through daily decisions and operations are executed by distributed teams.

Governance provides the connective architecture that allows these dimensions to remain coherent. It ensures that strategic ambition reflects the organization's capacity to absorb risk, that emerging exposure becomes visible to leadership and that operational decisions remain consistent with the boundaries defined at the strategic level.

FIGURE 7.1 The governance alignment triangle

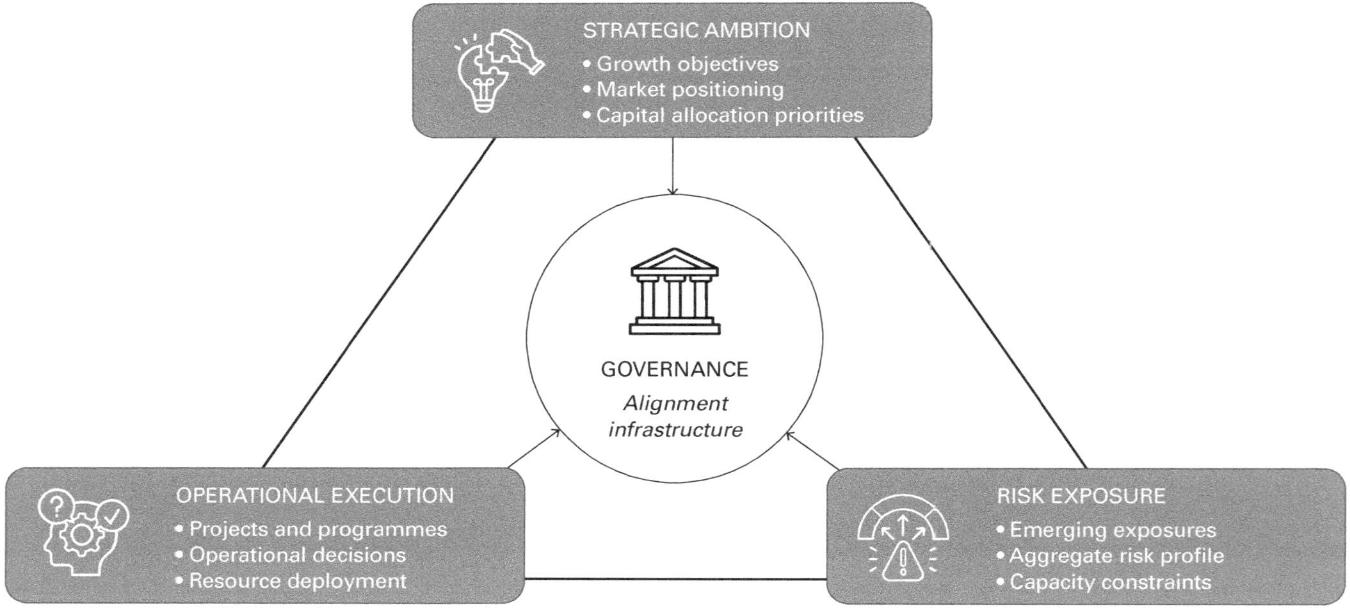

Governance maintains alignment between strategic ambition, operational execution and risk exposure as decisions accumulate across the enterprise.

Seen from this perspective, governance operates as organizational infrastructure. Like financial systems or information networks, it supports the continuous movement of signals and alignment with the strategic direction across the enterprise. It enables leaders to understand how individual decisions interact and how their cumulative effect influences the organization's resilience.

The consequences of weakened alignment

Effective governance maintains alignment between strategic ambition, risk exposure and operational execution. As long as these dimensions remain connected, leadership retains a clear view of how strategic decisions translate into cumulative exposure across the enterprise.

Strategic priorities evolve, operational activity expands and external conditions shift. In that context, governance must function as connective infrastructure that continually reconciles these dynamics.

When governance loses its connective function, several recurring symptoms tend to appear. These signals rarely emerge simultaneously, yet together they indicate that governance structures are operating in form while weakening in function (see Table 7.1).

As governance drifts from its purpose, the connection between strategic intent and operational reality becomes progressively weaker. As a result, organizations gradually commit resources to initiatives that exceed their capacity to manage growing exposure or sustain operational complexity. Governance does not necessarily permit obviously poor decisions. Instead, it allows a sequence of individual decisions that appear rational, to produce an outcome that is strategically inconsistent in aggregate.

Over time the gap between strategic intent and operational reality widens. Growth initiatives, transformation programmes, technology investments and cost reduction efforts begin to compete for the same resources and management attention. By the time leadership recognizes the resulting exposure, the organization may already have committed significant resources, capital and reputation to paths that are difficult to reverse.

Resilient organizations seek to prevent this form of drift. They design governance systems that preserve alignment between ambition, exposure and execution as conditions evolve. In doing so, they transform governance from a structure that monitors behaviour into one that continuously maintains strategic coherence across the enterprise.

TABLE 7.1 Signals of governance drift

Governance symptom	How it appears in practice	Implication
Retrospective focus	Boards and committees encounter risk primarily through reporting cycles that describe exposure after operational commitments have already been made. Governance explains outcomes rather than influencing the decisions that created them.	Governance becomes reactive rather than strategic.
Process over strategic coherence	Governance discussions concentrate on whether policies have been followed, reports have been produced and procedures respected. Compliance remains visible while the cumulative impact of strategic and operational decisions receives less scrutiny.	Formal compliance increases while strategic alignment weakens.
Information filtering*	Operational signals are summarized, aggregated and interpreted before reaching leadership forums. Large volumes of governance information circulate but clarity about emerging exposure diminishes.	Leadership visibility deteriorates despite extensive reporting.
Shadow decision-making	Critical choices are increasingly shaped through informal discussions, preparatory meetings or executive networks before formal committees convene. Governance forums become venues for confirmation rather than deliberation.	Formal governance structures lose influence over real decisions.

* Morrison, E (2014) Employee Voice and Silence, *Annual Review of Organizational Psychology*

Governance in an era of volatility

The effectiveness of governance systems has always depended on their ability to maintain alignment between strategic intent and organizational activity. In recent years, however, the conditions under which governance must operate have changed significantly. Strategic environments have become more volatile, regulatory expectations have expanded and organizational structures have grown increasingly complex.

These shifts place greater pressure on governance systems to ensure that leadership retains a coherent view of enterprise exposure as decisions accumulate across the organization.

Technological disruption, geopolitical instability and supply chain fragility have increased the pace at which organizations must adapt their strategic priorities. Investment cycles are shorter, competitive landscapes evolve rapidly and external shocks can alter operating conditions with little warning.

Governance structures designed for more stable environments often struggle to keep pace with this level of change. Decision cycles accelerate, while governance processes continue to operate according to established reporting rhythms and committee structures. What becomes harder to see is how these decisions interact once they begin competing for the same resources, management attention and operational capacity.

At the same time, supervisory expectations have shifted towards forward-looking oversight.[2] Regulators increasingly expect boards to demonstrate that they understand how emerging risks could affect the organization's resilience under different scenarios.

This expectation is reflected in supervisory frameworks such as stress testing regimes, operational resilience requirements and supervisory review processes. These mechanisms require organizations to examine how strategic choices interact with capital capacity, operational dependencies and external shocks.

The emphasis moves beyond retrospective reporting towards anticipatory governance. Boards are expected not only to monitor risk exposure but to demonstrate that governance structures enable them to recognize emerging vulnerabilities before they materialize.

A further challenge arises from the increasing complexity of modern organizations. Many enterprises now operate through distributed leadership structures, global supply chains and interconnected operational systems. Strategic initiatives are implemented simultaneously across multiple business units, geographic markets and technology platforms.

Under these conditions, the organization's overall risk profile takes shape through the interaction of many separate decisions rather than from a single strategic choice. Without governance mechanisms that integrate these signals, visibility of enterprise exposure can fragment across organizational silos.

Maintaining the connection between decisions and exposure therefore becomes significantly more difficult. Governance must not only oversee organizational activity but also reconcile decisions taken across multiple layers of the enterprise.

REAL-WORLD EXAMPLE

Portugal's fiscal governance reforms and policy alignment

The European sovereign debt crisis exposed weaknesses in the fiscal governance of several euro area countries, including Portugal. Years of expanding public expenditure and rising debt had gradually weakened the connection between fiscal policy decisions and long-term sustainability.

In response, Portugal implemented reforms aimed at strengthening the institutional framework governing fiscal decision-making. These included the creation of the Portuguese Public Finance Council to provide independent fiscal oversight,[3] closer integration with European fiscal governance mechanisms and improved transparency in the reporting of public finances.

These measures did more than increase monitoring. They strengthened the discipline applied to fiscal policy decisions by ensuring that budget proposals, spending commitments and economic forecasts were examined against the country's long-term fiscal capacity.

The effect was to reinforce alignment between policy ambition and fiscal sustainability.[4]

Governance reforms strengthen resilience when they ensure that strategic decisions remain consistent with the system's capacity to absorb risk, not when they merely expand oversight mechanisms.

The adaptive governance architecture

Resilient organizations rely on governance systems that remain capable of maintaining alignment as strategic priorities evolve and operational decisions accumulate across the enterprise.

This requires governance to function as an adaptive architecture rather than a fixed hierarchy of oversight bodies. Its purpose is to connect the layers of leadership through which strategic intent is translated into operational action.

In practice, governance connects three broad leadership layers. Boards establish strategic direction and define the boundaries within which strategic ambition must remain. Executive leadership translates those boundaries into organizational priorities, investment decisions and resource allocation choices. Operational leadership converts those priorities into day-to-day decisions while signalling emerging pressures that may challenge strategic assumptions.

The resilience of the governance system depends not only on the presence of these layers but on the mechanisms that connect them. Strategic intent must travel downward with sufficient clarity to guide decision-making. Equally, operational signals must travel upward with sufficient speed and accuracy to challenge assumptions when conditions change.

Three mechanisms, shown in Figure 7.2, are particularly important.

When these mechanisms function effectively, governance operates as a dynamic system of alignment loops. Strategic direction informs enterprise priorities, operational signals influence leadership decisions and exposure remains visible as the organization evolves.

Governance therefore becomes more than a hierarchy of approvals. It becomes the architecture through which organizations continuously reconcile ambition, exposure and execution.

PRACTITIONER PULSE

Governance friction often emerges through decision flow[5]

In a LinkedIn poll of risk and governance professionals, 52 per cent identified decision flow as the area where governance creates the greatest friction. Committee cycles received 20 per cent of responses, while alignment and escalation each accounted for less than 14 per cent. The findings suggest that governance challenges often arise less from formal oversight structures and more from the speed and clarity with which decisions move across the organization.

FIGURE 7.2 The mechanisms of adaptive governance

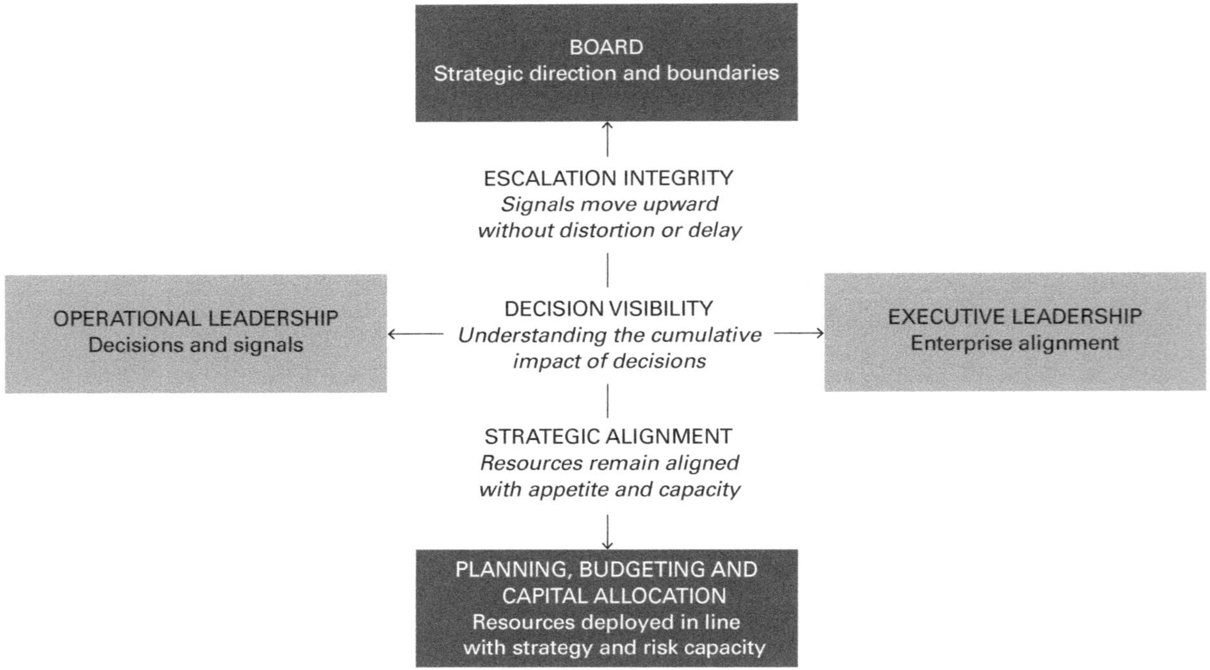

Why governance systems drift

The presence of the governance structures like reporting or committees does not guarantee that governance effectively functions. Over time, layered committees and reporting mechanisms can blur accountability[6] or create the appearance of oversight without strengthening the connection between strategic intent and operational decisions.

As governance systems become more complex and layered, it becomes harder for information, accountability and decisions to reach the right place in an organization. Under these conditions, the effectiveness of governance increasingly depends on the behaviours through which information is interpreted, decisions are challenged and risks are escalated.

When these behaviours shift, governance may continue to operate procedurally while losing its ability to maintain strategic alignment.

Several recurring dynamics contribute to governance drift. These dynamics do not necessarily appear simultaneously but together they can weaken the effectiveness of governance structures over time (see Table 7.2).

TABLE 7.2 Behavioural dynamics that contribute to governance drift

Governance dynamic	How it appears in practice	Effect on governance
Information filtering	Risk signals are summarized, softened or delayed as they move upward through organizational layers. Managers may attempt to resolve issues locally before escalating them.*	Leadership receives incomplete or delayed signals, reducing the ability to intervene early.
Incentive pressure	Performance frameworks emphasizing growth, efficiency or short-term results discourage escalation of emerging risks.	Individuals become reluctant to highlight constraints that may slow strategic initiatives.
Committee overload	Additional committees and oversight forums are created in response to emerging risks.	Decision authority becomes fragmented and governance discussions circulate without clear resolution.
Authority ambiguity	Boundaries between board oversight, executive authority and risk function responsibilities become unclear.	Uncertainty about decision rights weakens accountability for critical decisions.

* Detert, J and Edmondson, A (2011) Implicit Voice Theories: Taken-for-granted rules of self-censorship at work, *Academy of Management Journal*

Resilient organizations recognize that governance effectiveness depends as much on adaptation as on structure. Governance maturity is not a fixed condition. As organizational strategies evolve, operating environments become more volatile and institutional complexity increases, governance frameworks must evolve accordingly while continuing to fulfil their primary objectives.

Rather than relying solely on established structures, resilient organizations periodically reassess whether their governance architecture continues to support decision visibility, escalation integrity and strategic alignment. These reviews often occur as part of annual governance effectiveness assessments, strategic planning cycles or following significant organizational change. They clarify authority as organizational structures change, ensure escalation pathways remain credible under operational pressure and adapt governance forums so that strategic decisions are examined with a clear view of enterprise exposure.

In doing so, governance becomes a living system rather than a static framework. Its purpose is not only to supervise organizational activity but to ensure that leadership retains the capacity to reconcile ambition, exposure and execution as conditions evolve.

REAL-WORLD EXAMPLE

Sony's governance transformation and the restoration of strategic discipline

During the past decade, Sony has faced several episodes that exposed weaknesses in the relationship between governance, risk oversight and strategic decision-making. Cyber incidents, operational disruptions and periods of financial underperformance raised questions about the effectiveness of the company's governance structure and its ability to respond to complex risks in a rapidly changing technology environment.

In response, Sony undertook a significant transformation of its governance framework.[7] The company strengthened the independence of its board by increasing the number of external directors and reinforcing the role of board committees responsible for oversight of audit, risk and compensation. At the same time, executive accountability was clarified so that strategic and operational decisions could be examined against clearly defined responsibilities.

A further objective of these reforms was to improve the connection between risk oversight and strategic management. Rather than treating risk as a separate compliance function, Sony sought to integrate risk considerations more directly into strategic discussions[8] and business planning processes.

These changes reflected a broader shift in how governance was expected to operate. The objective was not simply tighter control over management activity but stronger alignment between strategic ambition, operational execution and the organization's ability to manage emerging risks.

The result was a governance structure better equipped to support strategic clarity during periods of disruption. Greater independence at board level strengthened challenge and oversight, while clearer executive accountability improved the organization's capacity to translate strategic priorities into coordinated action.

Sony's experience illustrates an important governance principle. Governance reforms create resilience not merely by increasing oversight but by strengthening the connection between leadership decisions, organizational exposure and the structures responsible for managing risk.

In this sense, governance design shapes how effectively an organization can respond to disruption. When governance structures reinforce alignment between strategy, exposure and execution, leadership retains the ability to adapt as conditions change.

Board and executive implications

Governance is often described as a system of oversight designed to monitor organizational performance and ensure compliance with established policies. In resilient organizations, however, governance performs a broader strategic function. It provides the mechanisms through which leadership maintains alignment between strategic ambition, organizational exposure and operational execution.

Boards play a central role in ensuring that governance structures provide meaningful visibility into how strategic initiatives translate into the organization's evolving risk profile. This responsibility extends beyond reviewing periodic reports or approving governance frameworks. Boards must actively examine whether governance mechanisms allow leadership to understand how decisions taken across the organization shape its evolving risk profile and whether authority for those decisions remains clearly defined across leadership levels.

Several questions are particularly important:

- Do strategic discussions integrate exposure and organizational capacity considerations alongside performance expectations?

- Do escalation pathways ensure that emerging risks reach the board early enough to influence strategic decisions?
- Do committee structures reinforce alignment across oversight functions or fragment governance across multiple forums?
- Are decision rights between boards, executives and risk functions sufficiently clear to maintain accountability for strategic decisions?

These questions shift governance discussions from procedural oversight towards strategic visibility. When boards examine how strategy, exposure and execution interact, governance becomes a mechanism through which leadership maintains organizational alignment rather than a structure that reviews outcomes after they have already materialized.

This perspective also has important implications for executive leadership. If boards expect governance discussions to outline how strategic choices affect enterprise exposure, executives must ensure that governance mechanisms remain closely connected to operational decision-making. Strategic planning, capital allocation and performance management processes must align with the strategic boundaries established through governance rather than operate independently of them. Maintaining this connection also requires clarity of authority across leadership levels so that decisions taken within business units remain consistent with enterprise priorities.

Risk leaders play an important supporting role in sustaining this alignment. By improving enterprise visibility into emerging exposure, maintaining credible escalation channels and translating complex risk signals into decision-relevant insights, risk functions help ensure that governance discussions remain grounded in the organization's evolving operational reality.

Effective governance ultimately requires continuous alignment between board oversight and executive action. Boards maintain visibility over the organization's evolving exposure, while executives ensure that strategy, operational priorities, escalation pathways and capital allocation decisions remain consistent with the organization's resilience capacity as conditions change.

Practical playbook

Strengthening governance resilience requires deliberate leadership attention. Governance frameworks can appear structurally sound while gradually losing their ability to guide real decision-making. With that in mind, strengthening governance requires mechanisms that keep strategy, organizational exposure and operational execution aligned as conditions evolve.

The following actions help organizations reinforce governance as a strategic capability and ensure that decision visibility, escalation integrity and strategic alignment remain effective in practice.

Boards

1. **Ensure strategic discussions integrate exposure and organizational capacity**
   Boards should require that major strategic initiatives explicitly consider how they affect the organization's cumulative exposure and resilience capacity. This assessment should accompany major investments, acquisitions and transformation programmes so that strategic ambition is examined alongside the organization's ability to absorb disruption. Boards should also ensure that governance reporting highlights the most material signals rather than overwhelming decision forums with excessive information.
2. **Periodically review governance structures to maintain alignment**
   Committee structures and governance forums should be reviewed whenever organizational strategy, operating scale or regulatory expectations change materially. Regular governance reviews help ensure that oversight responsibilities remain clear and that decision visibility is not diluted by excessive layering or fragmented mandates.
3. **Clarify decision authority across leadership levels**
   Boards should ensure that the boundaries between board oversight, executive authority and risk leadership remain explicit and understood across the organization. Clear decision rights reduce ambiguity during periods of operational pressure and help ensure that accountability remains visible when strategic initiatives encounter resistance or resource constraints.

Executives

1. **Integrate governance expectations into enterprise planning**
   Strategic planning, budgeting and performance management processes should reinforce the strategic boundaries defined through governance. When planning cycles and governance discussions operate independently, organizations risk committing resources to initiatives that collectively exceed their resilience capacity or create conflicts between competing priorities.

2 **Maintain visibility over cumulative exposure**
Executives should regularly review how multiple strategic initiatives interact across business units, technology platforms and operational capabilities. Monitoring cumulative exposure helps prevent organizational expansion from gradually increasing vulnerability and allows leadership to rebalance investment when operational complexity begins to exceed available capacity.

3 **Ensure escalation pathways function in practice**
Escalation mechanisms should enable operational signals to reach leadership forums early enough to influence decisions. Executives must ensure that organizational culture supports escalation rather than discouraging it through performance pressure or reputational concerns.

Chief risk officers and risk leaders

1 **Strengthen enterprise risk visibility**
Risk functions should develop integrated reporting that connects strategic initiatives, operational developments and emerging exposures. Effective reporting helps leadership understand how individual risks interact and influence the organization's overall trajectory while avoiding excessive reporting that obscures the most important signals.

2 **Protect escalation integrity**
Chief risk officers must ensure that critical signals can be escalated without dilution or delay. Independent escalation channels and direct access to senior leadership help maintain the credibility of governance discussions and reinforce a culture where raising emerging risks is recognized as responsible leadership rather than organizational resistance.

3 **Translate risk insight into strategic context**
Risk analysis should inform strategic discussions, capital allocation decisions and transformation programmes. By translating risk signals into decision-relevant insights, risk leaders help ensure that governance discussions remain connected to the organization's evolving operational reality.

KEY TAKEAWAYS

- **Governance is an alignment capability, not simply an oversight function.** Its purpose extends beyond monitoring performance and compliance. Effective governance maintains alignment between strategic ambition, enterprise exposure and operational execution as decisions accumulate across the organization.
- **Governance drift rarely results from the failure of formal structures.** Committees continue to meet, reports continue to circulate and responsibilities remain defined. Drift occurs when governance loses visibility of how individual decisions interact and collectively reshape the organization's exposure.
- **Resilient governance depends on three reinforcing mechanisms.** Decision visibility helps leadership understand the cumulative impact of strategic and operational choices. Escalation integrity ensures that emerging pressures reach decision makers before exposure materializes. Strategic alignment connects planning, capital allocation and execution to the organization's defined boundaries and capacity.
- **Governance effectiveness is shaped by behavioural dynamics as much as structural design.** Information filtering, incentive pressures, fragmented decision forums and unclear authority can weaken governance even when formal frameworks appear robust. Resilience depends on how information moves, how challenge occurs and how accountability is maintained under pressure.
- **Governance maturity requires continual adaptation.** As organizations grow, transform and respond to changing conditions, governance systems must evolve while preserving their core purpose. Resilient organizations regularly reassess whether their governance architecture continues to support visibility, challenge and alignment across the enterprise.

Reframing forward

Governance determines whether strategic risk boundaries remain visible as organizations evolve. Boards may define risk appetite and leadership teams may articulate strategic priorities, yet these boundaries influence outcomes only when governance systems ensure that decisions taken across the organization remain aligned with them.

In practice, strategic initiatives, operational pressures and external disruptions continually reshape organizational exposure. Without governance mechanisms that connect these developments to leadership oversight, signals remain fragmented across functions and strategic decisions gradually drift away from the intent originally established by leadership. Growth may continue, yet complexity increases and exposure accumulates in ways that remain difficult to detect.

Resilient organizations prevent this drift by treating governance as an alignment infrastructure rather than a periodic oversight exercise. They design governance systems that maintain shared visibility across leadership levels and preserve the integrity of escalation pathways. When these mechanisms function effectively, boards, executives and risk leaders can recognize emerging pressures and adjust direction before misalignment becomes disruption.

Yet governance alignment alone cannot sustain resilience. Strategic visibility must be supported by operational systems capable of translating leadership decisions into consistent performance under pressure.

The next chapter examines how resilient organizations design operational systems and control environments that reinforce confidence, adaptability and execution discipline across complex organizational structures.

Because resilience is not created when governance frameworks are defined; it is created when strategy, decisions and systems remain aligned as conditions change.

Endnotes

1 Tricker, B (2019) *Corporate Governance: Principles, Policies, and Practices* (4th edn.), Oxford University Press, Oxford

2 Basel Committee on Banking Supervision (2015) *Corporate Governance Principles for Banks.*

3 Conselho das Finanças Públicas (2023) *Public Finance Council: Institutional role and fiscal oversight in Portugal*

4 European Commission (2023) *Portugal Stability Programme and Fiscal Governance Review*

5 Haye, J (2026) Where does governance slow things down most? LinkedIn poll, 18 December, www.linkedin.com/feed/update/urn:li:activity:7407329766216753152

6 OECD (2015) *G20/OECD Principles of Corporate Governance*

7 Sony Group Corporation (2015–2023) *Corporate Governance Report and Integrated Report*, www.sony.com/en/SonyInfo/IR/library/governance

8 Kaplan, R and Mikes, A (2012) Managing Risks: A new framework, *Harvard Business Review*

08

Resilient systems and controls

Developing structures that build confidence and agility

> CHAPTER OBJECTIVES
>
> - Explain how control environments contribute to organizational resilience by shaping the interaction between structural, operational, technological and behavioural systems.
> - Demonstrate how controls translate governance intent into operational behaviour, decision-making and coordinated response.
> - Show why resilience depends not only on the presence of controls but on how organizational systems function together under changing conditions.
> - Equip leaders with practical principles for designing control environments that support visibility, adaptation and effective response under stress.

Controls sit at the heart of organizational activity. They shape how decisions are made, how risks are managed and how organizations maintain consistency across increasingly complex environments. From approval processes and monitoring mechanisms to escalation pathways and reporting structures, controls influence almost every aspect of day-to-day operations.

The true value of a control depends on the broader system it serves. While individual safeguards are essential, their impact is determined by how well they align with the organization's structures, processes and culture.

Organizations function through interconnected systems that extend beyond technology. These include structural arrangements that define accountability, operational processes that shape execution, technological infrastructure that enables activity and behavioural dynamics that influence how individuals respond to emerging risk. Technology is only one component of this architecture. Resilience depends equally on how information flows, how decisions are taken and how accountability is exercised.

In this context, architecture refers to the overall design of the organizational environment through which decisions are made, information flows and activities are coordinated. It encompasses structural arrangements, operational processes, technological infrastructure and behavioural dynamics, together with the controls that connect them. Resilience depends not on any individual component but on how the architecture functions as an integrated system when conditions change.

Controls operate within this architecture as mechanisms that stabilize these systems and translate governance intent into operational behaviour. Their effectiveness depends not only on their design but on how they function as conditions evolve.

This chapter examines how control environments influence system behaviour under pressure. It explores how organizations design controls that support visibility, coordination and adaptation without introducing rigidity.

Resilience therefore depends not on the presence of controls alone but on how organizational systems and controls interact as disruption develops.

From control frameworks to resilience architecture

Policies define acceptable practices, procedures guide operational activity and monitoring mechanisms verify whether those procedures are followed. Risk functions analyse emerging exposures while internal audit reviews whether controls operate as designed. Together, these mechanisms create discipline within complex organizations, helping ensure that activities remain within approved boundaries and that deviations are identified and corrected.

However, this design reflects a particular assumption about how disruption occurs. Control systems are primarily structured to detect deviations from predefined procedures. They are effective when risks arise through identifiable errors or breaches of process. They are less effective when disruption emerges from the interaction of complex and interconnected systems.

Many of the disruptions organizations face today originate in this way. Supply chains fail through dependencies that remain invisible until external conditions change. Digital infrastructures create interconnections through which local failures propagate across multiple services. Strategic decisions reshape risk exposure across the enterprise long before their effects appear in formal reporting.

Under these conditions, the critical question is no longer whether procedures have been followed but how organizational systems behave as conditions change. Controls, monitoring systems and escalation mechanisms provide the signals that reveal emerging vulnerabilities.

This distinction explains why organizations with extensive control frameworks may still encounter significant disruption. The issue rarely lies in the absence of controls but in how those controls are designed and interpreted.

Studies of high-reliability operations such as aviation, nuclear energy and complex medical environments show that control mechanisms are interpreted not only as enforcement tools but also as signals that reveal emerging stress within operational systems (Roberts, 1990[1]; LaPorte and Consolini, 1991[2]; Weick and Sutcliffe, 2015[3]). These environments maintain reliability by sustaining continuous attention to small operational anomalies and weak signals that may indicate the early stages of system drift. Alerts, limits and monitoring thresholds therefore provide more than confirmation that procedures are being followed. They reveal how operating conditions are evolving and allow specialists and leadership to respond before local disturbances escalate into wider disruption.

In a resilience-oriented architecture, controls are treated not only as constraints but also as sensors. They enable rapid organizational awareness by ensuring that signals reach those responsible for interpreting and responding to emerging risk.

In technology and supply chain environments, controls often function as both constraints and information pathways. Monitoring mechanisms reveal unusual activity, emerging dependencies and potential points of disruption, allowing organizations to respond before local disturbances spread more widely.

Understanding this broader role requires shifting attention from individual controls to the organizational systems within which they operate. Governance defines strategic intent and establishes risk boundaries. Organizational systems, including structures of accountability, operational processes, technological infrastructure and behavioural dynamics, determine how information moves and how decisions are taken under uncertainty. Control environments connect these elements by translating governance intent into operational discipline while maintaining visibility into emerging risk.

This architecture introduces inherent trade-offs. Measures that strengthen resilience often require redundancy, monitoring capability or decision capacity that may appear inefficient during stable periods. Systems designed exclusively for efficiency may perform well under predictable conditions yet struggle when assumptions change.

Resilient organizations recognize this tension. They design control environments that preserve visibility and coordination, allowing leadership to detect emerging stress and respond before local disruptions escalate.

Resilience therefore does not arise from the number of controls an organization maintains. It emerges from the alignment between governance intent, organizational systems and the controls that shape how those systems operate under pressure.

Interconnected systems and amplified operational risk

Several structural developments have increased the importance of understanding how organizational systems behave under changing conditions. These developments do not simply introduce new risks. They alter the way disruptions emerge and propagate across organizations, making it more difficult for traditional control frameworks to detect early signs of system stress.

Cloud platforms, digital service architectures and algorithmic decision systems now underpin many operational processes. While they create efficiency and scale, they also introduce interdependencies that may remain largely invisible during normal operations. Research has highlighted the systemic implications of technological concentration, particularly where critical services depend on a small number of shared cloud providers (Financial Stability Board, 2023).[4] A disruption affecting one provider can therefore affect multiple activities simultaneously across an organization and the wider ecosystem. By the time these disturbances appear in conventional risk reporting, organizations are often already managing the consequences of disruption.

Regulatory initiatives such as the European Union's Digital Operational Resilience Act (DORA[5]) reflect this systemic perspective by requiring organizations to examine how disruptions affecting critical technology providers could affect the continuity of essential services. Technology infrastructures are not the only systems where hidden dependencies create resilience challenges.

The global semiconductor shortage affecting the automotive industry between 2020 and 2022 illustrates how structural dependencies can remain largely unnoticed until disruption occurs. Automotive manufacturers had organized production around highly specialized semiconductor components supplied by a limited number of manufacturers. Procurement strategies prioritized cost-efficiency and stable supply under normal conditions. When demand for semiconductors increased sharply during the Covid-19 pandemic, driven in part by rapid growth in consumer electronics production, automotive manufacturers discovered that their access to critical components depended on manufacturing capacity that had already been reallocated elsewhere. Production lines across multiple manufacturers slowed or halted, not because a single supplier had failed, but because the broader supply system had become structurally constrained.

The consequences were substantial. Industry estimates suggest the shortage reduced global vehicle production by approximately 9 to 11 million units in 2021 alone, affecting manufacturers including Volkswagen, Toyota, Ford, General Motors and Stellantis, many of which temporarily halted or slowed production at multiple plants (AlixPartners, 2021[6]). The disruption persisted into 2022 before semiconductor supply conditions gradually stabilized.

This episode highlighted that vulnerability did not arise from a procedural failure within procurement processes; it emerged from the configuration of the supply system itself. Dependencies that appeared manageable under stable conditions proved fragile once external demand patterns shifted.

Regulatory expectations have evolved in response to these structural realities. In several sectors, regulators now require organizations to demonstrate their ability to maintain critical services during disruption rather than simply confirm that risk controls and governance procedures are in place. Operational resilience frameworks increasingly emphasize the identification of important business services, the mapping of dependencies across technology, suppliers and operational processes, and the ability to respond when disruption occurs. The focus therefore shifts from documenting controls to understanding how organizational systems sustain essential activities under stress.

Expectations from customers, investors and society more broadly have evolved in parallel. Organizations that provide financial services, digital platforms, healthcare, energy or logistics operate within infrastructures that many individuals depend upon daily. When these services fail, the consequences extend beyond internal operational disruption to affect customers, markets and communities. Stakeholders therefore evaluate organizations not only by their efficiency during stable periods but also by their ability to sustain essential services when unexpected events occur.

As technological, operational and supply systems become more interconnected, the consequences of disruption increasingly reflect how those systems interact under stress. In such environments, resilience depends less on the number of procedures defined during stable conditions and more on the organization's ability to detect emerging signals, coordinate expertise and adapt operational responses as circumstances evolve.

The architecture of resilient organizational systems and controls

Organizational resilience results from the interaction between the systems through which decisions are made, activities are executed and information flows across the enterprise. Control environments operate within these systems. Their effectiveness depends on how those systems are designed and how they behave under changing conditions.

A practical way to understand this interaction is to consider four interconnected organizational systems. Each system shapes a different dimension of how the organization anticipates, absorbs and responds to disruption. Controls operate across all four, reinforcing alignment between governance intent and operational reality. Figure 8.1 illustrates the relationship between governance intent, control environments and the organizational systems through which resilience is created and sustained.

> WHEN CAPABILITY EXISTS ONLY ON PAPER
>
> Many organizations mistake documented capability for operational capability. Firms often enter a crisis with detailed recovery plans, governance frameworks and escalation procedures. Yet the first hours of disruption may still be spent clarifying ownership, authority and decision rights. Resilience is demonstrated through how systems, people and governance structures behave when normal conditions disappear. (Adapted from insights shared during interviews conducted for this book.)

Structural systems

Structural systems define how responsibility and authority are distributed across the organization. They include organizational design, reporting lines, decision rights and accountability frameworks.

FIGURE 8.1 Governance, controls and organizational systems

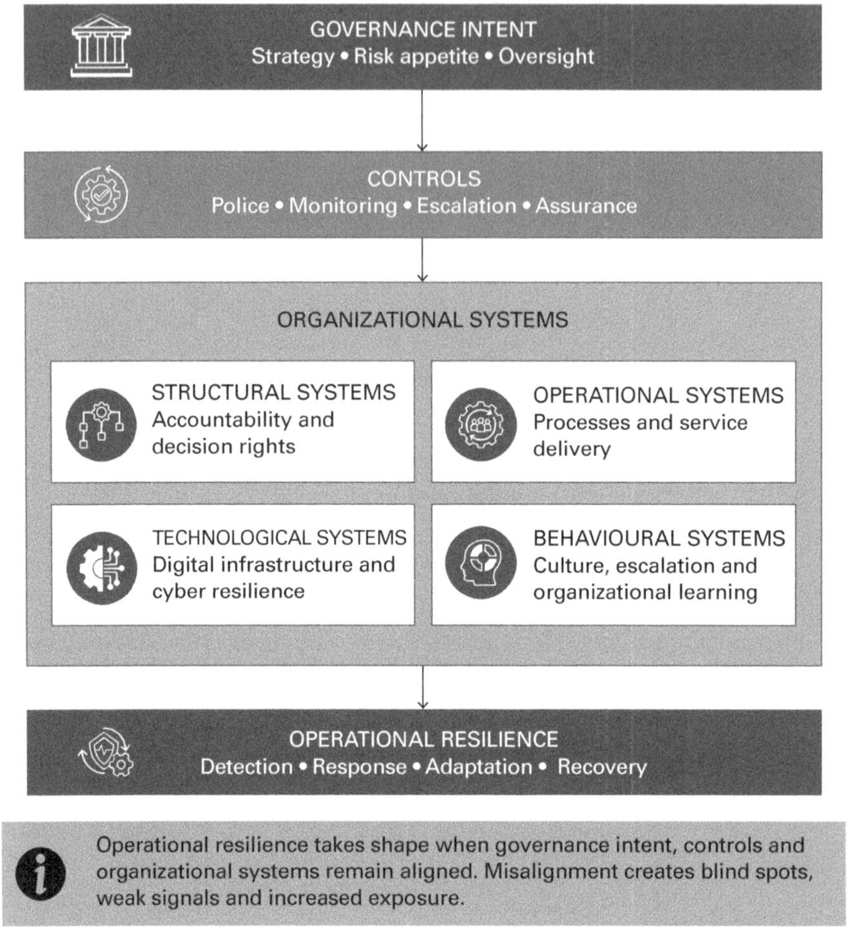

As discussed in Chapter 7, governance influences how decisions are escalated, challenged and acted upon. Structural systems embed these governance principles into the organization's operating model. In stable conditions, they provide clarity and coordination. Under stress, they determine whether decisions can be taken quickly and by the individuals best positioned to act. Where responsibility is fragmented or authority remains unclear, emerging issues may circulate across multiple functions without ownership, delaying response.

Resilient structural systems align accountability with decision authority. Individuals responsible for critical services or material risks are also empowered to act when conditions change, through predefined decision rights, clearly defined escalation thresholds and the authority to initiate containment or recovery actions without waiting for hierarchical approval, particularly where delays would compromise the continuity of critical services. Escalation pathways are clear and decision-making authority adapts to the nature of the disruption rather than remaining constrained by hierarchical boundaries.

Controls within structural systems therefore do more than define responsibilities. They ensure that ownership is explicit, that decision rights are understood and that accountability remains actionable when disruption occurs.

Operational systems

Operational systems consist of the processes through which products and services are delivered. These processes are typically designed for efficiency, consistency and control during normal operating conditions.

Under disruption, however, rigid adherence to predefined procedures becomes a source of fragility. When conditions deviate from the assumptions embedded in process design, employees face a practical dilemma. They can continue to follow procedures that no longer reflect operational reality or they can adapt in ways that may later be questioned if outcomes deteriorate. In many organizations, the perceived risk of being held accountable for deviation discourages timely action, even where procedures are no longer appropriate.

Effective operational systems address this tension explicitly. They are designed with controlled flexibility, where deviation from standard procedures is not left to individual discretion alone but is anticipated, framed and authorized in advance. This includes defining the conditions under which deviation is expected, the thresholds that trigger it and the principles that guide decision-making when standard processes no longer apply. Experience from high-reliability environments shows that effective response under pressure depends on allowing decision-making to shift towards those with the most relevant situational awareness as conditions evolve.

This does not imply the absence of discipline. It reflects a different form of discipline, where adaptation is guided by clearly articulated boundaries, escalation expectations and situational awareness rather than fixed sequences of steps. Individuals remain accountable, yet they are supported by a framework that recognizes that conditions may evolve beyond those assumed in process design.

Controls within operational systems support this balance. They define critical parameters, trigger escalation when conditions change and provide visibility into process performance. Crucially, they also legitimize informed deviation where strict adherence would undermine the continuity of critical services, ensuring that adaptation is recognized as part of disciplined execution rather than as a failure of compliance.

Technological systems

Technological systems now underpin a significant proportion of organizational activity. Digital platforms, data architectures, cloud infrastructures and cybersecurity capabilities form the backbone through which services are delivered and monitored.

These systems introduce both capability and exposure. They enable scale, speed and automation, while also creating dependencies that may amplify disruption when failures occur. As illustrated earlier, concentration within shared technology providers or data infrastructures can transform local incidents into wider operational disruptions.

Resilience within technological systems depends on visibility, redundancy and coordinated response. Organizations must be able to detect anomalies, understand dependencies and respond across interconnected platforms. This requires more than technical controls in isolation. It requires integration between monitoring systems, incident management processes and decision-making structures.

Controls within technological systems serve a dual function. They protect infrastructure from failure or compromise and they generate signals that allow the organization to understand how its digital environment is evolving under stress. These signals include indicators of performance degradation, unusual system behaviour and emerging stress within critical dependencies. Their value lies not only in prevention but in enabling timely coordination between technical specialists, operational teams and leadership during incidents.

Behavioural systems

Behavioural systems reflect the cultural and psychological environment within which individuals interpret risk, communicate uncertainty and take decisions. They include leadership behaviour, incentive structures, psychological safety and informal norms.

Even well-designed structural, operational and technological systems depend on how individuals behave in practice. When employees feel unable to escalate concerns, when incentives discourage transparency or when deviation from procedures is penalized regardless of context, early warning signals may be suppressed.

Conversely, environments that encourage open communication and learning allow weak signals to surface before they develop into material incidents. Near misses, anomalies and informal workarounds become sources of insight rather than indicators of failure to be concealed.

Controls within behavioural systems are less visible but equally important. They include escalation frameworks, feedback mechanisms and performance incentives that reinforce desired behaviours. Their effectiveness depends on whether individuals perceive that raising concerns supports organizational objectives rather than creating personal risk.

Yet behavioural dynamics become most visible when controls no longer reflect operational reality. Understanding how individuals adapt under these conditions provides important insight into the strengths and weaknesses of the broader control environment.

Integrating the systems

These four systems interact continuously as the organization functions. Structural clarity shapes how decisions are taken. Operational systems determine how those decisions are executed. Technological infrastructure governs the speed and visibility of information flows. Behavioural dynamics influence whether emerging signals are recognized and acted upon.

Control environments connect these systems. They translate governance intent into operational discipline while maintaining visibility into how risk evolves across the organization. When controls are aligned across structural, operational, technological and behavioural systems, they enable timely response and coordinated action under stress.

When misalignment occurs, this connection breaks down and vulnerabilities tend to emerge at the boundaries between systems, where ownership, visibility or control may be unclear and therefore remain unaddressed until disruption occurs. Controls may exist within individual systems yet fail to provide a coherent view of risk or support effective decision-making. Organizations may appear well controlled while remaining exposed to disruptions that develop across system boundaries.

The role of controls becomes clearer when considered across the organizational systems through which they operate (see Table 8.1).

TABLE 8.1 How controls enable response across organizational systems

System	What the system governs	How controls operate	Consequence of misalignment
Structural systems	Accountability, authority and decision rights	Define ownership, establish escalation thresholds and trigger shifts in decision authority	Decisions are delayed, ownership is unclear and response fragments across functions
Operational systems	Execution of processes and delivery of services	Define parameters, enable controlled deviation and trigger escalation when conditions change	Teams follow procedures that no longer fit conditions or hesitate to act, increasing disruption
Technological systems	Infrastructure, data flows and system interdependencies	Detect anomalies, generate signals and support coordination across systems and teams	Failures propagate before they are understood and response is reactive rather than coordinated
Behavioural systems	Culture, incentives and communication dynamics	Reinforce escalation, support transparency and legitimize action under uncertainty	Early warning signals are suppressed and issues escalate before becoming visible

REAL-WORLD EXAMPLE

Cyber resilience in telecommunications and the alignment of response systems

Telecommunications providers, such as Orange S.A. and Vodafone Group, operate critical national infrastructure where service disruption can affect millions of customers and impair access to essential services. As digital dependency has increased, so has exposure to cyber incidents capable of disrupting network availability at scale.

A series of publicly reported cyber incidents and service disruptions across the sector highlighted a recurring pattern. Technical controls for threat detection and system protection were often well developed, yet response effectiveness was constrained by fragmentation across organizational systems. Signals generated within technological systems were not consistently translated into coordinated operational action, ownership of response remained distributed and escalation pathways were not always aligned with the urgency of the situation.

In response, these organizations strengthened their resilience by redesigning how these systems interacted.

Technological systems were enhanced to provide a shared view of infrastructure performance, network activity and emerging threats, enabling signals to be interpreted collectively rather than in isolation.

Operational systems were adapted to link defined system conditions to predefined response actions, allowing teams to adjust processes and prioritize continuity of critical services as disruption unfolded.

Structural systems were clarified by aligning accountability for critical services with decision authority, supported by escalation thresholds that triggered immediate response and reduced reliance on hierarchical approval during incidents.

Behavioural systems were reinforced through regular simulation exercises and cross-functional incident scenarios, strengthening coordination between cybersecurity specialists, infrastructure teams and executive leadership while encouraging timely escalation and action under pressure.

Sector analysis supports the effectiveness of this approach. The ENISA Telecom Security Report[7] (2024) highlights that organizations adopting integrated incident response structures and regular simulation exercises improve detection and response efficiency and reduce the duration and impact of cyber-related service disruption.

The resulting improvement in resilience did not arise solely from stronger technical controls. It reflected the alignment of technological, operational, structural and behavioural systems, allowing signals to move more rapidly from detection to coordinated decision and action.

The lesson extends beyond telecommunications. In technology-dependent environments, resilience depends not only on the strength of individual controls but on how effectively those controls connect organizational systems. Where systems remain fragmented, controls generate information without enabling response. Where they are aligned, controls become part of an integrated capability to detect, interpret and act on evolving risk.

When controls collide with behaviour

When discussing behavioural systems earlier in the chapter, the focus was on the cultural and psychological conditions that influence how individuals interpret risk, communicate concerns and respond to uncertainty. Controls are designed to shape those behaviours, yet organizational performance often depends on individuals adapting when controls no longer reflect operational reality. The effectiveness of a control environment therefore depends not only on technical design but on how people interpret, apply and respond to controls under changing conditions.

When systems align with operational reality, controls guide behaviour and support consistent decision-making. When they become rigid or misaligned, individuals encounter situations where following procedures no longer enables effective execution. Behaviour then adapts.

These adaptations are typically practical workarounds rather than deliberate breaches. When formal processes encounter real-world constraints, employees adjust their actions, bypass steps or reinterpret procedures to maintain continuity and meet performance expectations.

Organizations expect adherence to defined processes yet rely on individuals to sustain performance when those processes no longer function as intended. For the individual, the choice becomes constrained: follow the process and risk operational failure or adapt the process and assume personal accountability.

Organizational workarounds as resilience signals

Workarounds are often treated as control failures. In practice, they frequently indicate that systems no longer reflect operational conditions. They typically result from recurring factors:

- excessive process complexity
- misaligned incentives

- impractical escalation mechanisms
- perceived risk in raising concerns.

How organizations respond to these behaviours determines whether they weaken or strengthen resilience.

Where deviation is treated solely as a breach, individuals conceal it. Signals of system stress are suppressed and issues remain invisible until disruption occurs. Controls may increase in number while becoming progressively less connected to operational reality.

Where workarounds are treated as diagnostic signals, they provide insight into how systems behave under real conditions. They reveal where processes fail, where escalation does not function effectively and where authority does not align with responsibility.

The conditions that shape behaviour

Whether these signals surface depends on the conditions within which individuals operate. Structural and operational systems may define authority and escalation. Technological systems may provide visibility. Yet individuals act only if they believe that doing so is expected and supported.

Where escalation leads to scrutiny without support or deviation is penalized regardless of context, individuals are more likely to remain within procedural boundaries even when those boundaries no longer reflect reality. Where environments support timely escalation and informed judgement, individuals are more likely to raise concerns and act within defined boundaries as conditions evolve.

This explains why structural empowerment alone is insufficient. Decision rights may exist in design yet remain unused in practice.

From compliance to system awareness

Control environments that support resilience extend beyond enforcement. They enable information about system behaviour to surface and be acted upon.

In practice, this involves:

- recognizing that adaptations often signal underlying constraints
- ensuring escalation mechanisms remain usable under pressure
- aligning incentives with timely risk recognition
- reinforcing leadership behaviours that prioritize learning over attribution.

Under these conditions, controls contribute to organizational awareness. Individuals, systems and governance processes remain connected as conditions evolve.

Resilience depends not on eliminating deviation, but on understanding what it reveals and responding accordingly.

Design principles for effective control environments

The four organizational systems described earlier provide the environment within which controls operate. Designing effective control environments requires a set of principles that help maintain alignment across these systems as conditions change.

Figure 8.2. illustrates how these principles interact to translate governance intent into effective operational response.

Principle 1: Clarity of ownership

Controls must be owned by individuals who have both responsibility and the authority to make and implement decisions that affect risk exposure and service continuity, such as initiating escalation, containing emerging issues, reprioritizing activities or adapting standard procedures within defined boundaries. Where ownership is fragmented or unclear, signals may circulate across functions without triggering response. Clear ownership ensures that emerging risks are interpreted and translated into timely decisions. It links structural design directly to operational decision-making.

Principle 2: Practical usability

Controls must remain usable under stress. Processes that are overly complex, time-consuming or dependent on multiple approvals are unlikely to be applied when conditions deteriorate. Usability ensures that controls function in practice, not only in design. It enables individuals to apply judgement within defined boundaries when standard procedures no longer reflect current conditions.

Principle 3: Alignment with incentives and objectives

Employees must perceive that acting on risk signals supports organizational objectives. Where incentives prioritize short-term performance or discourage

FIGURE 8.2 Design principles for effective control environments

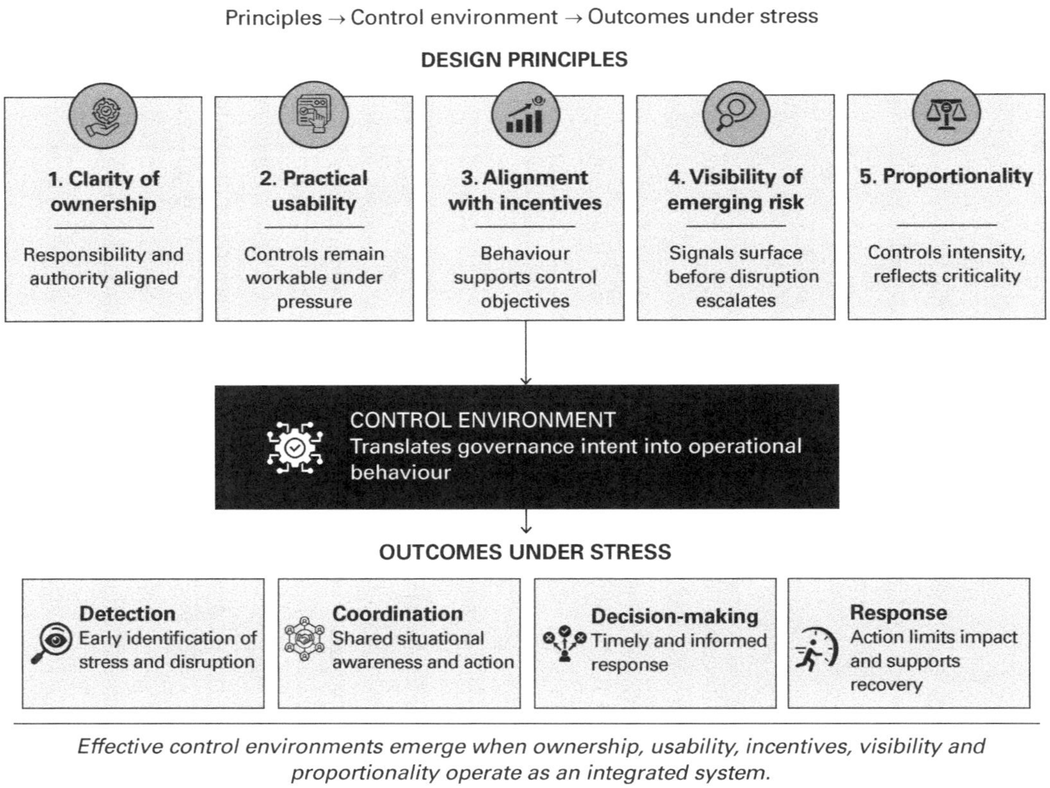

escalation, early warning signals may be ignored or delayed. Alignment ensures that behaviour reinforces rather than undermines the intent of the control environment.

Principle 4: Visibility of emerging risk

Control environments must prioritize early detection of operational stress. This includes identifying weak signals, monitoring deviations from expected conditions and ensuring that information flows to those responsible for interpretation and action. Visibility enables organizations to respond before disruption fully materializes.

Principle 5: Proportionality

Control intensity should reflect the criticality of the underlying activity. Excessive controls applied to low-impact processes create friction without improving resilience. Insufficient controls applied to critical services increase exposure to disruption. Proportionality ensures that control environments remain focused, efficient and aligned with organizational priorities.

Integrating the principles

These principles rarely fail in isolation. Weakness typically arises when they are applied unevenly across the organization.

Visibility may improve through enhanced monitoring, yet without clear ownership, the resulting signals do not translate into action. Decision authority may be defined, yet remain unused where escalation carries perceived personal risk. Processes may be designed for flexibility yet prove unusable under pressure due to complexity or competing incentives.

Under these conditions, control environments appear robust in design while remaining ineffective in practice. Individual components function as intended but their interaction fails to support timely and coordinated responses.

The effectiveness of a control environment therefore depends less on the strength of individual controls than on the consistency with which these principles are applied across organizational systems.

Board and executive implications

Boards and executive teams play a central role in shaping how organizational systems perform under stress. Traditional oversight often focuses on verifying the presence of control frameworks, policies and reporting structures. Resilient oversight focuses on how organizational systems behave when conditions move beyond the assumptions embedded within those frameworks.

For boards, this requires a shift in the nature of oversight discussions. Rather than focusing primarily on completeness of frameworks or adherence to processes, attention moves towards the interaction between structural, operational, technological and behavioural systems.

Several questions are particularly important:

- Where are the potential single points of failure across organizational systems, including technology, processes and decision structures?
- Which controls directly influence operational decision-making? And which exist primarily as reporting or assurance mechanisms?
- Which risks only become visible once disruption has already materialized?
- How quickly can emerging failures in critical services be detected, interpreted and escalated?
- Where do employees adapt or bypass procedures in order to perform their roles? What does this reveal about system design?
- Where are employees routinely adapting our processes in order to achieve the outcomes those processes were designed to support?

These questions help boards understand not simply whether controls exist but whether they support early detection, timely intervention and coordinated response.

For executive teams, the challenge is alignment. Ownership of critical services and risks must align with decision authority. Escalation mechanisms must function under pressure rather than only in design. Technological systems must provide timely and interpretable signals, while behavioural conditions must support early escalation and informed adaptation.

Risk functions support this alignment by helping organizations identify where signals are delayed, where escalation pathways are ineffective and where controls fail to translate into decision-making. Their role extends beyond framework design to ensuring that governance mechanisms remain connected to operational reality as conditions evolve.

Practical playbook

Effective control environments do more than enforce compliance. They help organizations detect emerging stress, coordinate response and adapt as conditions change. The following actions help boards, executives and risk leaders strengthen the connection between controls, organizational systems and operational resilience.

Boards

Boards shape the conditions within which control environments operate.

1. **Focus oversight on critical services rather than individual controls**
   Boards should ensure that governance discussions concentrate on the resilience of critical services and operational capabilities. This requires understanding how technology, processes and third-party dependencies interact to support service continuity rather than reviewing controls in isolation.
2. **Challenge complexity within control frameworks**
   Excessive layering of controls can obscure the most important signals and reduce usability under stress. Boards should challenge whether control frameworks remain proportionate and whether they support rather than hinder timely decision-making.
3. **Integrate resilience scenarios into governance discussions**
   Scenario analysis should extend beyond financial stress testing to include operational and technological disruption. Boards should examine how organizational systems behave under stress and whether escalation pathways and decision authority function as intended in those scenarios.

Executives

Executive teams ensure that control environments remain connected to operational reality.

1. **Map and maintain visibility over operational dependencies**
   Executives should ensure that dependencies across technology platforms, suppliers and internal processes are understood and regularly reviewed. This visibility helps identify where disruption may propagate across interconnected systems.

2 **Simplify escalation pathways for emerging risks**
Escalation mechanisms must function under operational stress. Executives should remove unnecessary layers and ensure that signals can reach decision makers quickly, particularly where delays may affect critical services.

3 **Align performance incentives with resilience objectives**
Performance management frameworks should reinforce behaviours that support early escalation and informed adaptation. Where incentives prioritize short-term outcomes, emerging risks may remain unreported until disruption occurs.

Chief risk officers and risk leaders

Risk leaders help ensure that control environments remain effective as organizational systems evolve.

1 **Integrate operational resilience within enterprise risk management**
Risk functions should connect operational resilience considerations with enterprise risk frameworks, ensuring that technological, operational and behavioural risks are assessed in a consistent and integrated manner.

2 **Use informal adaptations as indicators of system stress**
Workarounds and deviations should be examined as signals of misalignment between system design and operational reality. Risk functions should use these signals to inform improvements in control design and escalation mechanisms.

3 **Strengthen scenario testing across systems**
Scenario testing should examine how structural, operational, technological and behavioural systems interact under stress. This includes testing escalation pathways, decision authority and coordination across functions, not only technical recovery capabilities.

KEY TAKEAWAYS

- **Controls do not operate in isolation**. Their effectiveness depends on the organizational systems within which they operate and the behaviours they influence.

- **Organizational resilience is shaped by four interconnected systems.** Structural, operational, technological and behavioural systems determine how organizations detect, interpret and respond to disruption.
- **Controls translate governance intent into operational behaviour.** They influence how information flows, how decisions are made and how organizations respond when conditions change.
- **Vulnerabilities often emerge at the boundaries between systems.** Disruption rarely results from the failure of a single control. It develops through interactions between processes, technologies, structures and people.
- **Resilient control environments remain aligned with operational reality.** Organizations strengthen resilience when controls support visibility, coordination and decision-making under pressure rather than simply verifying compliance.

Reframing forward

This chapter examined how control environments support resilience by shaping the way organizational systems behave under pressure. When structural, operational, technological and behavioural systems remain aligned, organizations are better able to detect emerging stress, coordinate response and maintain continuity of critical services.

Yet resilience depends on more than responding effectively once stress becomes visible. Many of the risks that shape organizational performance develop gradually through shifts in technology, market conditions, geopolitical forces and interconnected systems. Their earliest signals are often weak, fragmented and difficult to interpret.

Resilient organizations extend beyond response capability. They develop the ability to identify and interpret weak signals before disruption becomes visible within operational systems.

The next chapter explores how organizations build this foresight capability. It examines how weak signals are detected, how emerging patterns are interpreted and how early insight can be translated into strategic and operational action.

Endnotes

1 Roberts, K H (1990) Some characteristics of high reliability organizations, *Organization Science*, 1 (2)
2 LaPorte, T R and Consolini, P M (1991) Working in Practice But Not in Theory: Theoretical Challenges of 'High-Reliability Organizations,' *Journal of Public Administration Research and Theory*, 1 (1)
3 Weick, K E and Sutcliffe, K M (2015) *Managing the Unexpected: Sustained performance in a complex world* (3rd edn), Jossey-Bass, San Francisco, CA
4 Financial Stability Board (2023) Enhancing Third-Party Risk Management and Oversight, FSB
5 European Union (2022) Digital Operational Resilience Act (Regulation (EU) 2022/2554)
6 AlixPartners (2021) Semiconductor shortage cost the auto industry $210 billion in revenue in 2021, AlixPartners Global Automotive Outlook
7 European Union Agency for Cybersecurity (ENISA) (2024) *ENISA Threat Landscape for Telecommunications Sector 2024*, Publications Office of the European Union, Luxembourg

PART FOUR

Tools, practices and pathways

09

Foresight in action

Anticipating disruption before it happens

> CHAPTER OBJECTIVES
>
> - Explain how foresight enables organizations to detect, interpret and translate emerging developments into decisions.
> - Demonstrate how integrating foresight into governance, strategy and capital allocation strengthens organizational resilience.
> - Show how organizations can act on uncertainty before changing conditions begin to constrain performance.

Emerging developments are continuously visible across organizations. Changes in customer behaviour, supply conditions and system performance provide early indications that underlying conditions are evolving. The value of these signals lies in how they are interpreted and how they influence decisions.

Organizations generate forward-looking insight through scenario analysis, horizon scanning and ongoing monitoring of their operating environment. These activities provide visibility into how conditions may develop and how current strategies may be affected.

Foresight becomes effective when this visibility is translated into decision-making. Signals, scenarios and emerging developments shape outcomes when they are connected to the choices that define strategy, operations and resource allocation.

This introduces a broader perspective on foresight as a capability that connects emerging developments to decisions, ensuring that organizations adjust direction as conditions evolve.

Previous chapters examined how organizations build resilience through governance structures and interconnected systems that enable coordination and response under changing conditions. These mechanisms provide the architecture through which resilience is executed.

This chapter introduces foresight as the input that allows this architecture to operate proactively. It examines how organizations identify and interpret emerging developments, how scenarios are used to explore evolving conditions and how foresight is translated into decisions that shape strategy, operations and capital allocation.

Foresight is not prediction

Foresight is increasingly positioned as part of risk management. Scenario analysis, stress testing and emerging risk frameworks are expected to provide forward-looking insight and strengthen preparedness for disruption. Within most risk functions, however, foresight is rarely defined as a decision capability in its own right.

Forward-looking activities exist in practice. Organizations analyse emerging trends, develop scenarios and assess potential exposures with the expectation that these efforts will improve their ability to anticipate disruption. In effect, foresight is treated as an extension of analysis, positioned alongside reporting and monitoring within existing risk frameworks. This interpretation appears intuitive. If organizations can describe possible future states, they should be better prepared for them.

However, research across high-reliability and complex systems provides a consistent insight. Early signals of disruption are often present within organizational systems, yet their significance is not always translated into decision-making. Studies of high-reliability environments show that maintaining resilience depends on sustained attention to small anomalies that may indicate emerging system stress.[1,2] Where these signals are not acted upon, local disturbances can escalate into wider disruption.

This pattern is reinforced in analyses of major organizational failures. Investigations into disasters such as NASA's Space Shuttle Challenger demonstrate that risks may be recognized yet progressively normalized, with decision-making remaining unchanged despite increasing evidence of exposure.[3] Over time, the absence of immediate consequences reduces the perceived urgency of action.

As we established before, foresight is frequently positioned as an analytical activity rather than as a decision capability. Scenario outputs are produced and reviewed yet remain disconnected from the processes through which strategy is defined, capital is allocated and operational priorities are set. As a result, foresight informs understanding without altering outcomes.

This dynamic reflects how information is generated and interpreted. Risk functions are typically structured around historical data and observable trends. Weak signals remain fragmented, difficult to quantify and often lack ownership within existing governance structures. As a result, organizations may recognize emerging developments without defining how they should influence current choices.

A further limitation arises from the assumption that risks can be treated uniformly. In practice, different types of uncertainty require different responses. Some risks are visible and well understood yet remain unaddressed. These are often described as 'grey rhinos': developments that are recognized but repeatedly deferred due to competing priorities, inertia or perceived cost. Other risks are known but remain unspoken, either because they challenge prevailing assumptions or because raising them carries perceived personal or organizational consequences. These dynamics are sometimes characterized as 'black elephants', reflecting the tension between awareness and acknowledgement.[4]

In many organizations, the challenge is not visibility but legitimacy. As earlier chapters explored, the decision to act is shaped as much by perceived personal costs as by available information.

Other risks emerge through complex system interactions and remain largely invisible until they manifest. For example, a disruption affecting a shared technology provider may trigger failures across multiple organizations before the underlying dependency is recognized. These developments arise from dependencies that are not fully understood or from conditions that evolve outside established monitoring frameworks. In contrast, rare events may fall outside expected distributions altogether, often described as 'black swans', where historical data provides limited guidance.

These distinctions highlight how foresight fails in different ways. Visible risks persist when organizations lack mechanisms or incentives to act. Unspoken risks remain unaddressed where escalation is constrained. Systemic risks develop where interdependencies are not recognized. Rare events expose the limits of historical analysis.

Treating these risks as equivalent leads to a misallocation of attention. Organizations invest in analytical sophistication while limiting the conditions that enable action.

Therefore, reframing foresight as a decision capability requires a different starting point. The focus shifts from describing possible futures to understanding how emerging signals influence present choices.

This perspective changes the role of scenarios and analysis. Their value lies in exposing assumptions, revealing vulnerabilities and highlighting the conditions under which current strategies may no longer remain viable. Foresight becomes valuable when it alters direction before changing conditions impose it.

Its effectiveness is measured by the extent to which it influences decisions. Signals that shape action strengthen resilience by enabling earlier and more deliberate responses to change.

When disruption outpaces risk frameworks

The limitations of foresight become more visible as the environment within which organizations operate continues to evolve. Several structural developments are reshaping how risk emerges and how disruption unfolds. These developments alter the conditions under which signals are generated, interpreted and acted upon.

Building on the themes of interdependency and concentration risk explored throughout earlier chapters, one important driver is the growing influence of advanced technologies, including artificial intelligence and data-driven decision systems. These technologies introduce non-linearity that is difficult to capture within traditional risk models. Outputs may change rapidly as underlying data evolves, and interactions between systems can produce outcomes that are neither predictable nor easily explainable. Research on model risk highlights how such environments can amplify small deviations into material consequences, particularly where dependencies are not fully understood or where human oversight is limited.[5]

Workforce dynamics introduce a further dimension of change. Shifts in employee expectations, hybrid working models and evolving labour markets affect how organizations access and retain critical capabilities. These developments happen gradually, creating signals that may seem operational in isolation yet collectively affect resilience, engagement, knowledge continuity and execution capacity.

Regulatory expectations have evolved in parallel. Supervisory frameworks increasingly focus on the ability to maintain critical services under stress, extending beyond financial exposure to include technology, third-party dependencies and operational continuity. This reflects a broader shift towards understanding how systems behave under changing conditions.

These developments generate signals that are distributed across systems and time horizons. Their implications are often difficult to interpret within existing frameworks. This is reflected in recurring organizational patterns. Disruptions are described as unexpected, while underlying conditions have been evolving over time. Scenario exercises are conducted, though their outputs are primarily used to assess the resilience of current strategies rather than to challenge their underlying assumptions. Risk reporting provides visibility into defined exposures, while offering limited insight into how underlying conditions affect strategic assumptions.

The perception of sudden shock reflects the accumulation of signals that were present but not integrated. Information exists across functions and systems yet remains fragmented. Without mechanisms to connect these signals and translate them into decision-relevant insight, organizations experience disruption as abrupt rather than as the result of gradual change.

The underlying dynamic is not new. The Challenger launch decision demonstrated how recognized risks can remain trapped within technical and organizational boundaries without altering strategic direction.

Boards receive information without a clear view of how that information should influence decisions. Risk reporting describes current exposure and performance against defined metrics yet provides limited insight into how underlying conditions are evolving or when existing assumptions may no longer hold. As conditions evolve, organizations continue to make decisions within established parameters even when the environment that originally justified those parameters has begun to change.

The foresight-to-decision loop

The limitation identified earlier lies in the absence of a mechanism that connects signals to decisions. Foresight requires a structured process through which emerging developments are detected, interpreted and translated into action. This can be understood as a continuous loop linking signal, interpretation, scenario, decision and feedback, as shown in Figure 9.1.

This need becomes more pronounced in complex environments, where cause and effect are not immediately visible and decisions are taken without complete information. Frameworks, such as Cynefin, as mentioned in Chapter 2, highlight how understanding emerges through interaction, while decision models such as OODA emphasize the role of interpretation in shaping action.

FIGURE 9.1 The foresight-to-decision loop

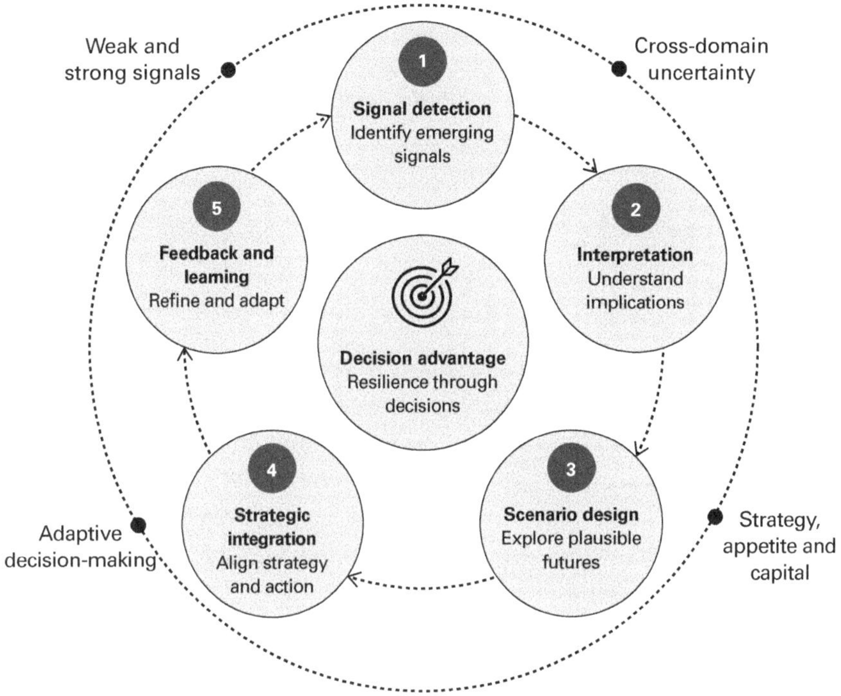

The foresight-to-decision loop shows how organizations translate emerging signals into decisions through a continuous cycle of detection, interpretation, scenario design, integration and learning.

Signal detection

Foresight begins with identifying signals that indicate potential change. Some signals are visible and measurable. Others are partial, ambiguous and fragmented. Both are necessary. Visible signals confirm that change is underway, while weak signals indicate where it may emerge.

Yet signals rarely arrive as complete narratives. They take shape through isolated observations, operational anomalies, changes in behaviour or shifts in external conditions. Their value lies not in their visibility but in the ability to connect them into a broader pattern.

Interpretation

Interpretation is rarely neutral. Existing incentives, prior successes and prevailing assumptions influence which signals are amplified, challenged or dismissed. It is shaped by assumptions, biases and organizational context. Signals that do not align with prevailing expectations may be deprioritized.

Scenario design

Effective scenarios are designed to explore plausible futures rather than predict probable outcomes. Their purpose is to test how conditions may evolve and to expose the assumptions underlying current strategies.

Disruption emerges through the interaction of operational, human, technological, regulatory and external factors, requiring scenarios to extend beyond financial exposure.

Decision integration

Decision integration is the point at which foresight either creates value or becomes an academic exercise. Signals and scenarios influence outcomes only when they alter choices regarding strategy, investment, risk appetite or operating models.

Scenarios influence outcomes when they are connected to strategy, risk appetite and capital allocation. Without this linkage, they remain analytical outputs rather than decision inputs.

Feedback and learning

Outcomes generated by decisions provide new signals that refine interpretation and scenario design. Over time, this creates a learning system.

Exposure to stress becomes a source of insight. Rather than treating disruption solely as a failure of planning, resilient organizations use it to refine assumptions, improve scenarios and strengthen future decisions. In this way, uncertainty becomes a source of adaptation rather than simply a source of risk.

Foresight in conditions of complexity

In complex environments, disruption results from the interaction of multiple factors rather than a single event. It emerges through the interaction of multiple signals that appear unrelated when viewed in isolation. Foresight therefore depends less on predicting individual events and more on understanding how structural, operational and external developments combine to reshape future conditions.

The foresight-to-decision loop provides a mechanism for interpreting these dynamics and translating them into action before effects become fully visible.

REAL-WORLD EXAMPLE

Foresight in banking and the integration of structural risk into decision-making

MUFG Bank operates in an environment shaped by long-term structural change. Japan's ageing and declining population affects demand for traditional lending and savings products, while digital platforms are reshaping how customers access financial services.

These dynamics have been visible for decades. The challenge has not been their identification but their translation into decisions. Traditional performance indicators remained broadly stable, even as underlying customer behaviour and long-term growth dynamics began to shift. Structural risk accumulated without triggering immediate corrective action.

In response, MUFG moved to integrate these trends directly into strategic planning and capital allocation.[6]

This has translated into concrete decisions. The bank has expanded internationally to offset domestic demographic pressure, accelerated investment in digital capabilities and acquired platforms, such as WealthNavi,[7] to position itself in automated, technology-driven wealth management, particularly in anticipation of the intergenerational transfer of wealth from an ageing population to digitally oriented clients. At the same time, it has reduced exposure to lower-return client segments and reallocated resources towards activities aligned with long-term structural viability.

Scenario analysis supports this process by linking structural trends to strategic choices. Demographic projections, behavioural shifts and digital ecosystem developments are used to assess how different business models perform over time. This does not produce a single forecast. It forces explicit trade-offs between defending existing revenue streams and investing in emerging capabilities before decline becomes visible in headline performance. In practice, this requires leadership to decide which elements of the existing model can be sustained and which must be reshaped or exited.

These decisions are not without tension. Shifting resources away from currently profitable activities requires acting before financial pressure becomes explicit. This is reflected in the bank's focus on improving return on equity, with targets of approximately 9 per cent by FY2026,[8] linking structural adaptation directly to performance outcomes.

The resulting improvement in foresight does not arise from predicting the timing of disruption. It reflects the integration of structural variables into decision-making, allowing the organization to adjust its direction as conditions evolve.

The lesson extends beyond banking. Structural risks are often visible well in advance, yet remain underacted upon when they are treated as background trends. Foresight becomes effective when such risks shape how capital is allocated and how strategic choices are made.

Why signals do not travel: Human and cultural dynamics

Translating signals into decisions depends on how information moves through the organization.

Signals rarely enter decision-making unchanged. They are reframed to align with existing priorities, adjusted to fit reporting structures and sequenced alongside competing demands for attention. This does not prevent foresight from occurring. It alters how and when it is applied.

Three dynamics are particularly relevant:

- **Ambiguity competes with urgency.** Signals that do not yet support a clear course of action are often deferred in favour of issues that are more immediate and measurable. Over time, this creates a bias towards acting on visible problems while emerging developments remain under-weighted.
- **Interpretation is distributed but decision-making is concentrated.** Signals are generated across the organization, yet decisions are often made within a narrower set of forums. This creates a gap between where information is observed and where action is taken, increasing the risk that signals are simplified or delayed before they influence decisions.
- **Timing is structurally constrained.** Acting on early signals requires decisions to be made before outcomes are fully visible. This introduces trade-offs between short-term performance and long-term positioning, which are not always resolved in favour of early action.

Organizations frequently become aware of change before they become willing to respond to it. The distance between awareness and action determines whether foresight creates advantage or merely provides hindsight in advance.

Embedded insight: When signals are deferred

Operational teams identify early indicators of change, such as increasing supplier dependency, shifts in customer behaviour or emerging constraints within systems. However, moving from observation to action requires these signals to become decision-relevant.

This transition is often unclear. Emerging developments do not carry an obvious instruction for action. Their significance depends on whether those observing them can interpret their implications and connect them to broader organizational objectives, performance expectations, risk appetite and underlying assumptions. In that context, the same signal may be treated as routine monitoring in one organization and as a trigger for strategic review in another.

Foresight becomes effective when organizations establish clear conditions under which emerging developments prompt reassessment rather than observation. Without these conditions, signals remain informative but not influential.

Implication

For signals to influence decisions, organizations require more than the ability to detect and interpret emerging developments. They require conditions that enable those developments to be translated into action.

In practice, the difference lies in how signals are positioned within decision-making. Some organizations treat emerging developments as contextual information to be monitored. Others define the conditions under which those same signals trigger escalation, challenge assumptions or prompt adjustment.

The conditions outlined in Table 9.1 determine whether signals remain informational or become decision-relevant.

THE FORESIGHT QUESTION BOARDS RARELY ASK

What are we most likely to be seeing too late because the signals are dispersed, ambiguous or trapped inside organizational silos?

The question shifts attention from risk identification to signal visibility. In many organizations, early indicators of disruption already exist within operational data, customer interactions, supplier relationships or frontline observations. The challenge is often not the absence of information, but the organization's ability to connect fragmented signals before disruption becomes visible. (Adapted from insights shared during interviews conducted for this book.)

TABLE 9.1 From signal to decision: Required conditions

Condition	What it requires	What it looks like in practice	If absent
Decision relevance	Signals are explicitly linked to strategy, performance and risk appetite	Emerging developments are framed in terms of impact on revenue, cost, capacity or strategic assumptions	Signals remain informational and are not prioritized
Ownership	Clear accountability for interpreting signals and triggering escalation	Named individuals or functions responsible for assessing implications and bringing signals into decision forums	Signals circulate without leading to action
Action thresholds	Defined triggers that distinguish monitoring from decision	Predefined indicators or conditions that require escalation or decision before outcomes are fully visible	Signals are repeatedly reviewed but not acted upon
Legitimacy of early action	Acceptance that decisions may be taken under uncertainty	Leadership supports action based on partial information where potential impact justifies early response	Action is delayed until evidence becomes conclusive, reducing available options

Embedding foresight into governance and decision-making

The conditions outlined in the previous section define when signals can influence decisions. Embedding foresight requires translating these conditions into governance and decision-making practices.

Embedding foresight requires governance forums to move beyond reviewing scenarios as analytical outputs. The focus shifts to how emerging developments affect strategic assumptions, resource allocation and risk boundaries. The question is no longer whether a scenario is plausible but whether current decisions remain appropriate if conditions evolve.

This changes the nature of oversight. Boards require visibility of developments that may affect long-term positioning before their impact becomes visible through traditional performance measures. Challenge extends beyond reviewing outcomes to examining whether the assumptions underpinning strategy remain valid as conditions change.

The same principle applies across executive decision-making. Strategic planning, investment decisions and transformation initiatives are assessed not only against expected outcomes but also against the conditions under which those outcomes may no longer be achieved. Foresight therefore becomes part of how priorities are established, resources allocated and trade-offs evaluated.

This also changes the role of the risk function. Rather than focusing solely on identification and reporting, risk leaders help translate emerging developments into decision-relevant implications. Signals are connected to strategic assumptions, potential constraints and areas where existing risk boundaries may come under pressure. In this way, foresight becomes integrated into decision-making rather than operating alongside it as a separate analytical activity.

The circle of control: Translating foresight into action

Foresight expands visibility into emerging developments, though visibility alone does not change outcomes. Organizations cannot control demographic shifts, technological disruption, geopolitical events or changing customer behaviour. They can only control how they respond. The circle of control defines the set of decisions through which organizations influence their future direction despite uncertainty.

These decision levers form a circle linking risk appetite, capital allocation and strategic trade-offs. Together, they determine how organizations respond to changing conditions. Risk appetite influences the level of uncertainty leaders are willing to accept. Capital allocation determines where resources are invested, protected or withdrawn. Strategic trade-offs determine which priorities receive sustained attention and which are deferred.

This is what makes the circle of control significant. Emerging developments become decision-relevant when they challenge one or more of these levers. A signal that does not affect appetite, resource allocation or strategic priorities may remain informative. A signal that alters any of them begins to influence the future direction of the organization.

Signals are therefore not assessed in isolation. Their significance depends on how they affect the choices through which organizations shape outcomes. Foresight becomes operational when emerging developments influence what leaders are willing to pursue, where resources are deployed and which priorities are advanced, protected or deferred.

This creates a direct link between foresight and action. As conditions evolve, organizations continuously adjust the elements within their circle of control, ensuring that emerging developments influence decisions before disruption becomes visible through traditional measures.

For these decision levers to respond to emerging developments, foresight must be integrated into existing governance structures. Decision forums incorporate forward-looking signals alongside performance metrics. Escalation pathways connect emerging developments to define decision thresholds. Strategic reviews revisit underlying assumptions rather than focusing solely on outcomes.

This integration ensures that foresight becomes part of how decisions are made rather than an activity conducted alongside them.

Embedding foresight ultimately depends on consistency. The foresight-to-decision loop provides the structure through which signals are detected, interpreted and translated into action. The conditions identified in the previous section ensure that signals become decision-relevant. Governance brings these elements together, enabling organizations to adjust their circle of control as conditions evolve.

REAL-WORLD EXAMPLE

Foresight in critical infrastructure and the institutionalization of long-term resilience planning

The French nuclear energy sector, led by EDF and overseen by ASN, operates within a system where long-term resilience is inseparable from national energy security. Nuclear generation represents a significant share of electricity supply, creating exposure to evolving technical, regulatory and geopolitical conditions over extended time horizons.

These risks emerge through the interaction of infrastructure ageing, energy policy, environmental constraints and system interdependencies. The challenge lies in incorporating them into decisions that shape the system over decades.

Following the Fukushima Daiichi nuclear disaster, stress-testing exercises were expanded to consider extreme scenarios beyond original design assumptions. This led to the introduction of the 'noyau dur' or hardened safety core, comprising dedicated backup systems designed to remain operational under severe conditions. This represents a direct translation of foresight into infrastructure design.

Foresight also informs how environmental and policy signals are interpreted. Rising river temperatures, linked to climate change, have introduced constraints on plant cooling, requiring adjustments to operational planning and at times, reductions in output to maintain ecological limits.

At a strategic level, foresight has shaped long-term investment decisions. The Grand Carénage programme,[9] representing a multi-decade investment to extend the life of existing reactors, reflects an assessment that maintaining and upgrading the current fleet is necessary to meet future energy demand and transition objectives.

A defining feature of this approach is its integration into governance. Foresight is embedded within regulatory requirements, investment planning and system design, ensuring that long-term developments are consistently reflected in decisions affecting safety, capacity and infrastructure.

The resulting improvement in resilience does not arise from predicting specific events. It reflects the institutionalization of foresight, where emerging developments are systematically translated into design choices, operational adjustments and strategic investment.

The lesson extends beyond the energy sector. Institutionalized foresight forces decisions to be made against long-term conditions rather than short-term performance. It embeds trade-offs between cost, safety and system resilience within everyday decision-making, ensuring that long-term risks shape present choices.

Board and executive implications

The value of foresight lies in influencing decisions before changing conditions begin to affect performance, operations or strategic outcomes.

For boards, this shifts oversight beyond current exposure and performance. Challenge increasingly focuses on the assumptions that underpin strategy, the conditions under which those assumptions may no longer hold and the signals that would justify reassessment. Visibility therefore extends beyond what is happening today to how the environment supporting current performance is evolving.

For executive teams, foresight becomes part of decision architecture. Strategic planning, investment decisions and transformation initiatives are assessed not only against expected outcomes but also against the conditions that could alter those outcomes over time. This requires greater attention to emerging developments that affect resource allocation, strategic priorities and risk appetite.

For CROs and risk leaders, the role extends beyond identifying emerging risks. It includes helping decision makers understand how changing conditions affect strategic assumptions, risk boundaries and the choices available to the organization. Foresight becomes valuable when it influences decisions rather than remaining within reporting, horizon scanning or scenario analysis activities.

Across all three groups, the common challenge is translation. Signals, scenarios and emerging developments create value only when they influence the decisions through which organizations shape their future direction.

Practical playbook

Foresight creates value when signals and insights influence decisions as conditions evolve. The following actions help ensure that foresight remains connected to governance and decision-making rather than becoming an analytical or reporting exercise.

Boards

1 **Require integration of scenarios into strategic decision-making**
Boards should require that scenario analysis is explicitly incorporated into strategic discussions, including market positioning, investment priorities and operating model design. The objective is not to review scenarios in isolation but to ensure that strategic choices are tested against a range of plausible conditions.

2 **Require visibility on decision-relevant signals**
Boards should require visibility on emerging developments that may affect strategic assumptions and future decisions. Oversight should focus on how these signals relate to strategy and the conditions under which they would trigger reassessment.

3 **Challenge assumptions, not just projections**
Governance discussions should examine the assumptions that underpin plans, including demand expectations, cost structures and external dependencies. This ensures that foresight informs how strategy is tested rather than how it is presented.

Executives

1 **Embed foresight into decision cycles**
Executives should introduce defined checkpoints within planning, transformation and investment processes where emerging developments and scenario implications are considered before decisions are finalized.

2 **Align capital allocation with forward-looking conditions**
Resource allocation should reflect not only expected performance outcomes but also exposure to structural change. This includes investing in capabilities that provide flexibility under alternative scenarios.

3 **Integrate foresight into transformation decisions**
Transformation initiatives should be assessed based on how they position the organization under evolving conditions rather than solely on immediate efficiency or growth outcomes.

Chief risk officers and risk leaders

1 **Establish mechanisms for signal detection**
Risk functions should ensure that emerging developments are identified across operational, customer and external environments. This requires continuous monitoring of weak signals, dependencies and behavioural shifts that may indicate changing conditions before they are formalized within risk frameworks.

2 **Translate scenarios into decision-relevant insights**
Scenario analysis should clarify implications for strategy, risk appetite and operational capacity, ensuring that scenarios inform decisions rather than remain analytical outputs.

3 **Develop structured scenario libraries**
Organizations benefit from maintaining a curated set of scenarios reflecting recurring patterns of disruption. These scenarios should be clearly defined, with explicit assumptions, boundaries and impact considerations, allowing decisions to be tested consistently across different contexts.[10]

FROM SIGNAL TO DECISION

Illustrative scenarios

Effective scenarios are defined by clear assumptions, boundaries and decision implications, ensuring that they inform choices rather than remain illustrative.

Talent flight

- **Weak signal**: declining engagement and rising attrition in critical roles
- **Scenario**: loss of institutional knowledge during transformation, affecting delivery capacity and continuity
- **Decision lever**: retention strategy, leadership intervention and succession planning

Supplier collapse

- **Weak signal**: concentration risk and financial fragility within key suppliers
- **Scenario**: disruption to critical operations and service delivery, with limited substitution options
- **Decision lever**: supplier diversification, contingency planning and contractual redesign

AI model failure

- **Weak signal**: model drift, unexplained outputs and reduced reliability
- **Scenario**: systemic decision errors affecting operations or customer outcomes across multiple processes
- **Decision lever**: governance, validation processes and oversight mechanisms

KEY TAKEAWAYS

- **Foresight is a decision capability rather than a forecasting activity**. Its value lies not in predicting specific events but in influencing decisions before changing conditions begin to affect performance, operations or strategic outcomes.
- **Signals of change are often visible long before disruption becomes apparent**. The challenge lies less in identifying emerging developments than in interpreting their significance and translating them into decisions that alter organizational direction.
- **Different forms of uncertainty require different responses**. Visible risks may be ignored, unspoken risks may remain unchallenged, systemic risks may emerge through hidden interdependencies and rare events may

expose the limits of historical assumptions. Treating these uncertainties as equivalent weakens foresight and misdirects attention.

- **Foresight becomes effective when it is connected to decision-making.** Emerging developments create value when they influence the organization's circle of control, shaping risk appetite, capital allocation and strategic trade-offs before options become constrained.
- **Resilient organizations institutionalize foresight.** They embed signal detection, interpretation and adaptation within governance and decision processes, ensuring that changing conditions influence strategic direction before disruption becomes visible through traditional measures.

Reframing forward

Developing foresight capability enables organizations to identify and interpret emerging developments before disruption becomes visible within operational systems. When signals are detected, connected and translated into scenarios, organizations gain earlier visibility into how conditions may evolve and how current strategies may be affected. Yet this capability addresses only part of the resilience challenge.

Foresight makes uncertainty visible. It does not ensure that organizations act on it. In practice, many organizations already possess more visibility than they use. Signals are identified, scenarios are developed and emerging risks are discussed, yet decisions often remain unchanged.

Resilient organizations do not rely solely on their ability to anticipate disruption. They ensure that anticipation is translated into decisions, ownership and performance. This requires connecting foresight to the mechanisms through which organizations define priorities, allocate resources and evaluate outcomes.

Without this connection, foresight remains informative rather than directive. It expands understanding without altering direction.

The next chapter examines how organizations design accountability systems that ensure resilience is measured, governed and sustained over time. It explores how decision ownership is defined, how performance is aligned with resilience objectives and how governance structures reinforce consistent action under changing conditions.

Endnotes

1 Weick, K E and Sutcliffe, K M (2015) *Managing the Unexpected: Sustained performance in a complex world* (3rd edn), John Wiley & Sons, Hoboken, NJ

2 Roberts, K H (1990) Managing high reliability organizations, *California Management Review*, 32 (4), 101–13

3 Vaughan, D (1996) *The Challenger Launch Decision: Risky technology, culture, and deviance at NASA*, University of Chicago Press, Chicago, IL

4 Sweidan, A (2013) The Black Elephant in the Room, (online video), www.youtube.com/watch?v=GLYb8l4P3x8

5 Bank of England (2023) Model risk management principles for banks, Bank of England, London, www.bankofengland.co.uk/prudential-regulation/publication/2023/may/model-risk-management-principles-for-banks

6 Mitsubishi UFJ Financial Group (2024) Medium-Term Business Plan (FY2024–FY2026), MUFG, Tokyo, www.mufg.jp/english/ir/strategy

7 Mitsubishi UFJ Financial Group (2023) MUFG to make WealthNavi a consolidated subsidiary, www.mufg.jp/english

8 Mitsubishi UFJ Financial Group (2024) Medium-Term Business Plan 2024, Mitsubishi UFJ Financial Group, www.mufg.jp/dam/ir/presentation/investorday/2024_en.pdf

9 EDF (2023) Grand Carénage programme: Extending the life of France's nuclear fleet, EDF, Paris: EDF, www.edf.fr/en/the-edf-group/producing-a-climate-friendly-energy/nuclear-energy/grand-carenage

10 Aevitium LTD (2024) Resilience Scenario Toolkit Blueprint: A strategic overview for risk leaders, www.aevitium.com/resilience-scenario-blueprint

10

Accountability that builds trust

Measuring and reporting resilience performance

> CHAPTER OBJECTIVES
>
> - Explain how accountability contributes to organizational resilience by ensuring that visibility, ownership and consequence translate signals into timely decisions.
> - Demonstrate how accountability depends on the interaction between reporting, decision-making and governance rather than on reporting structures alone.
> - Show how boards and executives align oversight, incentives and decision authority so that changing conditions lead to timely and coordinated action.

Reporting describes conditions. Accountability governs decisions.

Comprehensive reporting provides organizations with a clear view of exposure and performance. This creates a false sense of security that risks are understood, even when decision readiness is uncertain.

When conditions begin to change, this view no longer holds. Signals may be visible yet decisions are delayed, ownership becomes unclear and escalation does not consistently lead to action. Structured accountability can mask a gap between visibility and decision readiness.

Resilience is reported yet not consistently governed.[1] Organizations produce extensive dashboards across risk, performance and operations. The effectiveness of resilience is determined by how it connects to ownership, how it translates into decisions and how those decisions shape outcomes and future behaviour.

Leaders must design accountability as a system that ensures early warnings lead to timely and consistent decisions as conditions evolve. Consequence extends beyond corrective action because it shapes performance, incentives and learning across the organization.

This chapter examines how organizations design accountability systems that translate measurement into decision and decision into action. It explores how boards and executives align reporting, incentives and governance structures so that resilience influences how decisions are taken rather than how performance is described.

Why accountability fails despite reporting

Most organizations operate under a reassuring assumption: if risks are reported, they are being handled. Structured reporting creates the false confidence that exposure is understood and governance is working as intended. From a distance, this creates a coherent picture of control.

Yet accountability arises from the translation of information into decisions and from the clarity of who acts when conditions change. In most organizations, reporting describes states rather than choices. It answers what is happening, where exposure sits and how indicators have evolved. It rarely answers the more demanding question: what decision does this require, by whom and within what timeframe?

As a result, reporting operates as a parallel system to decision-making rather than an integrated one. Information flows upward, while decisions are distributed, delayed or implicit. Accountability becomes inferred rather than explicit.

Three structural drivers reinforce this gap.

1 **Metrics describe exposure, not decision readiness.**
Risk indicators are calibrated to measure exposure and its evolution over time. They provide comparability and consistency. They do not indicate whether the organization is prepared to act. A risk may be clearly identified and tracked, while the organization remains uncertain about the decision it would take if that risk materializes. Visibility without readiness creates a false sense of control.

2 **Accountability is distributed without clear ownership.**
Modern organizations operate through interconnected systems. Risks cut across functions, products and geographies. In response, accountability is often shared across risk, operations, technology and finance. Shared accountability creates alignment in principle. In reality, it often diffuses responsibility. When multiple functions contribute to a risk, ownership of the resulting decision often becomes unclear. The system reports collectively, while accountability for action remains ambiguous.

3 **Reporting cycles lag behind decision timelines.**
Boards and executive committees operate on structured reporting cadences. Monthly and quarterly cycles provide rhythm and oversight. Strategic risks and operational disruptions evolve on very different timescales. Market conditions shift in days. Technology failures propagate in minutes. Cultural markers build up gradually and then accelerate. When reporting is tied to fixed cycles, it captures a version of reality that has already moved on, forcing decisions to rely on conditions that may no longer exist.

The consequence is not the absence of information. It is the misalignment between information and action. Organizations see risks emerging, track their evolution and yet miss the moment where intervention is still possible.

REAL-WORLD EXAMPLE

Decision-oriented reporting in retail and the alignment of accountability systems

Retail organizations, such as Marks & Spencer,[2] operate increasingly complex and interconnected business models, where digital platforms, supply chains and customer experience are tightly linked. As digital transformation accelerates, changes in one domain can affect performance across multiple systems, often with limited delay.

A systemic misalignment surfaced during large-scale transformation programmes across the sector. Reporting frameworks provided accurate visibility within individual domains, yet this visibility was fragmented. Technology performance, operational stability and customer outcomes were monitored separately. Indicators generated within these domains were not consistently translated into integrated decision-making, ownership of outcomes was distributed, and escalation pathways were not always aligned with the speed at which conditions evolved.

Reporting described system performance, while accountability for decisions across those systems remained unclear. Trade-offs between transformation speed, operational resilience and customer experience were not consistently framed or governed at the point where intervention was possible.

In response, organizations strengthened accountability by redesigning how reporting and decision systems interacted.

Reporting systems were enhanced to provide an integrated view of transformation progress, operational performance and customer impact. This enabled signals to be interpreted collectively rather than within functional boundaries.

Decision systems were adapted to link defined performance conditions to predefined decision pathways. For example, when acceleration in digital deployment increased pressure on fulfilment capacity and customer experience, thresholds were established linking latency, service levels and customer indicators to transformation pace. When these thresholds were approached, escalation was triggered and specific decision options were required, including adjusting deployment speed, reallocating operational capacity or revising service expectations.

Structural systems were clarified by aligning accountability for transformation outcomes with decision authority. Ownership of trade-offs between growth, stability and customer experience was made explicit at executive level, reducing ambiguity when thresholds were breached.

Behavioural systems were reinforced by embedding decision discipline into governance forums. Leadership discussions shifted from reviewing performance indicators to evaluating decision options and associated trade-offs, supported by clearer escalation expectations and reduced reliance on retrospective analysis.

The resulting improvement in accountability did not arise from increased reporting. Instead, it reflected the alignment of reporting, decision, structural and behavioural systems, allowing early warnings to move from observation to decision within defined timeframes.

In environments characterized by interdependency and rapid change, accountability depends not on the volume of information available but on how effectively reporting systems are connected to decision pathways.

The challenge is to design reporting systems that connect signals to decisions and decisions to ownership rather than producing more data. Table 10.1 illustrates the distinction between reporting that describes conditions and reporting that is designed to trigger action.

TABLE 10.1 From descriptive reporting to decision-oriented accountability

Descriptive reporting	Decision-oriented reporting
What is happening	What decision is required
Functional metrics	Cross-functional impact
Historical trends	Forward thresholds
Shared ownership	Clear ownership
Periodic review	Trigger-based action

Accountability under external and internal pressure

Accountability in resilience is no longer an internal design choice. It is shaped by external expectations and internal constraints that expose the limits of traditional reporting and governance structures.

Across sectors, regulatory frameworks have evolved from assessing the presence of controls to evaluating the effectiveness of outcomes. Supervisors now expect organizations to demonstrate that critical services can be maintained under stress, that decision-making remains effective during disruption, and that governance structures translate risk visibility into timely action.[3] This shift places greater emphasis on how accountability is exercised rather than how risk is documented.

Investor expectations have developed in a similar direction. Resilience is now interpreted as a proxy for long-term value protection. Operational disruption, technology failure and supply chain fragility are no longer viewed as isolated incidents but as indicators of governance effectiveness. Disclosure requirements have expanded to include operational resilience, sustainability and broader ESG considerations, increasing scrutiny on how organizations manage interconnected risks and trade-offs over time.

Public tolerance for failure in sectors where services are critical has reduced significantly. Disruption is no longer assessed solely on financial impact but on its consequences for customers, communities and broader societal functioning.

The widespread disruption to digital banking services at TSB Bank[4] illustrated this shift, where the impact was measured not only in financial terms but in prolonged customer disruption and loss of trust, highlighting the consequences of misaligned accountability during system change. These external pressures interact with internal dynamics that further constrain accountability.

Escalation occurs after conditions have already deteriorated. Relevant insights are available, often well before disruption materializes, yet the connection between that intelligence and decision-making is disjointed. Reporting cycles capture the evolution of risk, while escalation pathways do not consistently translate that evolution into timely intervention.

At the same time, performance management frameworks continue to prioritize short-term outcomes. Growth, efficiency and delivery against immediate targets are the dominant measures of success. Resilience, by contrast, is often assessed retrospectively, following disruption. This creates a structural misalignment between what is incentivized and what is required to sustain performance over time.

As organizational systems become more interconnected, this misalignment is amplified. Dependencies across technology, operations, supply chains and customer channels increase the speed at which local disruptions can propagate. Accountability structures designed for more stable and segmented environments struggle to keep pace with this level of complexity.

At the centre of these dynamics sits a persistent asymmetry. Executives are rewarded for achieving short-term growth and performance objectives but are penalized disproportionately when resilience failures occur. This asymmetry encourages decisions that optimize visible performance while deferring or under-prioritizing actions that strengthen resilience but may constrain short-term outcomes.

Rebalancing this dynamic requires accountability structures that make resilience visible in decision terms, assign clear ownership for trade-offs and ensure that signals lead to timely and consequential action.

The resilience accountability system

Reporting, ownership and escalation are present in most organizations and often well developed in isolation. Yet accountability depends less on the existence of these mechanisms than on the way they operate together. Reporting defines what is visible, governance structures define who is responsible, escalation processes determine how decisions are triggered, and performance frameworks shape how outcomes are reinforced.

A more effective approach is to consider accountability as a system through which insights are translated into decisions and decisions into outcomes. Within this system, four conditions determine whether accountability is realized in practice:

1. the organization's ability to surface relevant observations
2. the clarity of ownership attached to those observations
3. the consequences that follow when conditions change
4. the way experience is incorporated into future decisions.

Together, these four conditions determine whether visibility is translated into action and action into learning. Accountability depends on how effectively they operate as a connected system rather than as separate governance mechanisms.

Visibility – from performance reporting to system awareness

Visibility determines whether emerging conditions are recognized while outcomes can still be influenced.

Visibility is structured around performance reporting. Metrics describe activity, utilization and compliance within defined domains. This provides a consistent view of performance yet it remains limited in its ability to capture how conditions evolve across interconnected systems.

Effective visibility extends beyond individual metrics to reflect how pressures develop within the system as a whole. It incorporates forward-looking indicators, highlights interdependencies across functions and processes, and surfaces early warning signals that precede observable impact. This allows leadership to interpret not only what is happening but how current conditions may affect future stability.

This requires a shift in the type of indicators that are prioritized. Alongside traditional performance metrics, organizations increasingly monitor signals such as capacity strain across critical processes, concentration of dependency on key suppliers or systems, workforce fatigue in high-risk functions and escalation frequency or near-miss patterns. These indicators do not describe failure. They indicate conditions under which failure becomes more likely.

The value of these insights lies in their ability to reveal how pressures build up across the system. For example, stable operational performance may coexist with increasing supplier concentration and rising workforce strain, creating a level of exposure that is not visible through isolated metrics.

Visibility becomes meaningful when these insights are interpreted collectively rather than independently.

Resilience dashboards reflect this broader perspective. They bring together strategic, operational and cultural indicators into a single view, allowing signals to be interpreted in relation to one another. Metrics are organized around conditions that require attention rather than presented as isolated data points. This enables earlier recognition of emerging stress and supports more timely intervention.

Ownership – aligning responsibility with decision authority

Visibility does not in itself create accountability. It must be connected to clearly defined ownership.

In complex organizations, outcomes are produced through the interaction of multiple functions. Technology, operations, finance and customer-facing teams all contribute to performance. Responsibility is often distributed across these domains.

While this distribution supports coordination, it can reduce clarity at the point where decisions are required. When signals indicate that conditions are changing, the absence of clearly defined ownership can delay action or lead to inconsistent responses.

Effective accountability requires alignment between responsibility for outcomes and the authority to act, ensuring that those accountable can make or trigger decisions when conditions change. Ownership must be defined at the level where decisions can be taken, ensuring that those accountable for an outcome are also able to influence it when conditions change.

This alignment extends across governance structures. Audit provides assurance on effectiveness, Risk interprets forward-looking exposure and remuneration committees shape incentives. When aligned, these functions reinforce accountability. When disconnected, they fragment it.

ACCOUNTABILITY DIAGNOSTIC

Ownership and decision authority

For each critical risk or performance condition:

- Is there a clearly identified owner responsible for the outcome?
- Does that owner have the authority to act within the required timeframe?

- Are decision thresholds defined or does action depend on interpretation?
- Is it clear who decides when conditions deteriorate across multiple functions?
- Do escalation pathways specify how quickly decisions must be taken?
- Are incentives aligned so that acting early is rewarded rather than deferred?

Consequence – linking signals to decisions

The effectiveness of accountability is determined by whether defined conditions trigger clear and timely decisions (consequences).

Many organizations confuse discussion with intervention. Signals are reviewed, debated and monitored, yet no decision follows. Accountability is not demonstrated when risks are visible. It is demonstrated when visibility changes behaviour.

Effective systems define in advance how the organization responds when conditions change. Thresholds establish when attention is required and decision pathways clarify what actions follow. These pathways clarify responsibility and define the decisions required within a given timeframe. This reduces reliance on interpretation under pressure and supports more consistent decision-making.

Consequence also extends into performance management. When resilience signals influence how performance is assessed, they become part of how priorities are set. Where this link is absent, signals are informational and are less likely to shape behaviour.

Feedback – adapting the system over time

Accountability systems evolve through experience. As organizations encounter disruption and near-misses, the assumptions embedded within reporting, ownership and decision pathways are tested. Feedback mechanisms ensure that these experiences are incorporated into how the system operates.

Metrics, thresholds and decision pathways are refined as governance structures evolve to address areas where accountability was unclear or delayed. Near misses are particularly valuable because they reveal where accountability functioned too late rather than not at all. This creates a continuous learning process through which the organization strengthens its ability to respond to future conditions.

REAL-WORLD EXAMPLE

Resilience reporting in healthcare and the alignment of accountability systems

Healthcare organizations in Germany, including large hospital groups operating within federal and regional coordination structures, operate in highly interdependent environments where clinical capacity, workforce availability and supply chains must function in alignment.

During the Covid-19 pandemic, reporting frameworks were heavily centred on capacity indicators such as intensive care bed availability, hospital occupancy rates and patient throughput. In Germany, this visibility was supported by the DIVI Intensive Care Register,[5] which provided near real-time data on ICU capacity across the country and became a central coordination tool for managing system pressure.

These metrics provided a clear view of system utilization and were widely used to monitor capacity constraints. However, sector analysis and post-pandemic reviews highlighted a recurring limitation. Capacity indicators alone did not fully capture the sustainability of operations under prolonged stress. Workforce fatigue, staff availability and supply chain disruption often developed ahead of observable deterioration in capacity metrics.

This tension became visible in practice. Measures such as the suspension of Pflegepersonal-Regeluntergrenze (minimum staffing levels) were introduced to increase available capacity. While this supported short-term system throughput, it also increased pressure on clinical staff and raised concerns about longer-term sustainability and quality of care.

In this context, signals were present across multiple parts of the system, yet they were not always integrated into a single decision framework. Reporting provided visibility into capacity, while indicators of workforce strain and operational sustainability were less consistently embedded in decision-making. Ownership of response was distributed across clinical, operational and administrative structures, and escalation pathways varied across regions and institutions. As a result, reporting described activity, while accountability for maintaining system stability under sustained pressure was less clearly defined.

In response, healthcare organizations and coordinating bodies expanded the scope of reporting and clarified coordination mechanisms. Reporting systems increasingly incorporated indicators related to workforce availability, staff absence, supply constraints and escalation activity, providing a broader view of system conditions beyond capacity alone. Decision processes were progressively structured around defined escalation levels, linking system pressure indicators to coordinated actions such as resource reallocation, patient transfers and prioritization of critical services. Governance structures were adapted to clarify responsibility for service continuity, aligning operational coordination with decision authority at regional and institutional levels. Furthermore, operational practices were reinforced through coordinated response protocols and cross-functional collaboration between clinical leadership, hospital management and public health authorities, improving the consistency of response under pressure.

The resulting improvement in resilience did not arise from increased reporting. It reflected the broader integration of system-level indicators with clearer coordination and decision structures, allowing earlier and more consistent responses under sustained pressure.

The lesson extends beyond healthcare. In complex and interdependent environments, accountability depends on how effectively reporting is connected to decision pathways.

The reality of accountability

Accountability is tested at the point where a decision must be taken under constraint. It is at that moment that structural clarity meets behavioural reality.

High-performing organizations treat accountability as an active discipline. Visible signals lead to informed choices, ownership remains clear when trade-offs emerge and escalation results in timely action. Yet the presence of these mechanisms does not guarantee that accountability will be exercised consistently under pressure. Several recurring behaviours explain why.

First: Redefinition of the decision itself[6]

When conditions deteriorate, the question shifts. A decision about whether to pause an initiative becomes a discussion about whether performance remains within tolerance. An indicator that should trigger intervention is treated as a trend to be monitored. The decision is not avoided but it is reframed in a way that reduces immediate impact. This extends the time available for performance recovery while allowing exposure to increase.

Second: Diffusion of accountability at the point of trade-off

In interdependent systems, decisions require coordination across functions. Trade-offs between growth, stability and customer outcomes rarely sit within a single domain. When ownership of these trade-offs is not explicitly defined, responsibility becomes collective in principle and unclear in practice. Decisions are escalated, revisited or redistributed, creating delay without resolving the underlying tension.

Third: Substitution of explanation for action

As conditions deteriorate, the response often shifts towards further analysis. Additional data is requested and assumptions are revisited, creating a sense of progress while the underlying decision remains unchanged. As explored earlier, extending analysis does not improve the decision once the key assumptions are understood. It delays commitment while exposure continues to evolve.

Fourth: Gap between defined thresholds and applied tolerance

Thresholds may be established within governance frameworks, yet their application depends on judgement. When conditions approach these thresholds, they are often interpreted in context rather than acted upon directly. Signals are absorbed locally, particularly when performance is close to target or when escalation carries visible consequences. The result is a divergence between formal design and actual response.

These behaviours are shaped by how incentives, ownership and decision pathways interact under pressure. In each case, the visible signal is not ignored; it is absorbed into a process that delays commitment and preserves flexibility. Accountability weakens not because organizations fail to see the issue but because they postpone the moment at which a choice must be made.

ACCOUNTABILITY IS SHAPED BY CONSEQUENCE

Accountability often weakens when the consequences of acting become unclear. Under pressure, some individuals escalate issues prematurely while others remain silent. Although these responses appear different, both reflect uncertainty about what will happen if judgement is exercised and the outcome proves unpopular or incorrect. This highlights an often-overlooked aspect of accountability. Authority and ownership may be clearly defined, yet decision quality deteriorates when individuals become more focused on the consequences of acting than on the conditions requiring action. (Adapted from insights during interviews conducted for this book.)

Board and executive implications

For a board, accountability is reflected in the distance between a signal and a decision.[7] When this gap extends, exposure develops in the period between recognition and action.

This gap is not immediately visible. Reporting is comprehensive and ownership appears defined, yet decisions remain delayed or reframed as conditions change. What appears as structured governance can therefore mask a disconnect between design and execution.

Effective oversight places a different emphasis. It examines whether accountability functions in practice, particularly when signals require decisions to be taken under constraint. The objective is not only to confirm that responsibilities are assigned but to understand whether signals lead to timely action, whether ownership is exercised at the point of decision and whether consequences are applied consistently.

For boards, this requires a shift in the nature of oversight discussions. Rather than focusing primarily on the completeness of reporting or the clarity of organizational structures, attention moves towards how visibility, ownership and decision pathways interact when conditions deteriorate.

Several questions become particularly important:

- Where does visibility fail to translate into action, despite signals being available?
- Which risks or conditions lack clearly defined ownership at the point where decisions are required?
- Where are decisions delayed, reframed or redistributed rather than resolved?
- Which thresholds trigger action under stress? Which remain within reporting cycles?
- How consistently are consequences applied when conditions change, particularly where trade-offs are required?

These questions allow boards to move beyond confirmation of reporting towards an understanding of how accountability operates under pressure. They provide insight into whether governance mechanisms support timely intervention or allow exposure to develop between signal and action.

This perspective has direct implications for executive leadership. If boards expect accountability to be exercised through decisions, executives must ensure that organizational systems support that expectation under all conditions. This requires aligning visibility, ownership and decision pathways so that signals generated across the organization lead to clear and timely action.

Executives are responsible for ensuring that:

- ownership of risks and outcomes aligns with decision authority at the point where action is required
- decision thresholds are defined in a way that triggers action rather than continued observation
- escalation mechanisms lead to decisions within relevant timeframes, not extended review cycles
- performance and incentive structures reinforce early intervention rather than delayed response.

This alignment ensures that accountability is not a formal attribute of governance, but operates as a system through which decisions are taken and reinforced over time.

Risk functions play a critical role in enabling this shift. They define the frameworks and indicators that make accountability visible, yet their contribution extends beyond design. They support the organization in identifying where signals do not lead to decisions, where ownership is unclear and where escalation does not result in action. By examining how accountability operates across the organization, they help ensure that governance structures are connected to decision-making rather than reporting alone.

PRACTITIONER PULSE

Ownership remains the weakest link in accountability

In a LinkedIn poll[8] of risk and governance professionals, 47 per cent identified ownership as the area where accountability is weakest. Behaviours received 25 per cent of responses, followed by follow-through at 19 per cent, while roles and responsibilities accounted for 9 per cent.

The findings suggest that accountability challenges often arise less from organizational design and more from whether individuals take responsibility for decisions and outcomes.

Practical playbook

Accountability frameworks are often defined through roles, reporting and escalation pathways. Their effectiveness is determined by whether they translate signals into decisions when conditions change. The following actions help organizations ensure that accountability supports timely and consistent decision-making under pressure.

Boards

1. **Define resilience as a governance outcome**
   Boards should position resilience as an outcome of governance rather than a property of individual frameworks. Their focus should be on whether signals trigger timely intervention and whether trade-offs between performance and stability are addressed explicitly.
2. **Require integrated, decision-oriented dashboards**
   Oversight should be supported by dashboards that connect risk signals, operational conditions and strategic objectives. In reality, many organizations have strengthened visibility across these domains, yet the link to decision-making remains uneven. Boards should ensure that reporting highlights when decisions are required rather than simply presenting performance indicators, and that thresholds are linked to defined actions.
3. **Align committee oversight around decision accountability**
   Audit, risk and remuneration committees should operate with a shared understanding of how accountability is exercised. Boards should ensure that assurance, forward-looking risk assessment and incentive structures reinforce consistent decision-making, particularly where resilience requires trade-offs across functions.

Executives

1. **Assign ownership at the level where decisions are taken**
   Executives should ensure that accountability aligns with decision authority at the point where trade-offs are made. Ownership should not be distributed across functions and must sit with individuals who can act, including adjusting priorities or reallocating resources, so that signals lead to timely decisions rather than escalation or delay.

2 **Align incentives with resilience outcomes**
Performance frameworks should reflect the importance of early intervention and sustained system stability. Executives should ensure that incentives do not discourage escalation or delay decisions when resilience considerations require adjustment to short-term objectives.

3 **Embed escalation triggers into decision processes**
Escalation mechanisms should be linked to defined thresholds that trigger decisions rather than extended review. Executives should ensure that escalation pathways operate within relevant timeframes and that decision latency is visible and actively managed.

Chief risk officers and risk leaders

1 **Design dashboards that support decisions, not only reporting**
Risk functions should develop reporting that highlights when action is required and clarifies the implications of different decision options. This includes linking indicators to thresholds and ensuring that reporting supports interpretation and action rather than monitoring alone.

2 **Integrate data across functions to reflect system conditions**
Risk functions should ensure that indicators from operational, technological and behavioural domains are connected. This integration enables a more accurate view of how pressures develop across the system and supports earlier identification of conditions requiring intervention.

3 **Challenge reporting that does not lead to consequence**
Risk leaders should actively identify where reporting provides visibility without influencing decisions. This includes examining where signals remain within reporting cycles, ownership is unclear or escalation does not result in action, and using these insights to strengthen accountability mechanisms.

KEY TAKEAWAYS

- **Accountability is a decision capability rather than a reporting process.** Its value lies not in the visibility it creates but in its ability to translate signals into timely decisions when conditions change.
- **Visibility alone does not create accountability.** Reporting can identify emerging exposure, yet risks continue to accumulate when ownership,

decision authority and escalation pathways are not aligned with the point at which action is required.

- **Accountability depends on the interaction of visibility, ownership, consequence and feedback.** These elements operate as a connected system that determines whether signals lead to action, whether decisions are reinforced through incentives and whether experience strengthens future responses.
- **Behavioural dynamics often weaken accountability under pressure.** Decisions may be reframed, delayed or redistributed, while thresholds are interpreted rather than acted upon. Accountability weakens not because organizations fail to recognize signals but because they postpone the moment at which a choice must be made.
- **Resilient organizations embed accountability within governance and decision-making.** They connect signals to decisions, decisions to ownership and outcomes to learning, ensuring that resilience is actively governed rather than inferred from reporting structures alone.

Reframing forward

Measuring resilience creates visibility. Designing accountability creates discipline.

When visibility, ownership and consequence are aligned, organizations move from reporting risk to governing resilience. Signals are not only observed; they lead to decisions that shape outcomes while conditions can still be influenced. Accountability turns resilience into an active practice rather than a static structure, yet this capability addresses only part of the resilience challenge.

Accountability operates within the organization. It defines how decisions are taken, how trade-offs are managed and how performance is sustained under changing conditions. Its effectiveness is revealed when signals require action under pressure.

In reality, resilience is not assessed internally alone. Markets, regulators and society provide an external perspective on whether organizations can maintain performance as conditions deteriorate. Disruption, failure and recovery expose where accountability holds and where it breaks down.

What appears effective within governance structures is tested against expectations that extend beyond the organization itself.

This introduces a broader dimension to resilience. It is shaped not only by internal alignment but by how organizations respond to external scrutiny, evolving expectations and systemic pressures.

The next chapter examines how these external forces shape resilience. It explores how regulatory expectations, market dynamics and societal scrutiny reveal gaps in governance and redefine what effective leadership requires.

Resilience is therefore not only defined by how organizations see and act.

It is defined by how those actions are tested, challenged and judged beyond their own boundaries.

Endnotes

1. Committee of Sponsoring Organizations of the Treadway Commission (2017) Enterprise Risk Management: Integrating with Strategy and Performance, COSO, New York
2. Marks & Spencer Group plc (2024) Annual Report and Financial Statements 2024, Marks & Spencer, London
3. Bank of England, Prudential Regulation Authority and Financial Conduct Authority (2021) Operational Resilience: Impact Tolerances for Important Business Services
4. Financial Conduct Authority and Prudential Regulation Authority (2022) Final Notices: TSB Bank plc, FCA and PRA, London, www.fca.org.uk/publication/final-notices/tsb-bank-plc-2022.pdf
5. DIVI Intensive Care Register (2021) Intensive Care Capacity Monitoring Reports
6. Kahneman, D (2011) *Thinking, Fast and Slow*, Penguin, London
7. Institute of Directors (2024) Guidance for Boards on Corporate Governance and Resilience, IoD, London
8. Haye, J (2026) Where is accountability weakest today? LinkedIn poll, 23 September, www.linkedin.com/feed/update/urn:li:activity:7427639901661057024?utm_source=share&utm_medium=member_desktop&rcm=ACoAAACPfFMB6H2gmXmX07V0yupet72E9uvZ5kQ

11

External pressures and industry lessons

What markets, regulators and society reveal about resilience

CHAPTER OBJECTIVES

- Examine how market, regulatory and stakeholder reactions influence the timing of organizational response.
- Explain how small gaps in coordination, dependencies and decision-making can be amplified once external actors begin to act.
- Demonstrate how signals that appear manageable internally can extend across systems, counterparties and stakeholders as conditions evolve.
- Show how leaders can position decision authority, governance and response capabilities so that action is taken within the timeframe imposed by external reactions.
- Highlight that resilience is determined not only by internal preparedness but also by the organization's ability to respond at the speed required by its environment.

Two organizations face the same supply chain disruption. A critical supplier fails and deliveries are at risk.

One organization activates predefined contingency pathways. Decision authority is clear at the point of disruption. Alternative sourcing is initiated within the same operating cycle, and communication with customers and regulators follows immediately.

The other organization reports the disruption and prepares escalation. The issue is escalated across functions, additional analysis is requested and communication is delayed while the situation is assessed. During that time, customers adjust orders, suppliers reprioritize allocation and regulators seek clarification.

The disruption is identical. The outcomes diverge.

The difference sits in how decisions are taken once external actors begin to respond. Where decision pathways are clear and ownership is positioned at the point of action, the organization maintains continuity. Where decisions depend on escalation and alignment across forums, response is delayed and options reduce as conditions evolve.

This chapter explores how dependencies, decision pathways and governance structures determine whether organizations act within that timeframe or follow events once conditions have already shifted.

Resilience is an external test of internal decisions

Resilience is most often inferred from what appears in internal governance artefacts. Board packs summarize risk exposure, stress-testing outputs confirm scenario coverage, and control frameworks demonstrate that key processes are documented and monitored. In a quarterly risk committee, these materials create confidence that the organization understands its exposures and is managing them within acceptable boundaries. Because the reports look complete and structured, leadership believes the organization is ready to handle disruption. They treat visibility as a proxy for capability.

This assumption no longer holds when signals fall outside regular governance cadence. A metric shifts between reporting cycles, a dependency identified in a scenario materializes differently or a decision is deferred because the relevant committee will not convene for another two weeks. None of these events breach thresholds. They remain below escalation, outside agenda or between reporting intervals.

As outlined in Chapter 10, escalation follows predefined thresholds, reporting cycles and committee structures. That design provides clarity in stable conditions. It also fixes the timing of when issues are formally recognized. However, as conditions evolve, signals move faster than that structure allows. By the time escalation reaches formal discussion, the range of viable responses has already reduced.

External actors do not engage with the organization's internal representation of risk. Fragility builds in the gap between internal acceptance and external perception. A supervisor reviewing a disruption does not assess whether the relevant control was documented; they assess whether critical services continued. Similarly, a market counterparty does not consider whether escalation followed the defined pathway; it adjusts exposure based on their assessment of the organization's ability to act. In both cases, reactions are driven by perceived outcomes rather than internal governance narrative.

As we will discuss later in this chapter, amplification of risk begins with a gap that already exists, often recognized but not prioritized. It may sit in a board paper as a dependency with a mitigating action plan, or in a risk register with a residual rating deemed acceptable. Under normal conditions, the gap is manageable. But under stress, the same gap is exposed to forces that change its impact.

Regulatory scrutiny accelerates expectations into immediate requirements. Market participants adjust positions before full information is available. Investors reassess not only the issue but the organization's ability to respond to it. As the time available for internal coordination shrinks, what was previously a manageable exposure becomes a broader organizational challenge.

The amplification is also not linear. A control weakness that appears local within an operational process can trigger broader consequences when it intersects with external expectations. A delay of days in internal escalation can translate into immediate repricing or supervisory intervention. The consequence is not proportional to the original gap. It is shaped by the interaction between that gap and external response.

> This is the point at which resilience is defined. Not by the existence of frameworks but by the organization's ability to sustain decision quality when those frameworks are overtaken by events.

Leaders cannot rely solely on internal indicators of preparedness. They must understand how quickly external pressure could amplify a manageable issue into a broader organizational challenge.

Resilience, in this sense, is not an internal state. It is the outcome of an interaction. Internal structures determine what the organization can see and plan for. External pressure determines what it must confront and how quickly it must respond.

The rest of this chapter examines that interaction across different environments. Industries vary in their constraints, governance models and sources of pressure, but the amplification mechanism does not.

External forces are reshaping decision timing

The consequences of this shift are visible across financial markets, operational resilience exercises and major organizational failures. In each case, external actors influence the pace of events, sometimes, materially accelerating the time to major existential crisis.

The collapse of Silicon Valley Bank in 2023 illustrates this change in timing. Concerns about its balance sheet were established and visible so depositors, connected through real-time networks, withdrew funds simultaneously. Liquidity and governance processes designed for sequential withdrawals were overtaken by behaviour that developed within hours.

In a regulatory space, operational resilience regimes test how organizations act under disruption, not whether controls are documented. In scenario exercises, decisions are required before full information is available and outside established governance sequences. Divergence appears at the point where action must be taken. For instance, a market disruption is acted on by counterparties, suppliers and customers before it is captured in reporting cycles. Changes in liquidity, pricing and contractual terms occur immediately.

During the UK LDI (liability-driven investment) crisis in 2022, counterparties issued collateral calls within hours as gilt yields rose. Pension funds had not yet consolidated exposure across mandates. Liquidity decisions were driven by margin requirements rather than internal governance processes.

Investor response develops in parallel. Valuation and funding conditions adjust as signals are interpreted across the market. In the case of Credit Suisse in 2023, a series of disclosed losses and control failures accumulated into a broader assessment of capability. Funding costs increased and liquidity pressure intensified as markets acted on that assessment.

Societal response extends this further. Information is interpreted and circulated across networks in real time. A delay that appears operationally

TABLE 11.1 How external actors shape decision timing

External actor	What they act on	How they act	What this forces internally
Regulators	Service disruption, control breakdown	Intervention, supervisory pressure	Immediate decision-making under scrutiny
Markets	Price signals, liquidity indicators	Repricing, withdrawal of capacity	Rapid adjustment of exposure and funding
Investors	Performance signals, governance credibility	Reallocation of capital, valuation shifts	Justification of strategy and control effectiveness
Society/ networks	Interpreted signals, narratives	Rapid dissemination, coordinated behaviour	Real-time communication and response under uncertainty

justified internally is interpreted externally as a loss of control. Communication becomes a key part of the response at the point decisions are taken.

External actors determine both timing and sequence. Decisions must be taken within the timeframe set by their actions (see Table 11.1).

REAL-WORLD EXAMPLE

Operational resilience stress testing and the exposure of decision pathways

European banks subject to operational resilience stress tests are required to maintain critical services under severe disruption.

Prior to simulation, organizations typically invest significant effort in preparing scenarios, defining dependencies and agreeing response arrangements through governance processes.

During simulation, decisions are required under conditions of uncertainty. Information is incomplete, assumptions are challenged and priorities shift as the situation develops.

As discussed earlier in this chapter, resilience depends on whether decision authority exists before disruption occurs or must be established after the signal emerges. Operational resilience testing exposes this distinction under controlled conditions.

Once disruption begins, information remains incomplete and conditions continue to evolve. The exercise therefore reveals whether existing structures support timely judgement and action, or whether authority, ownership and response options must first be clarified before decisions can be taken.

Supervisory assessment extends beyond operational capability. It examines whether organizations can sustain decision quality when disruption places existing governance assumptions under pressure.

External amplification of internal conditions

Figure 11.1 shows how disruption unfolds once external actors engage with an organization's internal conditions. The starting point is not the event itself but the state of governance before it occurs. Decision ownership, clarity of escalation and the ability to act without delay determine how prepared the organization is when signals emerge.

A trigger event exposes the organization's underlying conditions. Whether financial, operational or reputational, the event itself is rarely decisive. What matters is how external actors respond once it becomes visible.

Regulators, markets, investors and society interpret the same signal through different lenses. Their reactions accelerate consequences and compress the time available for decision-making.

Outcomes depend on the organization's ability to respond within that narrowing window. Where governance clarity, decision ownership and cultural discipline are established in advance, disruption is more likely to be contained. Where they are not, the same event can propagate across stakeholders and systems, extending beyond its original scope.

REAL-WORLD EXAMPLE

Operating under inflation: Decision-making under continuous rate adjustment

During the inflation surge between 2021 and 2022, the Banco Central do Brasil increased its policy rate from 2 per cent to over 13 per cent within 18 months.[1] This shift was transmitted rapidly across lending markets, funding costs and customer expectations. Pricing decisions that had previously been reviewed monthly became outdated within days.

FIGURE 11.1 External amplification model

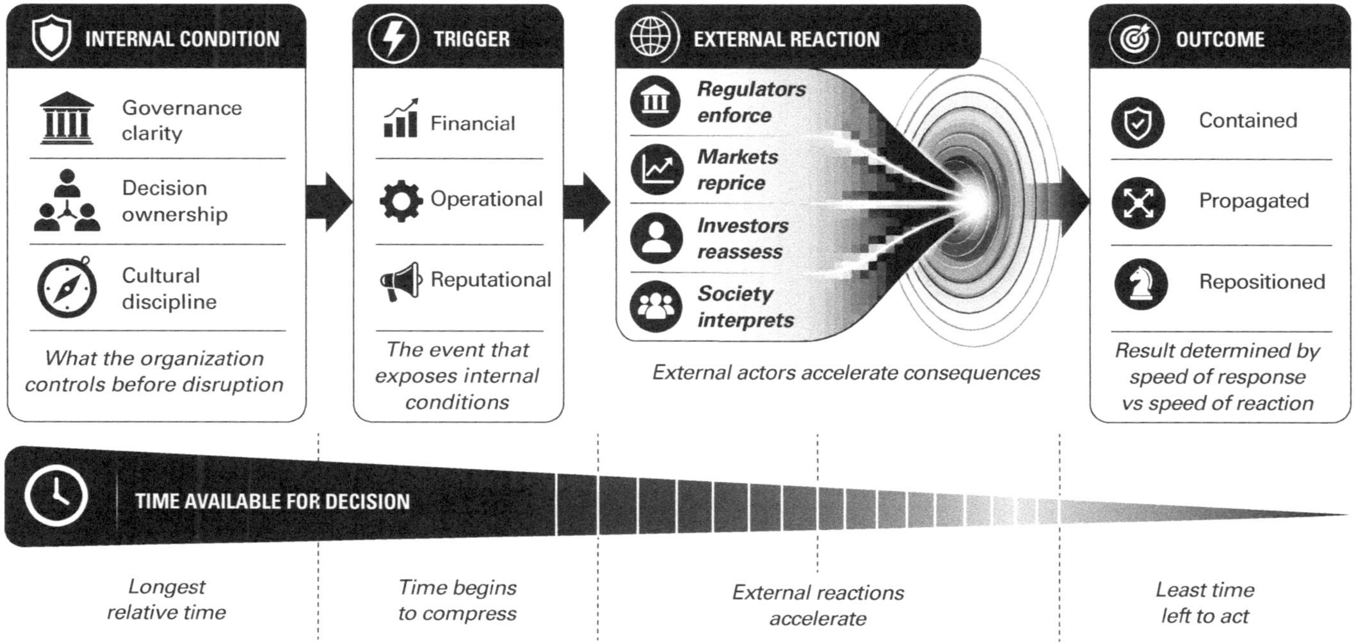

At several large Brazilian banks, credit and pricing decisions were no longer routed through standard committee cycles. Governance shifted from scheduled review to continuous adjustment. Lending rates were revised within the same week, sometimes within days, as market conditions evolved. Treasury and risk teams monitored liquidity and funding positions daily, enabling exposures to be adjusted as conditions evolved.

International institutions structured for more stable rate environments often updated pricing through governance cycles. Decisions require consolidation across functions before approval is granted. When rates move sharply, this sequence introduces delay. Funding costs and market pricing adjust during that interval, while internal decisions remain in process. By the time approval is secured, the conditions those decisions were based on have already changed and pricing is implemented after the market has moved.

During the same period, differences in governance flexibility became visible across the market. Local incumbents such as Itaú Unibanco and Bradesco adjusted credit models and retail pricing frequently as conditions evolved. Some foreign subsidiaries remained subject to monthly review cycles or head office approval processes. Funding costs adjusted immediately while lending rates lagged, creating pressure on margins and exposing the limitations of slower decision processes.

Through the lens of the external amplification model, the trigger was the rate shock. The amplification occurred through market mechanisms, as funding costs and pricing expectations adjusted immediately. Institutions able to act within the same operating cycle absorbed the impact. Those dependent on governance cycles responded after conditions had already shifted.

The following questions outlined in Table 11.2 focus on how decisions are taken once signals are acted upon externally. They examine whether ownership is defined at the point of action, whether decisions are taken within the same operating cycle, and where time accumulates between detection and response.

TABLE 11.2 Governance audit under external pressure

Decision area	Question	What to look for in practice
Decision timing	When a critical signal emerges, what determines the timing of the first decision: internal governance cycles or external reaction?	Decisions taken within the same operating cycle as the signal, not deferred to scheduled forums

TABLE 11.2 *continued*

Decision area	Question	What to look for in practice
Ownership clarity	At the point where conditions change, is decision ownership already defined or established through escalation?	Predefined ownership at trigger points, with no need to convene authority
Signal translation	When multiple indicators move simultaneously, how are they translated into a single decision?	Clear prioritization and convergence into action, rather than parallel discussions
Response sequencing	Which decisions must be taken before full information is available, and are these pathways defined in advance?	Pre-agreed decision options activated under defined conditions
Governance latency	Where does time accumulate between signal detection and decision approval?	Minimal delay between detection and action, with limited dependency on formal cycles
External interpretation	How would external actors interpret a delay in your response, and how quickly would that influence their actions?	Explicit consideration of external reaction in decision timing
Proportionality	How is the scale of response determined when impact is not proportional to the initial signal?	Decisions based on propagation potential, not just initial magnitude
Communication as control	At what point does communication become part of the response, and who owns it?	Communication integrated into decision pathways, not treated as a separate activity

How external reaction reshapes behaviour

External reaction changes how decisions are taken. As outlined in Chapter 10, signals change as they move through escalation. Under these conditions, decisions are formed while external reactions are underway. In leadership discussions, attention moves quickly toward a course of action that can be explained to investors, regulators or counterparties. Information is increasingly interpreted through that lens, while alternative explanations and response options receive less scrutiny. Specifically:

- **Evaluation and justification converge.** Decisions must address the issue and be explained to external actors at the same time.
- **Dissent reduces.** Challenge can be perceived as delay when response windows narrow.
- **Decision-making centralizes.** Authority concentrates around a smaller number of senior leaders as uncertainty increases.
- **Communication becomes part of the response.** External interpretation is managed while internal understanding continues to develop.

These behaviours occur within existing governance structures. Committees, reporting and escalation remain unchanged. Outcomes reflect how these processes are used once external actors begin to act.

Constraint-driven adaptation: Jugaad in fintech and non-profit organizations

In resource-constrained environments, such as early-stage fintech firms or non-profit organizations operating in volatile conditions and funding constraints, decisions are taken continuously to maintain delivery. Teams adjust fraud thresholds, pricing or service models within the same operating cycle, at the point where constraints are encountered.

This approach is often described as Jugaad,[2] a Hindi term referring to resourceful, problem-solving under constraint. Decisions are taken close to execution, allowing the organization to continue operating without waiting for alignment across governance forums.

As these adjustments are repeated, they extend beyond their original context. Decisions taken for specific situations are reused across different conditions and over longer periods. An informal operating model develops without defined ownership, escalation pathways or decision boundaries.

When external expectations increase, these practices are assessed collectively. Investor review in fintech and donor oversight in non-profit organizations requires consistency in how decisions are taken and monitored. Where ownership and coordination are not defined, actions remain effective in isolation yet inconsistent at scale.

Outcomes reflect whether these decisions are connected to governance through clear ownership and defined boundaries.

EXTERNAL CONDITIONS ARE BECOMING PART OF THE OPERATING ENVIRONMENT

Geopolitical instability is increasingly becoming part of the operating environment rather than an occasional disruption. Organizations now operate within conditions shaped by shifting alliances, regional conflicts, supply-chain dependencies and regulatory divergence. Their influence is often transmitted through suppliers, customers, markets and counterparties that respond before governance processes have concluded. (Adapted from insights shared during interviews conducted for this book.)

Impact of external factors across sectors

The amplification mechanism described in this chapter is consistent across sectors. What differs is the constraint through which it operates. Each industry encounters amplification in a specific way, shaped by how decisions are structured, how quickly signals propagate and how external actors respond.

In **financial services**, amplification operates through interconnectivity and standardization. Institutions are linked through funding markets, pricing mechanisms and counterparty exposure. Common regulatory frameworks and risk models lead participants to monitor the same indicators and act on them within similar thresholds. When conditions change, responses occur simultaneously across institutions. Liquidity is withdrawn, positions are reduced and exposure is reallocated within the same timeframe, extending the impact beyond the originating event.

STRUCTURAL PRINCIPLE

Regulation aligns behaviour and concentrates system response

Regulation defines how participants interpret signals and what actions are considered acceptable in response. By establishing common rules, thresholds and reporting expectations, it creates consistency in how conditions are assessed across the system.

This consistency changes how responses develop. When the same indicators are monitored and similar actions are expected, reactions occur within a similar timeframe and follow comparable paths. Adjustment becomes coordinated rather than dispersed.

The effect extends beyond timing. When rules are aligned, the range of permissible responses narrows. Participants are less likely to take divergent actions, even when conditions differ locally. Variation is reduced at the point where it would otherwise absorb part of the shock.

This reduces the system's buffering capacity. Instead of absorbing disruption through different responses, the system transmits it. Adjustment occurs through similar actions taken across multiple participants, concentrating impact rather than distributing it.

A comparable effect is observed in natural systems exposed to monoculture risk.[3] Forests composed of a single species respond to environmental stress, such as disease, in the same way as forests with numerous species. Variation cannot not buffer the impact. It is transmitted across the system, increasing the likelihood of widespread failure.

The amplification mechanism is consistent. When rules and structures align behaviour, responses converge in timing and direction. Resilience depends on variation. When variation is reduced, the system reacts as one.

In **non-profit organizations**, amplification operates through capacity and immediacy. Resources are limited and delivery is often tied directly to funding, access conditions and local infrastructure. In resource-constrained NGOs operating in volatile environments, changes in demand, funding or access affect multiple programmes at once. Decisions are taken at the point of delivery to maintain continuity, often before full information is available. The absence of buffer capacity increases the speed at which local disruption affects overall delivery.

In **startups**, amplification operates through scale and speed. As transaction volumes, user numbers and product complexity increase, the time between a signal and its impact reduces. Decisions that were previously contained at low scale extend immediately across the organization. Product, risk and operational adjustments must be made within the same operating cycle, as issues affect a growing number of users and activities at once.

In **government**, amplification operates through process and public scrutiny. Decisions follow defined procedures, consultation requirements and accountability structures. These processes remain in place as external conditions change and public response develops. Media coverage, stakeholder reaction and political accountability increase the visibility of delays, extending the consequences of decisions taken within formal timelines.

REAL-WORLD EXAMPLE

Systemic dependency and delayed adjustment: Supply chains after Fukushima

The disruption following the Fukushima nuclear disaster exposed how dependency had been structured across global supply chains.[4] In several sectors, critical components were sourced from a limited number of suppliers concentrated in the affected region.

In that context, the Renesas Electronics Naka facility supplied a significant share of automotive microcontrollers used globally. When production stopped, manufacturers reliant on those components were unable to maintain output. Assembly lines were suspended across multiple regions, including at Toyota and General Motors.

The impact reflected how sourcing decisions had been structured. Supplier concentration reduced cost and limited redundancy. When disruption occurred, substitution was not immediately available. Supplier concentration had reduced cost and complexity under stable conditions. Alternative sourcing and redundancy had been limited as they reduced efficiency. When disruption occurred, there was no immediate pathway to substitute supply.

The issue was not the absence of information because dependencies were known at an operational level. It was the governance of those dependencies. Dependency increased on a limited number of suppliers and alternative sourcing was not established. When the trigger occurred, adjustment options were constrained.

This is how amplification occurred. A localized disruption extended across industries because multiple organizations depended on the same point of failure. The system did not absorb the shock through variation. It transmitted it through shared dependency.

Board and executive implications

For boards, resilience is reflected in how decisions are taken when timing is set outside the organization. Signals are identified internally, yet consequences develop as external actors respond. Risk exposure arises in the period between recognition and action, particularly when decisions wait for the next forum or additional alignment while conditions continue to change.

Attention shifts to how specific decisions would be taken if conditions moved during the current operating cycle. Directors test whether action would occur immediately, who would take it, and whether governance structures would enable or delay response.

Key questions

- Where would external reaction expose the weakest assumption in our operating model?
- Which exposures remain acceptable within internal thresholds yet would trigger action when interpreted externally?
- What decision would be forced by market, regulatory or counterparty action? How quickly could it be taken?
- Where does time accumulate between signal detection and decision execution when conditions change?
- Which dependencies would constrain adjustment once external actors have acted?

These questions direct attention to how the organization acts when conditions change. They show whether decisions are taken within the same operating cycle or delayed while alignment is sought and conditions continue to move.

For executive leadership, the implication is operational. Decision-making must function at the point where signals are observed. When conditions shift, action cannot depend on escalation through multiple forums or extended analysis.

This requires that:

- decisions can be taken where the signal appears without waiting for the next committee
- thresholds trigger immediate action rather than further review
- dependencies are understood in terms of how they limit available options once conditions change
- communication is issued at the same time as action, where external interpretation affects outcome.

Risk functions support this by identifying where decisions are delayed in practice. This includes situations where signals are reported but not acted upon, where ownership is unclear at the point of action or where escalation leads to discussion rather than resolution. This provides a view of how decisions are taken under changing conditions and whether the organization is designed to lead the market or merely follow it.

Practical playbook

Embedding resilience requires ensuring that decisions can be taken within the same operating cycle as the signal, without waiting for extended escalation or alignment. The following actions help organizations ensure that decisions are taken in time and remain effective as conditions evolve.

Boards

1. **Test decisions against external timing**
   Boards should examine how specific decisions would be taken if conditions changed between meetings. This includes whether action would occur immediately or wait for the next scheduled forum, and whether the relevant decision makers are positioned to act without delay.
2. **Align commitments with execution capability**
   Public commitments on resilience, service continuity or risk appetite should be tested against how decisions are taken when conditions change. Boards should examine whether a commitment would hold if a key service were disrupted, whether the organization could act within the same operating cycle, and whether decision authority is positioned to support that response.
3. **Review dependencies as decision constraints**
   Oversight should include examining where dependencies would limit available options once external actors have acted. This includes supplier concentration, funding reliance or operational bottlenecks that reduce the organization's ability to adjust in time.

Executives

1. **Position decision authority at the point of action**
   Executives should shorten the decision cycle by ensuring that decisions can be taken where signals are observed. This reduces reliance on escalation through multiple forums and enables action within the same operating cycle.
2. **Link thresholds directly to action**
   Thresholds should initiate defined actions rather than additional review. When conditions move, the organization should move with them, without requiring further validation before acting.

3 **Integrate timing into strategic planning**
Strategic decisions should be tested against how conditions can change and how external actors may respond. This includes identifying which assumptions would be challenged first and which actions could be taken immediately to adjust the plan. A strategy remains viable only if it can be adapted within the timeframe imposed by external reaction.

Chief risk officers and risk leaders

1 **Translate external signals into decision triggers**
Risk functions should ensure that external indicators, such as market movements, regulatory signals or stakeholder behaviour, are connected to defined decision points. This allows the organization to act before conditions fully materialize internally.

2 **Identify where decisions are delayed in practice**
Risk leaders should examine where signals are reported but not acted upon within the same operating cycle. This includes identifying delays caused by escalation pathways, unclear ownership or reliance on scheduled forums.

3 **Connect signals across domains**
Risk functions should link regulatory, market, operational and behavioural indicators to reflect how conditions evolve across the organization. This supports earlier recognition of when decisions are required and how they should be coordinated.

KEY TAKEAWAYS

- **External actors shape resilience outcomes.** Organizations assess preparedness through governance, controls and scenarios. Resilience is ultimately determined by how effectively they respond once regulators, markets, investors, customers or counterparties begin to act.
- **External actors accelerate consequences.** Small gaps in coordination, decision-making or dependency management can remain manageable under normal conditions. External reactions amplify those gaps, reducing the time available for assessment and response.

- **Outcomes depend on decision timing.** Exposure develops in the period between recognizing a signal and taking action. Organizations that can respond within the timeframe created by external reaction are more likely to contain disruption.
- **System design shapes resilience.** Dependencies, sourcing models, funding structures and decision authority determine which options remain available once conditions change. Resilience depends as much on these design choices as on individual decisions.
- **Resilience must be embedded in decision-making.** Organizations strengthen resilience when signals are linked to predefined actions, decision authority is positioned close to emerging issues and leaders understand where external actors may force a response.

Reframing forward

External actors set the timing of response. Markets adjust exposure, regulators intervene and stakeholders respond while decisions are still being formed. The organization is assessed in how it acts during that period.

This places a requirement on capability inside the organization. Outcome is determined by how individuals interpret those signals, take ownership and act within the same operating cycle.

Yet, the challenge sits in execution. Decisions are taken with incomplete information, under time constraint and with consequences already developing externally. The organization's performance reflects whether people can act under these conditions.

This directs attention to capability. Experience, judgement and decision confidence determine whether action follows the signal or waits for further alignment.

The next chapter examines how this capability is developed. It focuses on the people, skills and behavioural conditions that support decision-making when timing is constrained.

Resilience is determined by how people act when others have already begun to respond.

Endnotes

1 Banco Central do Brasil (2023) Historical series of the Selic rate, Banco Central do Brasil, www.bcb.gov.br/en/monetarypolicy/historicinterestrates

2 Radjou, N, Prabhu, J and Ahuja, S (2012) *Jugaad Innovation: Think frugal, be flexible, generate breakthrough growth*, Jossey-Bass, San Francisco, CA

3 Diamond, J (1997) *Guns, Germs and Steel*, W W Norton & Company, New York

4 OECD (2011) The Impact of the Japanese Earthquake on Global Supply Chains, OECD Policy Brief

12

Talent that sustains change

Developing skills and mindsets for lasting capability

CHAPTER OBJECTIVES

- Develop the capabilities required to sustain performance under pressure.
- Recognize how gaps in talent, engagement and learning shape resilience.
- Build adaptability and long-term value through people and culture.

Organizations invest heavily in transformation and leadership development, measuring progress through certifications and programme completion. These indicators suggest that knowledge has been transferred and capability improved. Yet execution still breaks under pressure.

As discussed in Chapter 10, individuals often calibrate behaviour against perceived personal consequences rather than formal accountability arrangements. As uncertainty increases, behaviour shifts from action to validation. Individuals seek additional input or escalate decisions rather than committing to a path. This response is rational: acting concentrates responsibility, while validation distributes it. The result is defensive decision-making, where choices are shaped by personal exposure rather than the requirements of the project.

Momentum stalls as decisions bounce between teams and resources are swallowed by rework. Because this is often misdiagnosed as a lack of information, organizations respond with more analysis and tighter controls. These actions improve oversight, but they don't change how people act under pressure.

This chapter examines how organizations close that gap. It focuses on how talent, learning and culture shape behaviour under pressure, and how these conditions determine whether individuals act, challenge and take ownership when execution depends on it.

Capability is not defined by what the organization knows. It is defined by how people act when conditions are uncertain and consequences are real.

Closing capability gaps in resilience execution

Decision-making slows when teams pass decisions upward instead of taking them where the work is done, particularly under uncertainty when information is incomplete and trade-offs are not fully defined. Performance then reflects whether individuals act, defer or transfer decisions.

Three behaviours consistently indicate where capability is not applied.

1 **Hesitation under uncertainty** arises when individuals seek additional validation before acting. Decisions remain open while further input is requested, even where sufficient information is already available. This extends decision cycles and delays downstream activity.
2 **Escalation dependency** develops when decisions are routinely moved upward rather than resolved at the point of ownership. What begins as support becomes a default mechanism. Decisions accumulate at senior levels, reducing capacity and slowing execution across the organization.
3 **Lack of confidence in decision-making** affects how trade-offs are assessed and applied. Where confidence is low, decisions are revisited after initial commitment or reversed once outcomes begin to materialize. This introduces rework and increases coordination effort across teams.

These behaviours are embedded in how work progresses. Their impact becomes visible through execution breakdowns:

- Delivery timelines extend without a clear root cause.
- Similar issues are revisited across teams.
- Decisions appear repeatedly in governance forums without resolution.
- Senior attention is drawn into operational detail.

Strategic initiatives take longer to deliver, outcomes become less consistent and more resources are required to achieve the same results, reducing the expected return on investment. To make this relationship explicit, Table 12.1

TABLE 12.1 From capability gap to execution failure

Capability gap	Behaviour under pressure	Execution impact	Economic consequence
Low decision confidence	Delay and validation loops	Slower execution	Increased delivery cost
Weak trade-off judgement	Rework and reversals	Inefficiency	Margin erosion
Escalation dependence	Decisions transferred upward	Bottlenecks	Senior capacity overload
Lack of ownership	Issues remain unresolved	Fragmented execution	Increased coordination cost

links observable behaviours under pressure to their execution impact and economic consequence.

The table shows how capability gaps translate into operational dynamics that affect cost, speed and consistency. Each behaviour reflects a situation where decisions are not resolved at the point of ownership. As these patterns repeat, they create cumulative impact across programmes and functions.

Closing these gaps requires changing how decisions are prepared and reinforced across the organization. This includes developing judgement through scenario-based learning, aligning decision rights with where work is performed and creating conditions where individuals can act without unnecessary escalation.

Without these changes, decision-making capability is not strengthened through repeated application. Decisions continue to be delayed, transferred or revisited, and execution absorbs the cost through time, coordination and rework.

Talent as a resilience lever

Organizational responsiveness under stress depends on who is able to take decisions and coordinate action when conditions change. Roles that carry this responsibility determine whether the organization responds within the required timeframe or extends decisions through escalation and delay.

Two roles are critical.

1 **Decision makers** resolve issues where they arise. They assess incomplete information, make trade-offs and commit to action without waiting for full validation. Their effectiveness determines whether decisions are taken within the same operating cycle or deferred.

2 **Coordinators** across functions connect decisions that depend on each other. They align priorities, resolve conflicts and ensure that actions taken in one area do not create disruption in another. Their role determines whether execution remains aligned or fragments across teams.

Where these roles are clearly defined and supported, decisions are taken more quickly and with greater consistency. Where these roles are unclear or underdeveloped, decisions are repeatedly referred between teams, coordination effort increases and issues take longer to resolve.

A recurring risk is the concentration of decision-making in a limited number of individuals. In such situations, decisions depend on specific people rather than defined roles. When those individuals are unavailable or overloaded, decisions are delayed or transferred and execution becomes uneven.

Many organizations possess the expertise they need. The challenge is that the same individuals are repeatedly relied upon to resolve complex issues, absorb regulatory change, support transformation programmes and guide critical decisions. Over time, resilience becomes dependent on a small number of people rather than a distributed organizational capability.

This dependency increases when only a small number of individuals can take critical decisions. When decision-making capability, including judgement, trade-off assessment and the ability to act under uncertainty, is not developed across the organization, decision-making cannot be sustained as demand increases or conditions change. New situations are escalated to a small group of experienced individuals, creating bottlenecks and reducing responsiveness.

CAPACITY LIMITS RESILIENCE BEFORE BUDGET DOES

Many organizations view resilience through the lens of funding, technology or resources. However, capacity often becomes the more significant constraint. They frequently run out of capacity before they run out of budget. The challenge is rarely whether change can be funded. It is whether the organization can absorb and implement multiple demands simultaneously. Resilience depends not only on resources but also on the capacity of people and teams to adapt without degrading performance. (Adapted from insights shared during interviews conducted for this book.)

Organizational performance increasingly depends on where decisions can be taken rather than where they arise. When decision-making capability is concentrated in a small number of individuals, coordination effort increases, responsiveness declines and the organization's capacity to absorb change becomes constrained. In that context, talent becomes a resilience lever when decision-making capability is distributed across roles rather than concentrated in key individuals.

REAL-WORLD EXAMPLE

Inditex: Talent and decision-making at the point of demand

Inditex[1] operates in an environment where demand changes rapidly and supply chain decisions must be adjusted within short timeframes. Execution depends on converting changes in customer behaviour into timely action across a global network.

Store managers and frontline teams observe demand directly. They identify changes in customer preferences, product performance and local trends. These roles are expected to translate observation into action, including adjusting orders, influencing product allocation, and feeding information back into design and production.

This model relies on individuals who adjust decisions as conditions change. Demand signals are used to refine product allocation and distribution, allowing teams to respond without waiting for central direction.

Decisions are resolved where information is observed. Adjustments to inventory, product mix and distribution are made within the same operating cycle, reducing reliance on escalation and allowing the organization to respond before demand shifts further.

The ability to make decisions is reinforced through rapid feedback. Sales data and customer response provide immediate indication of whether decisions were effective. Smaller production runs limit exposure, allowing incorrect decisions to be identified and adjusted quickly. This reduces the cost of error and supports continuous refinement of judgement.

The model operates within defined boundaries. Production capacity, supply chain constraints and brand positioning set limits on local decisions. These guard-rails ensure that distributed decision-making remains aligned with overall objectives.

The impact is reflected in execution. Faster decision cycles support shorter production runs, reducing inventory risk and limiting exposure to demand variability. Product alignment improves as decisions reflect current customer behaviour rather than historical assumptions.

This case shows how capability is built and applied at scale. Decision-making is positioned at the point where information is observed, reinforced through continuous feedback and supported by clear boundaries. Adaptability is developed through repeated application of judgement, allowing performance to improve as conditions change.

Learning as an execution capability

Learning influences execution only when it changes how decisions are made. Most organizations invest in training to build knowledge, tracking course completion, certifications and attendance as indicators of progress. While these measures confirm exposure to content, they do not show whether individuals can act under pressure.

When decisions must be made with incomplete information, some act while others delay, escalate or defer. This difference reflects how individuals have learnt to assess trade-offs, commit to action and accept consequence.

Learning that supports execution has three characteristics:

1. **It is contextual.** It reflects the situations in which decisions are taken. Individuals develop judgement by working through real scenarios, not abstract examples. This includes exposure to uncertainty, conflicting priorities and time constraints.
2. **It is experiential.** It requires individuals to take decisions, not observe them. Simulations, role-based exercises and live problem-solving develop the ability to act when outcomes are uncertain.
3. **It is reinforced.** It is anchored in daily work. Feedback is linked to how decisions are made, including where outcomes required adjustment or where escalation replaced resolution. This strengthens how judgement is applied over time.

TABLE 12.2 Training vs applied capability

Learning model	Focus	Outcome
Classroom training	Knowledge transfer	Knowledge without application
Scenario-based learning	Decision-making under pressure	Reduced hesitation under pressure
Post-decision review and reinforcement	Reviewing real decisions and outcomes	Consistent execution under stress

Where learning reflects real decision conditions, individuals are more likely to act because they have already practised making decisions under uncertainty. Where this exposure is absent, they rely on validation or escalation to reduce uncertainty, separating knowledge from execution. To make this distinction explicit, Table 12.2 contrasts different learning approaches and their effect on execution.

Learning contributes to decision-making capability when it increases an individual's ability to assess trade-offs, make timely decisions and act despite uncertainty. Training that remains detached from day-to-day decision-making may increase knowledge, yet individuals continue to seek validation, defer decisions or escalate issues that could be resolved locally.

Culture and engagement as economic drivers

Culture influences how individuals respond when decisions carry consequence. It shapes whether they act, challenge assumptions and take ownership, or avoid exposure and defer decisions.

Engagement reflects how individuals experience that culture. In engaged environments, individuals raise issues early, question assumptions and commit to decisions within their remit. This supports faster resolution and reduces the need for escalation.

Disengagement affects behaviour in a different way. Individuals limit exposure, avoid challenge and defer decisions where possible. Issues remain unaddressed until they affect delivery, at which point correction requires more time and coordination.

TABLE 12.3 Culture to economic impact

Cultural condition	Observable behaviour	Decision impact	Economic impact
High trust	Early challenge	Faster decisions	Lower cost
Low trust	Silence	Late correction	Cost increase
Disengagement	Minimal ownership	Delay	Reduced productivity

Trust shapes how information is used. In high-trust environments, individuals surface concerns as they arise and contribute to decision-making beyond their immediate responsibilities. In low-trust environments, information is withheld or delayed and decisions proceed without full visibility of risk. These behaviours affect execution directly.

Silence delays the identification of issues. Decisions proceed without challenge and require correction at a later stage. Escalation increases when individuals transfer responsibility rather than act, concentrating decisions at senior levels. Delay extends delivery timelines as decisions remain unresolved or are revisited after initial commitment.

The impact develops across activities. Early challenge reduces rework and shortens decision cycles. Silence and disengagement extend timelines, increase coordination effort and introduce variability in performance. To make this relationship explicit, Table 12.3 links cultural conditions to behaviour, decision impact and economic impact.

Ultimately, the economic impact of culture emerges through everyday decisions. Organizations that encourage challenge, ownership and early issue identification reduce rework, shorten decision cycles and improve coordination. Where trust and engagement weaken, delay, escalation and correction become embedded in how work is performed.

REAL-WORLD EXAMPLE

Google: Applying knowledge through challenge and contribution

Google[2] initiated Project Aristotle to understand why some teams sustained performance under changing conditions while others, with similar levels of expertise, did not. The focus was on how teams operated during execution rather than on technical capability.

Teams were composed of individuals with comparable experience, qualifications and access to information. Processes and structures were consistent. Differences in performance were observed in how individuals contributed to decisions.

In some teams, individuals raised concerns, challenged assumptions and contributed information as decisions were being formed. Issues were addressed early, reducing the need for later adjustment. Decisions were resolved with greater clarity and work progressed without repeated escalation or revision.

In other teams, individuals did not act on what they knew. Concerns remained unspoken, challenge was limited and decisions proceeded without full visibility of risk. Issues were addressed after initial commitment, requiring rework and increasing coordination effort.

The difference was behavioural. It reflected how individuals experienced accountability and consequence within the team. Where individuals felt able to contribute and challenge, they applied their knowledge during decision-making. Where they did not, knowledge remained unused and was introduced later, after decisions had already progressed.

Psychological safety shaped this behaviour. It determined whether individuals acted at the point where decisions were made or withheld input until later stages.

The impact was measurable. Teams with higher levels of contribution and challenge showed faster decision cycles, fewer revisions and more consistent execution. Performance reflected whether individuals acted on what they knew, not the level of knowledge itself.

Culture ROI asymmetry

Most investments produce visible results within a relatively short period. Leaders can usually identify a direct relationship between the investment and the result, whether through increased capacity, improved efficiency or stronger financial performance. Not with culture.

The costs of cultural weakness take shape through thousands of small decisions involving ownership, challenge, escalation and communication. Because the impact is dispersed across functions and time periods, leaders would typically attribute the resulting delays, rework and coordination effort to operational complexity rather than cultural conditions.

The benefits of a strong culture are equally difficult to isolate. A single act of challenge rarely changes organizational performance on its own. Its value is realized through the decisions, projects and initiatives it influences.

A concern raised early may prevent costly rework. Effective challenge may improve an investment decision. In all cases, the resulting benefits are typically attributed to the initiative itself rather than to the cultural conditions that enabled better decisions.

Culture therefore functions as a multiplier rather than a direct source of value. Strong cultural conditions improve the return generated by other investments, while weak cultural conditions impede it. This contribution is difficult to isolate because it is embedded within the performance of the initiatives it influences.

> Culture is often treated as one component alongside strategy, governance, technology, processes and people. Yet, in practice, it operates differently. Culture shapes how these elements interact, how decisions are made and how information flows across the organization. Rather than functioning as a standalone capability, it influences the effectiveness of all capabilities around it.

Jugaad as a capability

Chapter 5 introduced Jugaad as a cultural phenomenon. Organizations that encourage challenge, experimentation and psychological safety create conditions where individuals feel able to adapt established approaches when circumstances require it. Chapter 8 explored how Jugaad influences organizational resilience by enabling systems and teams to continue functioning when predefined processes or controls no longer provide a complete answer.

Yet, why are some individuals able to generate workable solutions under constraint while others become dependent on additional resources, revised procedures or external direction?

Jugaad describes a form of resourcefulness. Originating from India, the term is often associated with finding practical solutions under constraint. Within organizations, it reflects the ability to create workable options from the resources, information and authority that remain available rather than focusing on what is missing.

This capability becomes valuable when individuals encounter situations that do not fit established approaches. Rather than treating constraints as barriers, they treat them as design parameters. Limited resources, competing priorities, time pressure and changing conditions become factors to work with rather than reasons for inaction.

At its core, Jugaad combines three capabilities:

1 **Resourcefulness:** identifying alternative ways to achieve an objective using available resources.
2 **Adaptability:** adjusting approaches when assumptions, conditions or requirements change.
3 **Practical problem-solving:** developing solutions that are workable within real-world constraints rather than waiting for ideal conditions.

These capabilities influence how organizations respond when plans, processes or operating models no longer align fully with reality. Some individuals become dependent on additional resources, revised procedures or external direction before they can proceed. Others generate alternative approaches that allow progress to continue within existing constraints.

The significance extends beyond individual problem-solving. Repeated examples of local adaptation often reveal where assumptions embedded within existing processes no longer reflect operational reality. What begins as a workaround may highlight structural opportunities to improve products, services, controls or ways of working.

This creates an important leadership challenge. Not every adaptation should become standard practice. Some are appropriate responses to local circumstances. Others reveal better ways of achieving organizational objectives. Leaders therefore need mechanisms to identify which adaptations should remain local and which should inform broader organizational learning.

Viewed in this way, Jugaad is more than improvization. It is a capability that enables organizations to generate new options when existing ones become insufficient. Resilience depends not only on the ability to execute established responses but also on the ability to create alternative responses when circumstances demand them.

Antifragile talent

The capabilities discussed throughout this chapter help individuals make decisions, adapt to changing conditions and generate new responses when established approaches no longer work. Antifragile talent goes a step further. It improves because of these experiences.

Most development programmes assume that capability is built through training, coaching and planned experience. Antifragility recognizes that some of the most valuable development occurs through exposure to challenge itself. Difficult situations, unexpected setbacks and changing conditions become sources of learning rather than obstacles to avoid.

Antifragile individuals use their experiences differently. They examine why assumptions proved incorrect, how decisions influenced outcomes and what adjustments may be required in future situations. The value lies not in the setback itself but in the ability to extract learning from it and apply that learning to subsequent decisions.

Three characteristics are particularly important.

1 **Learning agility**
Individuals update their thinking as new information becomes available. Previous experience informs decisions without constraining them. Assumptions are reassessed as conditions evolve, allowing decisions to remain aligned with current realities rather than past expectations.

2 **Experimentation**
New options are tested within appropriate boundaries rather than remaining theoretical. Individuals observe outcomes, refine their approach and generate learning during action rather than only after completion. This allows capability to develop through application rather than observation alone.

3 **Constructive response to setbacks**
Outcomes that fall short of expectations are treated as sources of insight rather than reasons to avoid future action. Successes and setbacks both contribute to learning. The focus is on understanding what occurred, identifying what can be improved and applying those lessons to future decisions.

Together, these characteristics create a different relationship with uncertainty. Stress, complexity and change still create pressure. The difference is that capability increases through exposure rather than simply surviving it. To clarify these nuances, Table 12.4 contrasts how different talent profiles respond to stress and the outcomes that follow.

As uncertainty becomes a more permanent feature of the operating environment, organizations increasingly encounter situations that cannot be addressed through existing knowledge alone. Those that develop antifragile talent continually expand their ability to respond, adapt and improve as new challenges emerge.

TABLE 12.4 Fragile, robust and antifragile talent

Talent type	Response to challenge	Long-term outcome
Fragile	Capability deteriorates under stress	Reduced effectiveness
Robust	Capability withstands stress	Maintained effectiveness
Antifragile	Capability improves through stress	Increased effectiveness

Balancing improvisation and governance

Jugaad and antifragility both depend on the ability to adapt. Individuals must be able to test ideas, exercise judgement and respond to situations that were not fully anticipated when processes were designed. Yet adaptation without structure creates inconsistency in how decisions are made. Similar situations may be handled differently across teams, reducing consistency and making outcomes more difficult to predict.

At the other extreme, rigid governance limits the ability to respond. Decisions wait for approval, alignment or additional analysis, even where timely action is required. Work pauses while conditions continue to evolve, and options narrow as delays accumulate.

Therefore, effective governance depends on clear guard-rails that define how far individuals can act without escalation. These include:

- decision boundaries linked to risk and impact
- defined thresholds that trigger escalation
- clarity on where discretion applies and where it does not.

Escalation clarity is equally important. Individuals need to know when decisions must move beyond their remit and what information is required to support that transition. Where escalation is unclear, decisions are either retained beyond appropriate limits or transferred prematurely, reducing both responsiveness and accountability.

The objective is less about reducing improvisation and more about ensuring that it operates within defined conditions, supported by clear decision rights and feedback on outcomes. This allows individuals to act when required while maintaining consistency, accountability and alignment with organizational objectives.

Board and executive implications

The drivers of execution in this chapter – engagement, learning and talent distribution – are not directly visible in governance discussions. Boards receive signals through outcomes such as delivery timelines, escalation levels and performance variability. These signals reflect how people act under pressure, yet they are often interpreted without reference to the conditions that shape that behaviour.

This creates a gap in oversight. Performance is assessed through results, while the factors that determine whether individuals act, challenge and take ownership remain implicit. Engagement levels, learning effectiveness and reliance on specific individuals influence execution, yet they are rarely examined in connection with performance outcomes.

Making these drivers visible requires linking performance outcomes to behaviour. Table 12.5 links common performance signals to the underlying behavioural and talent drivers that shape execution.

The table shows that performance signals can be read as indicators of how individuals act within the organization.

Delays indicate that decisions are not resolved where they arise, often reflecting hesitation or unclear ownership. Escalation reflects where responsibility is transferred rather than assumed, increasing reliance on a limited number of individuals. Variability across teams indicates differences in engagement and learning, where similar conditions produce different responses. Dependency on specific individuals shows that experience is not

TABLE 12.5 From culture and talent signals to execution impact

Governance view	Traditional interpretation	Culture and talent interpretation
Delayed delivery	Planning or resource issue	Hesitation, low confidence or unclear ownership
High escalation	Risk awareness	Limited confidence or reliance on senior decision makers
Performance variability	Execution inconsistency	Differences in engagement and learning across teams
Key person dependency	Talent issue	Concentration of experience and lack of distributed capability

distributed, limiting the organization's ability to sustain execution as demand increases.

For boards, this interpretation allows outcomes to be assessed in terms of whether individuals across the organization are able to act when required. Performance reflects not only strategic direction but whether engagement, learning and role design support consistent action under pressure.

For executive leadership, the same signals indicate how execution develops across teams. Differences in delivery speed, coordination effort and rework reflect where individuals act and where they defer or rely on escalation.

Risk functions contribute by identifying these patterns across the organization. Silence where challenge is expected, delayed action where issues are known and repeated reliance on the same individuals indicate how engagement, learning and experience shape execution.

Interpreted in this way, governance gains visibility into the drivers of performance. Outcomes can be assessed not only in terms of what is delivered but how reliably execution can be sustained as conditions change.

Practical playbook

Building capability requires changes to how organizations select, prepare and support individuals who take decisions under stress. This includes how roles are defined, how behaviour is reinforced and how performance is assessed.

The focus is on ensuring that individuals can act, challenge and take ownership when conditions require it.

Boards

Boards oversee whether the organization can sustain execution under pressure. This requires visibility on how engagement, talent distribution and culture affect performance.

1. **Assess engagement as a risk driver**
   Boards should examine whether individuals raise concerns, challenge decisions and act within their remit. Low engagement reduces the flow of information and delays action, increasing exposure through late correction.
2. **Monitor concentration of decision-making**
   Oversight should include where critical decisions depend on a limited number of individuals. Concentration increases bottlenecks and reduces

the organization's ability to respond when demand increases or conditions change.

3 **Link culture to performance outcomes**
Boards should require evidence that cultural conditions are reflected in execution. This includes examining how behaviours such as challenge, ownership and escalation influence delivery timelines, rework and cost.

Executives

Executives determine how capability is developed and applied across the organization. This includes aligning incentives, learning and operating structures with decision-making requirements.

1 **Align incentives with decision ownership**
Performance measures should reinforce taking decisions at the appropriate level. Where incentives favour escalation or risk avoidance, decisions are transferred rather than resolved.

2 **Invest in experiential learning**
Development should focus on preparing individuals to make decisions under uncertainty. This includes scenario-based work and structured reviews of decisions taken during execution.

3 **Reduce structural barriers to action**
Execution slows where decision rights are unclear or where multiple approvals are required. Simplifying decision pathways enables individuals to act within defined boundaries.

Chief risk officers and risk leaders

Risk functions provide visibility on how behaviour affects execution and exposure. This requires integrating cultural and behavioural indicators into risk oversight.

1 **Identify cultural risk signals**
Risk leaders should monitor patterns such as silence, delayed escalation and repeated rework. These indicate where individuals are not acting on available information.

2 **Quantify the impact of disengagement**
Disengagement should be assessed through its effect on execution. This includes delays in decision-making, increased coordination effort and higher delivery cost.

3 **Integrate behavioural indicators into risk frameworks**
Risk frameworks should include measures of how decisions are taken. This provides a view of whether issues are addressed early or deferred until they affect delivery.

KEY TAKEAWAYS

- **Resilience depends on capability, not knowledge alone.** Training, experience and expertise create value only when individuals can apply judgement, make decisions and act under changing conditions. Capability is demonstrated through action rather than possession of knowledge.
- **Culture influences how effectively organizational capability is converted into outcomes.** Strong cultural conditions encourage ownership, challenge and information sharing. Their value is often embedded within the performance of decisions, projects and initiatives rather than appearing as a direct organizational output.
- **Learning strengthens resilience when it develops judgement.** Individuals build capability by applying knowledge, assessing trade-offs and learning from outcomes. Experience contributes to resilience when it improves future decisions rather than simply increasing familiarity with existing processes.
- **Jugaad reflects a capability for resourcefulness and adaptation.** It enables individuals to generate workable responses when established approaches become insufficient. This capability becomes increasingly important when organizations encounter situations that fall outside the assumptions embedded in existing processes.
- **Antifragile talent improves through exposure to challenge.** Learning agility, experimentation and constructive responses to setbacks allow individuals to strengthen capability over time. Resilience enables recovery. Antifragility enables growth through experience.
- **Governance should create the conditions for safe adaptation.** Effective governance does not eliminate improvisation. It provides the boundaries, decision rights and escalation mechanisms that allow individuals to exercise judgement while maintaining consistency, accountability and alignment with organizational objectives.

- **Talent, culture, learning and governance operate as an integrated system.** Organizations strengthen resilience when they develop people who can make decisions, adapt to changing conditions, learn from experience and act within clearly defined guard-rails. Sustainable performance depends as much on these human capabilities as it does on frameworks, processes and controls.

Reframing forward

If resilience depends on how people act under pressure, the next question is how this can be measured.

Most organizations track outcomes such as delivery timelines, escalation levels and performance variability. These indicators show what has happened. They do not show whether individuals were able to act, challenge and apply judgement when decisions were required.

This creates a delay in how issues are identified. Gaps in engagement, learning and talent distribution are recognized after they affect delivery rather than at the point where behaviour begins to shift.

Making resilience measurable requires focusing on the conditions that shape execution. This includes how individuals respond under pressure, how consistently learning is applied and how widely experience is distributed across roles.

Chapter 13 examines how these conditions can be assessed. It focuses on how organizations identify gaps in behaviour, learning and talent before they translate into delays, escalation and performance breakdown.

Endnotes

1 Ghemawat, P and Nueno, J L (2006) *ZARA: Fast Fashion*, Harvard Business School Publishing, Boston, MA

2 Rozovsky, J (2015) The five keys to a successful Google team, https://rework.withgoogle.com/blog/five-keys-to-a-successful-google-team

13

Measuring what matters

Tracking maturity, foresight and culture

CHAPTER OBJECTIVES

- Understand how resilience measurement influences attention and organizational behaviour.
- Recognize where traditional metrics create blind spots and decision latency.
- Connect signals to decisions to enable earlier intervention and stronger resilience.

Organizations rely on measurement to understand resilience. They track service availability, recovery performance, control effectiveness and regulatory adherence. These indicators provide a structured view of performance and support accountability across functions.

As conditions change, signals appear before impact becomes visible. Thresholds are breached, exception backlogs grow and decisions require additional review, creating delays between issue identification and action. Although signals are observed in operations and discussed in governance forums, they do not consistently lead to action.

Cultural dynamics, escalation behaviour and decision timing shape how resilience performs under stress. These conditions are visible but are not consistently incorporated into formal reporting. The result is a gap between visibility and action. Organizations strengthen their ability to explain performance after impact. They remain less consistent in acting on signals before outcomes are fixed.

This chapter examines how measurement can be used to close that gap. It reframes measurement as a governance mechanism that shapes attention, decision-making and outcomes. It focuses on how organizations track maturity, foresight and culture, and how measurement choices influence whether signals lead to timely decisions.

The illusion of measurement

In most organizations, resilience is assessed through performance metrics, control indicators and historical outcomes. These measures provide visibility into conditions that can be observed, evidenced and reported consistently over time.

This reflects how governance operates. Boards, regulators and auditors require evidence that controls are functioning, obligations are being met and identified issues are being addressed. As a result, measurement naturally concentrates on established conditions rather than emerging ones.

Data systems reinforce this approach. They capture events, incidents, exceptions and threshold breaches with precision. A control is performed or it is not. A limit is breached or it is not. These measures provide clarity on outcomes and performance.

Resilience, however, often begins to change before outcomes deteriorate. Decisions take longer to reach resolution. Escalation becomes more frequent. Ownership becomes less clear. Assumptions are challenged more often. These developments influence resilience long before they appear in traditional reporting.

What is measured receives attention, challenge and intervention. What remains outside established measures often receives less scrutiny until its consequences become visible.

Table 13.1 makes this distinction explicit. It contrasts what is formally measured with the conditions that often influence resilience before performance indicators begin to change.

The contrast highlights a gap between what is reported and what drives outcomes. That gap sits in how different types of metrics influence decisions.

Some metrics confirm outcomes after the fact. Others signal change earlier but remain disconnected from action. A smaller set reflects behaviour and judgement. For example, a risk committee may spend increasing amounts of time revisiting the same issue, decisions may require multiple rounds of review before approval, or accountability may shift between

TABLE 13.1 Measurement distortion: What gets seen vs what drives outcomes

Dimension	What is measured (visible)	What is not measured (structural)	Governance consequence
Outcomes	Incidents, losses, breaches	Near-misses, pattern formation	Failure is explained after impact
Controls	Completion rates, test results	Effectiveness under stress	Activity is mistaken for resilience
Decision-making	Escalations logged	Delays, deferrals, ownership gaps	Decision latency remains hidden
Culture	Survey scores (periodic)	Real-time behaviour under pressure	Cultural risk is underestimated
Coordination	Formal governance forums	Cross-functional friction	Fragmentation persists unnoticed

functions before ownership is accepted. These developments often indicate weakening resilience before any threshold is breached or performance metric changes. Such signals rarely enter formal reporting because they cannot be standardized or compared consistently. They depend on interpretation in context and vary by situation, team and decision moment.

They surface in meetings and influence how risk is assessed. They are rarely tracked or reported consistently over time. Without continued visibility, they do not accumulate sufficient attention to trigger intervention.

Decision-making follows what is structured, visible and repeatedly reported. Metrics that meet these conditions shape attention and timing. Metrics that remain contextual inform discussion without consistently changing outcomes.

Table 13.2 isolates this mechanism by distinguishing how different categories of metrics shape decision-making.

Leading indicators influence outcomes only when they trigger action. When they remain within reporting, they become descriptive.

Signals linked to behaviour and judgement sit further outside formal measurement. Delayed decisions, shifting ownership during escalation and hesitation at the point of commitment are visible in practice. They shape how resilience performs under pressure. They are not tracked in a way that accumulates weight or prompts intervention.

TABLE 13.2 Metric type vs decision value

Metric type	What it captures	What it misses	Decision implication
Lagging indicators	Events after impact	How exposure developed	Enables explanation, not prevention
Control indicators	Activity performed	Reliability under stress	Creates assurance without certainty
Leading indicators	Early signals (thresholds, trends)	Context and interpretation	Only valuable if linked to action
Cultural signals	Informal behaviour patterns	Consistency and visibility	Often excluded from formal decisions

Decision-making follows what is structured, visible and repeated. Reporting reinforces control over what has already been observed. It provides limited traction on how exposure is developing.

Decision latency in a forward-looking world

The limitations of measurement remain manageable in stable conditions, where underlying weaknesses do not materially affect outcomes. They become critical when the environment moves faster than the organization's ability to interpret and act on signals.

External expectations have shifted. Regulators require forward-looking resilience assessments that demonstrate how disruption is anticipated and managed before impact. Investors use non-financial risk and governance as indicators of how consistently performance can be sustained over time. Digital and interconnected systems increase the speed and scale at which failures propagate, reducing the time available to respond and amplifying second-order effects.

Under these conditions, the indicators being monitored continue to provide the information they were designed to provide. The challenge is that emerging pressures often appear outside established measures. Escalation becomes more frequent, decisions take longer to reach resolution and unresolved issues begin to accumulate. These developments affect how organizations respond to pressure yet they rarely form part of formal resilience measurement.

The consequence is decision latency. Time expands between signal recognition and action, allowing exposure to develop during that interval. Resilience depends on reducing that gap by linking early signals to decision thresholds, ensuring emerging risks trigger intervention before they become visible in outcomes.

The resilience measurement architecture

Organizations often have too many metrics and too little understanding of what those metrics actually reveal. Measures that describe outcomes are often combined with indicators intended to assess capability and signals that influence decisions under pressure. As the number of indicators grows, it becomes increasingly difficult to distinguish between what confirms performance, what indicates preparedness and what shapes execution. Maturity depends not on the quantity of measures being tracked but on whether organizations understand the different roles those measures play.

The three-domain measurement model

Resilience is captured through multiple categories of metrics. It is the product of the interaction of three domains that operate at different points in time and influence decisions in different ways.

1. OUTCOME (LAGGING)

Outcome metrics capture what has already occurred. They provide a record of impact and confirm how resilience has performed after the fact.

These include incidents, losses and breaches, along with service disruption metrics and financial impact. They are precise, auditable and comparable across reporting cycles. They support accountability and external reporting.

They do not explain how outcomes developed. They confirm the result once it is already fixed.

Example: A payment outage is recorded as a two-hour disruption affecting a defined number of customers. The metric captures duration and impact. It does not show how many earlier warnings were raised before the failure occurred.

2. CAPABILITY (LEADING)

Capability indicators reflect the organization's ability to respond before impact occurs. They shape how future outcomes will unfold under stress.

These include scenario readiness, control adaptability and resource flexibility. They indicate whether the organization can absorb disruption, adjust execution and sustain performance when conditions change.

Their value depends on how they are used. When linked to decision thresholds, they enable early intervention. When treated as static assessments, they become descriptive.

Example: Following the outage, resilience testing confirms that systems can be recovered within defined tolerance levels. The result demonstrates technical capability. It does not indicate whether, during the incident, decisions were taken quickly enough to activate that capability.

3. CULTURAL AND FORESIGHT SIGNALS (STRUCTURAL)

Cultural and foresight signals shape how the organization interprets and acts on information under pressure. They influence whether capability translates into effective action.

These include escalation behaviour, clarity of decision ownership and the ability to recognize and interpret signals as they emerge. They are visible in how teams operate, how decisions are taken and how issues move across the organization.

They are less structured than other metrics. They are also more determinative. They define whether signals lead to action or remain unaddressed.

Example: In the weeks before the outage, a recurring control weakness had been raised and discussed across teams. Resolution required multiple escalations before ownership was confirmed. The delay is visible in meeting discussions. It is not captured as a metric, yet it determined how the incident developed.

Figure 13.1 illustrates how different measures reveal different aspects of resilience. Most organizations place greatest emphasis on outcomes because they are precise, auditable and easy to compare over time. Capability indicators provide a view of preparedness, while cultural and foresight signals influence how effectively organizations interpret information and act under pressure. Together, these domains determine whether insight translates into action.

FIGURE 13.1 The three-domain measurement model

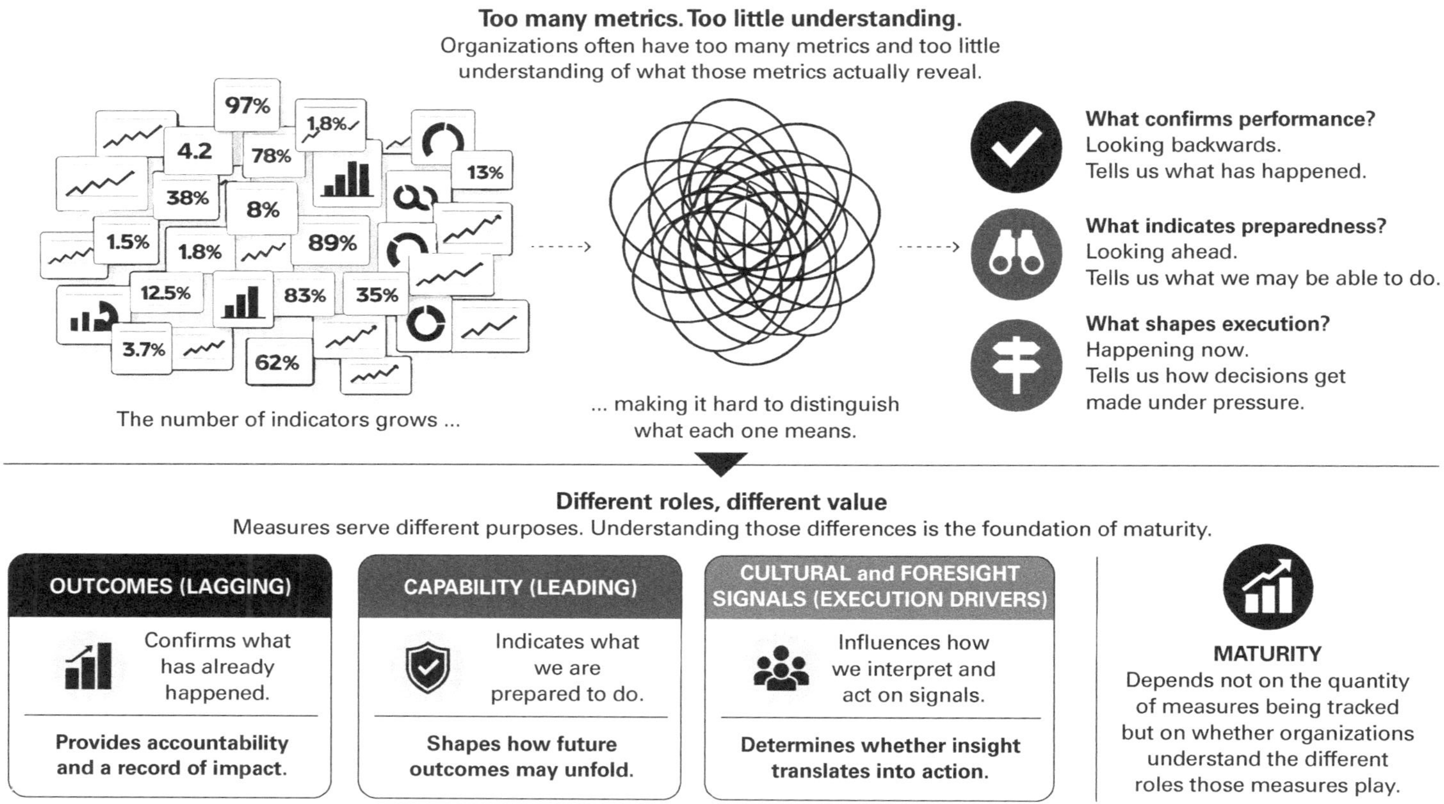

REAL-WORLD EXAMPLE

BNP Paribas and UK PRA: Measurement and resilience benchmarking

The regulatory focus on operational resilience has required financial institutions to demonstrate that critical services can remain within defined impact tolerances under stress. Frameworks introduced by the UK Prudential Regulation Authority and the Bank of England[1] require firms to identify important business services, map dependencies and test their ability to operate through disruption.

The transition period concluded on 31 March 2025. Firms are now expected to demonstrate that they can operate within their impact tolerances in live conditions, not only define them through mapping and testing.

Institutions, including BNP Paribas,[2] have developed comprehensive measurement frameworks in response. Critical services are mapped across systems, processes and third-party dependencies.[3] Scenario testing provides structured evidence of performance under stress. Reporting is aligned across functions and supports consistent interpretation of risk.

This approach improves visibility. Organizations gain a clearer understanding of where disruption may occur and how it can be measured. The framework establishes a shared reference point across technology, operations and risk.

The limitation appears when conditions begin to change. Measurement defines the service, the dependency and the tolerance for disruption. It does not define how signals are escalated, how decisions are taken or how coordination is managed once disruption begins.

Dependencies on external providers add complexity. Critical services often rely on third parties, including cloud infrastructure providers, where resolution requires coordination beyond the organization. Signals may be identified internally, while action depends on alignment across multiple entities. Decision timelines extend as coordination increases.

Accountability is formally assigned. Frameworks such as the Senior Managers and Certification Regime define ownership for resilience outcomes. Execution depends on how information is interpreted and acted upon across functions during disruption. Ownership is clear. Response varies.

Practically, organizations improve their ability to identify and measure disruption. They remain less consistent in how quickly signals lead to decisions and how effectively responses are coordinated under pressure.

Mapping critical services clarifies where failure occurs. It does not determine how signals are escalated or decisions are taken when disruption begins.

What to measure and what to avoid

Measurement choices direct attention. The question is not whether these metrics are useful, but what they enable the organization to see and act on. Table 13.3 and 13.4 distinguish between indicators that support timely decision-making and those that require discipline in how they are interpreted.

TABLE 13.3 Measurement focus: From activity to decision value

Category	What to prioritize	What it reveals	Governance value
Escalation	Speed and quality of escalation	How quickly signals reach decision makers	Reduces decision latency
Scenario response	Responsiveness under stress	Ability to adapt in real conditions	Confirms capability in practice
Decision-making	Clarity of ownership under pressure	Who can act and when	Enables timely intervention
Coordination	Cross-functional alignment	How work moves across boundaries	Prevents fragmentation

The indicators in Table 13.3 capture how the organization moves from signal to action.

TABLE 13.4 Measurement discipline: Where over-reliance distorts insight

Metric type	What it confirms	What it does not show	Risk if overweighted
Incident counts	Frequency of failure	How failure developed	Focus on outcomes only
Control completion	Process execution	Effectiveness under stress	False sense of assurance
Compliance indicators	Adherence to standards	Decision quality in practice	Static view of risk

The measures outlined in Table 13.4 remain necessary, yet over-reliance on them creates a false sense of security. They confirm that processes exist and operate. They do not establish whether those processes will hold in adverse situations or translate into timely decisions.

Measurement fails through imbalance. When organizations concentrate on outcomes and activity, they strengthen their ability to explain performance. When they extend measurement to capability and behaviour, they strengthen their ability to influence it.

Why signals do not become decisions

The value of an indicator is established at the point where it triggers a change in behaviour. Without that connection, measurement remains descriptive regardless of timing. Indicators only influence outcomes when they are recognized as signals requiring action rather than observations requiring explanation.

A signal raised at the point of execution is usually clear. It reflects direct exposure to the issue. As it moves upward, its framing changes. Language becomes more cautious. A concern requiring action becomes a topic for further discussion. The content remains; its urgency reduces.

REPORTING CAN REDUCE URGENCY

Information rarely reaches senior leadership in the same form in which it was first raised. Concerns that begin as operational frustrations or repeated exceptions are often discussed, clarified and summarized before they appear in reports. By that stage, much of the uncertainty has been removed and the issue feels more controlled than it did at the point where it was first experienced. Clear reporting helps leaders understand what is happening. It can also create distance from the conditions that triggered concern in the first place. Resilient organizations pay attention not only to what is reported but also to how the message has changed as it moved through the organization. (Adapted from insights shared during interviews conducted for this book.)

Incentives shape how that signal is handled. Acting on an early warning may require slowing delivery, reallocating resources or exposing uncertainty. These actions carry immediate cost. Performance objectives remain in place. The signal is acknowledged. The decision remains unchanged.

PRACTITIONER PULSE

Culture shapes whether signals trigger decisions

In a LinkedIn poll of risk and governance professionals, 51 per cent identified culture as the primary factor preventing data from influencing decisions. Clarity received 33 per cent of responses, while skills and capacity accounted for 12 per cent and 5 per cent respectively. The results suggest that organizations fail when signals remain visible without altering decisions. This reinforces the chapter's central argument that measurement creates value only when information changes behaviour.

Repetition alters how the signal is perceived. When thresholds are breached without consequence or issues are revisited without resolution, the condition becomes familiar. What was treated as an exception becomes part of normal operations. The organization adjusts to the signal rather than addressing it.

Together, these mechanisms create a predictable pattern. Signals are reframed, action is deferred and repeated deviations gradually lose their urgency. The signal remains visible throughout. Intervention does not. Figure 13.2 makes this sequence explicit.

Over time, the organization becomes less responsive to signals, allowing exposure to develop while decisions continue to be postponed.

This follows the logic of the Swiss Cheese Model[4] introduced in Chapter 5. Gaps remain contained when isolated. When they align, they allow failure to pass through multiple layers of control. In this context, the gaps sit in behaviour: how signals are escalated, how decisions are prioritized and how deviations are interpreted over time.

The ability to interrupt this sequence depends on cultural maturity. Signals must be acted upon at the point where they first appear.

Similarly, Clark's 4 Stages of Psychological Safety[5] we discussed in Chapter 3 provide a practical lens. Individuals contribute, question and act within their role. Resilience depends on the stage where individuals escalate risk and challenge decisions when required. Without that condition, signals continue to move through the organization without changing outcomes.

Outcomes are determined by whether individuals escalate, prioritize and act before the signal loses its force.

FIGURE 13.2 Signal degradation path

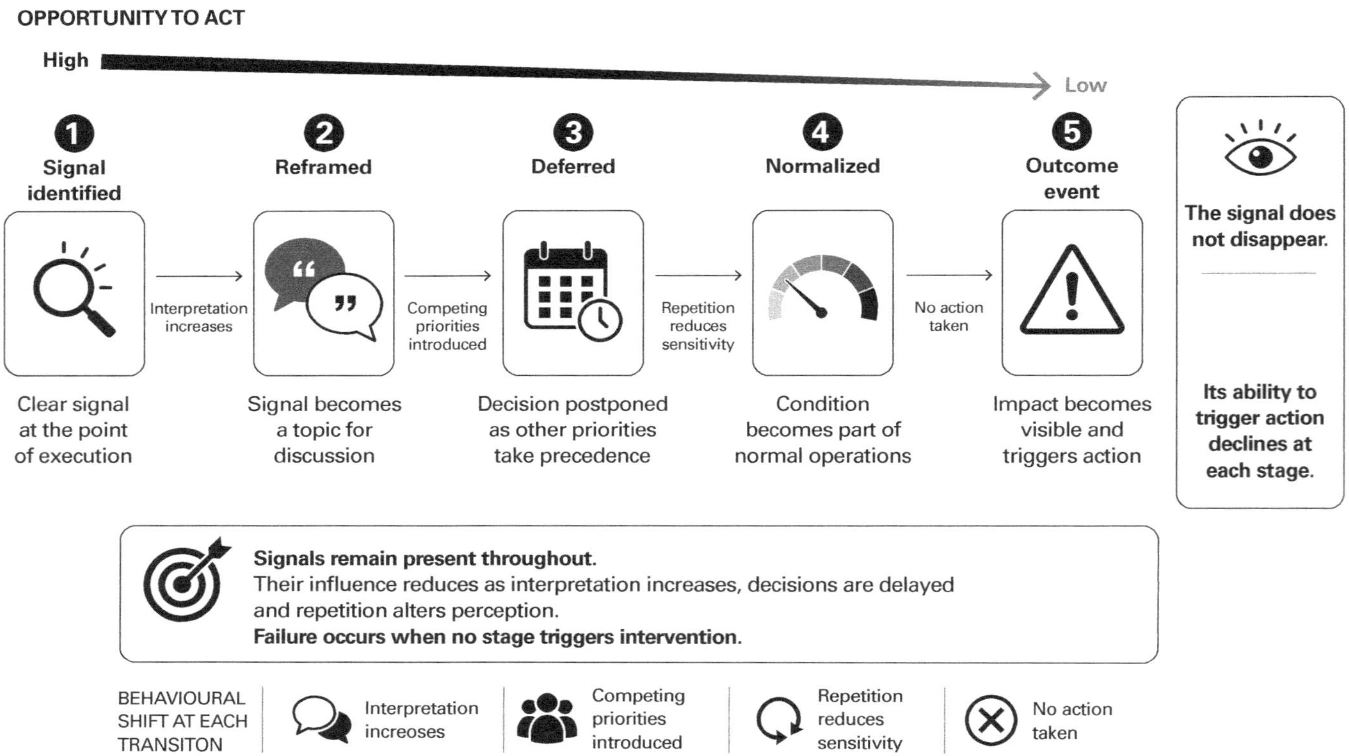

Comparing resilience maturity across industries: Uneven development

Resilience develops unevenly across industries. These differences are visible in what is measured, how signals are interpreted and how decisions are taken under stress. The comparison highlights where each sector is strong and where exposure remains. It does not identify a single model to replicate.

Financial services

Financial institutions rely on structured measurement. Risk metrics are defined, monitored and reported with precision. Stress testing provides a systematic view of performance under adverse conditions.

This approach creates clarity on exposure and supports regulatory accountability. Cultural and behavioural signals remain less integrated. Escalation dynamics, decision ownership and response speed are visible in practice. They are not consistently captured in formal measurement.

The result is strong visibility on quantified risk with less structure around how signals translate into decisions.

Public sector

Public sector organizations focus on scenario-based resilience. Planning incorporates long-term risks and system-wide dependencies. Preparedness is built through exercises and coordination across functions and agencies.

This approach supports continuity under complex conditions. Decision-making involves multiple stakeholders and defined governance processes. Movement from signal to action requires alignment across multiple decision layers. The result is broad anticipation of risk with longer decision cycles.

REAL-WORLD EXAMPLE

Japan: Scenario-based resilience and disaster preparedness

Japan operates in an environment where exposure to natural disasters is persistent. Earthquakes, tsunamis and extreme weather events require organizations and public authorities to prepare for disruption as a recurring condition rather than an exceptional event.

Resilience is structured through long-term, scenario-based planning. National frameworks,[6] such as the Disaster Management Basic Plan, define how different types of disruption are anticipated and managed. These scenarios are embedded into infrastructure design, urban planning and governance processes. Building standards incorporate seismic resilience. Transport systems are designed to maintain continuity or enable controlled shutdown. Early warning systems are integrated into public communication channels, allowing signals to be transmitted rapidly and consistently.

This approach connects planning with execution. Regular drills and simulations test how organizations and communities respond under realistic conditions. National exercises, such as Disaster Prevention Day on 1 September, reinforce this cycle, ensuring that scenarios are repeatedly tested across institutions and communities.[7] These exercises involve coordination across government agencies, emergency services and private operators. A disruption in one system triggers defined responses in others. For example, seismic signals can lead to the automatic suspension of high-speed rail services,[8] reducing exposure before damage occurs.

Decision-making is positioned close to the point of execution. Frontline teams operate within defined scenarios and are expected to act as conditions unfold. This reflects a strong emphasis on operational awareness at the point where signals are first detected. Signals are not only escalated; they are acted upon within established boundaries.

Measurement reflects this orientation. Indicators extend beyond past events to include preparedness for future conditions. Response times during simulations, coordination across agencies and the ability to operate within defined scenarios provide a view of how the system performs before disruption occurs.

The impact is visible in execution. Preparedness spans multiple scenarios. Coordination between planning and response is reinforced through repeated testing. Signals generated during exercises are incorporated into future planning, creating a continuous cycle of adjustment.

Resilience improves when measurement reflects future conditions and is directly linked to how decisions are taken at the point where signals emerge.

Startups and scale-ups

Startups and scale-ups operate with direct proximity to signals. Decisions are taken close to the point of execution. Adaptation occurs in real time as conditions change.

This approach enables speed and flexibility. Formal measurement remains limited. Indicators are often informal and not consistently tracked. As the organization grows, this creates variation in how decisions are taken across teams. Decision quality becomes more variable as informal signals

TABLE 13.5 Resilience maturity by sector

Sector	Measurement strength	Decision behaviour	Structural gap
Financial services	Quantitative metrics, stress testing	Structured, governed	Cultural signals weakly integrated
Public sector	Scenario planning, long-term view	Coordinated, multilayered	Slower decision cycles
Startups/scale-ups	Real-time signal use	Fast, decentralized	Limited formal measurement

are interpreted differently across teams. The result is strong responsiveness with limited structure to sustain consistency at scale.

Cross-sector insight

Each sector concentrates on a different dimension of resilience. Financial services emphasizes measurement and control. The public sector emphasizes preparedness and coordination. Start-ups emphasize speed and adaptation. This results in uneven development across resilience capabilities.

Benchmarking highlights these differences. It shows where resilience is developed and where it remains incomplete. It does not identify best practice. It reveals how measurement, capability and behaviour combine differently across sectors (see Table 13.5).

Board and executive implications

Boards receive assurance through measurement. Reports confirm that controls operate, incidents are tracked and thresholds are monitored. This provides visibility on performance. It does not establish whether the organization will act early enough to influence outcomes.

Oversight requires a shift in focus. The question is no longer limited to whether controls are functioning. It extends to whether signals lead to decisions before impact occurs.

This changes how information is interpreted at board and executive level. Outcomes, control metrics and indicators remain relevant. Their value depends on what they reveal about how decisions are taken across the organization.

Table 13.6 links common governance signals to how they should be interpreted in the context of resilience.

The table shows how governance signals can be interpreted as indicators of decision behaviour. Stable metrics indicate consistency in reporting. Low incident levels indicate limited observed failure. Repeated threshold breaches indicate that conditions are changing. Backlogs and escalation patterns provide a direct view of how decisions are taken. Accumulating exceptions indicate delayed resolution. Escalation indicates where ownership shifts rather than remains at the point where the signal is identified.

For boards, this interpretation shifts oversight towards the conditions that determine whether action is taken. The focus moves from confirming that processes operate to understanding how signals translate into decisions across the organization.

For executive leadership, the same signals indicate where decision-making slows. Delays in resolution, repeated discussion of the same issues and reliance on escalation reflect where signals are recognized but not acted upon.

Risk functions contribute by identifying these patterns across reporting and governance forums. Repeated signals without action, delayed escalation and concentration of decision-making authority show how measurement connects to behaviour.

TABLE 13.6 From measurement signals to decision dynamics

Governance view	Traditional interpretation	Decision-focused interpretation
Stable control metrics	Controls are operating effectively	Signals may not be triggering action
Low incident levels	Risk exposure is limited	Early signals may not be visible or acted upon
Repeated threshold breaches	Tolerances are being tested	Signals are present without intervention
Growing exception backlog	Operational pressure	Delayed decisions and unresolved ownership
High escalation volume	Risk awareness	Decisions not resolved at the point of origin

These patterns indicate resilience maturity in practice. Where decisions follow outcomes, the organization remains reactive. Where signals are visible but do not change behaviour, early warning exists without intervention. Where signals influence prioritization and trigger action, decisions move closer to the point where exposure can still be controlled.

The most important metric is not the number of incidents; it is the time between signal and decision. This interpretation brings measurement back to its purpose: influencing decisions before outcomes are fixed.

This interval determines whether the organization acts while outcomes can still be influenced or responds after impact has occurred.

Practical playbook

Improving resilience requires changes in how signals are translated into decisions. This includes how indicators are defined, how they are linked to action and how behaviour is reinforced across the organization.

The focus is not on increasing the volume of metrics. It is on ensuring that signals lead to timely intervention.

Boards

Boards oversee whether the organization acts on early warning signals before impact occurs. This requires visibility on how indicators influence decisions across the organization.

1. **Require forward-looking indicators**
   Boards should ensure that each material risk includes at least one indicator that reflects developing conditions. This provides visibility before outcomes are fixed.
2. **Challenge lagging-heavy reporting**
   Oversight should examine whether dashboards are dominated by outcome metrics. A concentration of lagging indicators limits the ability to identify emerging exposure.
3. **Track decision latency**
   Boards should monitor the time between signal identification and decision. Extended intervals indicate that signals are present without triggering action.

Executives

Executives determine how measurement is translated into operational decisions. This includes linking indicators to action and ensuring coordination across functions.

1 **Link indicators to decision thresholds**
Indicators should trigger defined responses. A threshold breach should lead to review, escalation or resource adjustment. Without this link, indicators remain within reporting.

2 **Integrate scenario testing into performance**
Scenario exercises should be used to assess how decisions are taken in adverse situations. Results should inform how teams are evaluated and developed.

3 **Monitor cross-functional dependencies**
Executives should track how signals move across functions. Delays often occur where ownership is unclear or coordination is required across multiple teams.

Chief risk officers and risk leaders

Risk functions provide visibility on how measurement connects to behaviour. This requires integrating indicators that reflect how decisions are taken in practice.

1 **Introduce cultural diagnostics into reporting**
Risk leaders should include indicators that capture escalation behaviour, decision ownership and response timing. These signals show how early warnings are handled.

2 **Design escalation-based metrics**
Metrics should reflect how issues move through the organization. This includes escalation speed, frequency of rework and resolution timelines.

3 **Align measurement with risk appetite triggers**
Indicators should be linked to risk appetite thresholds. Breaches should prompt defined action, ensuring that exposure is addressed before impact occurs.

KEY TAKEAWAYS

- **Measurement determines what organizations notice and when they respond**. Dashboards and metrics provide discipline and consistency. They also shape attention. What is measured becomes part of routine discussion, while signals that fall outside established reporting often receive less scrutiny. Resilience depends as much on what remains invisible as on what is formally tracked.
- **Outcome metrics explain performance**. They do not explain how outcomes developed. Most organizations measure incidents, losses and control activity with precision. These measures confirm what has already occurred. They provide accountability and comparability. They offer limited insight into how decisions, behaviours and responses evolved before impact became visible.
- **Resilience depends on the interaction of outcomes, capabilities and cultural signals**. Effective measurement extends beyond historical performance. Capability indicators show preparedness, while cultural signals influence how information is interpreted and acted upon. Weakness in any one domain limits the effectiveness of the others.
- **Early signals only create value when they trigger decisions**. Indicators are present across most organizations. Their significance is determined by whether they lead to intervention. A leading indicator that does not change behaviour ultimately behaves like a lagging indicator. Visibility alone does not prevent failure.
- **Signals lose influence as they move through organizations**. Interpretation, competing priorities and repeated exposure gradually reduce urgency. Signals remain visible throughout the organization yet their ability to trigger action declines. Failures often emerge because intervention is delayed rather than because information is absent.
- **Cultural maturity determines whether signals retain their force**. Escalation behaviour, decision ownership and psychological safety influence whether concerns are acted upon at the point of detection. Resilience is strengthened when individuals are willing and able to challenge, escalate and respond before conditions deteriorate.

- **The most important resilience metric is the time between signal and decision.** Boards and executives often focus on incidents and losses. Resilience is shaped earlier. The critical question is how quickly emerging signals lead to action. Organizations that connect signals to decisions strengthen their ability to prevent failure rather than explain it.

Reframing forward

Measurement shapes how resilience is understood and how organizations respond to emerging risk.

Indicators make conditions visible. Outcomes confirm what has already occurred. Signals show where exposure is developing. The difference lies in whether that visibility leads to action.

Most organizations have early warnings available. Signals appear in operations, escalation patterns and decision forums. They do not consistently translate into timely intervention. The gap sits between recognizing a signal and acting on it.

Closing that gap depends on leadership. Measurement creates visibility. Leadership determines whether signals are acted upon when they first appear or deferred until impact becomes visible.

The next chapter builds on this foundation. It examines how leadership influences decision-making and how organizations translate visibility into consistent action across teams and functions.

Endnotes

1 Bank of England (2021) *Operational resilience: Impact tolerances for important business services*, Bank of England, London
2 BNP Paribas (2023) *Universal Registration Document and Annual Financial Report*, BNP Paribas, Paris
3 Bank of England (2023) *Operational resilience: Critical third parties to the UK financial sector*, Bank of England, London
4 Reason, J (1997) *Managing the Risks of Organizational Accidents*, Ashgate, Aldershot

5 Clark, T R (2020) *The 4 Stages of Psychological Safety: Defining the path to inclusion and innovation*, Berrett-Koehler, Oakland, CA
6 Cabinet Office, Government of Japan (2023) *Disaster Management in Japan*, Cabinet Office, Tokyo
7 OECD (2020) *Strengthening the Governance of Disaster Risk Reduction in Japan*, OECD Publishing, Paris
8 International Bank for Reconstruction and Development/World Bank (2019) *Learning from Megadisasters: Lessons from the Great East Japan Earthquake*, World Bank, Washington, DC

14

The leadership and CRO playbook

> CHAPTER OBJECTIVES
>
> - Design decision conditions that strengthen organizational resilience.
> - Reinforce ownership and reduce decision friction.
> - Enable timely intervention and organizational agility.

Organizations rely on governance to maintain resilience. Governance provides structure, visibility and clear expectations about how decisions should be taken. Yet when conditions change, decisions often slow rather than accelerate.

The impact is visible in day-to-day activity. Delivery milestones slip and require replanning. Issues are often identified early, yet decisions rarely occur where they first emerge. Instead, additional validation and cross-functional alignment extend the time to intervention. Resolution extends across teams and forums rather than occurring where the issue first arises. This exposes a limitation in how decisions are enabled.

Governance defines structure. Resilience depends on whether people act within it. When ownership is clear and authority is exercised with confidence, issues are addressed where they arise. When they are not, decisions become dependent on coordination and alignment, extending the time to intervention.

A gap emerges between governance design and organizational behaviour. Organizations strengthen oversight and coordination, while timely action remains uneven. Closing this gap requires a shift in leadership focus.

Resilience depends on the conditions under which decisions are taken. These conditions shape whether issues are acted on early, ownership remains clear and authority is exercised when it matters most. This chapter sets out that approach. It defines the role of the CRO as an architect of agility and outlines actions that strengthen ownership, reduce decision friction and support timely intervention across the organization.

From oversight to intervention

Resilience is often strengthened through additional oversight. Organizations often respond to uncertainty by strengthening oversight in the hope that greater visibility will improve decision-making. Yet better information does not consistently lead to earlier action. Issues are identified with accuracy and discussed in detail, yet decisions frequently require further validation or alignment before intervention is taken. The constraint lies in how visibility is used.

Oversight mechanisms provide a clear view of performance and exposure, supporting monitoring, coordination and accountability, but their effectiveness depends on whether this information establishes ownership and prompts action when issues arise. When thresholds operate as reporting markers rather than decision triggers, visibility increases without changing how the organization responds. A dashboard may highlight a deteriorating trend in a critical process. The data is accurate and the discussion is constructive, yet ownership remains unclear. Because resolution depends on further alignment, the time to intervention extends despite improved information.

PROTECT THE SIGNAL, NOT JUST THE PROCESS

Organizations invest heavily in reporting, governance and escalation processes to improve visibility. These mechanisms strengthen oversight yet repeated refinement can unintentionally weaken the urgency that prompted the issue in the first place.

Resilience depends not only on whether issues are escalated but also on whether the original signal survives the journey to decision makers. Effective leaders protect the integrity of information as carefully as they protect the integrity of processes. Decisions improve when uncertainty remains visible rather than being diluted through repeated validation and presentation. (Adapted from insights shared during interviews conducted for this book.)

Resilience improves when this delay is reduced. This requires redefining how signals are treated at the moment they become visible. In more resilient systems, signals prompt decisions. Ownership is established early, authority is clear and intervention occurs before coordination complexity increases. This distinction can be understood through two operating models shown in Table 14.1.

In many organizations, the initial response is to review and align. Information is shared, additional analysis is requested and agreement is sought before action is taken. This approach improves understanding, though it extends the time to intervention.

In more resilient systems, the same information establishes ownership immediately. The accountable individual acts within defined boundaries as soon as the issue becomes visible. Alignment follows action rather than preceding it.

This shift changes what is required from leadership. Acting under pressure depends on clarity of ownership, confidence to proceed without full information and discipline to avoid unnecessary escalation. This is where the role of the CRO becomes practical.

A reporting-oriented CRO ensures that issues are visible and well understood. An intervention-oriented CRO ensures that those same issues lead to decisions. This is achieved by defining thresholds as action points, clarifying who is expected to act and structuring escalation so that it supports rather than delays intervention. The difference in design is limited but the difference in outcome is significant.

Resilience depends on how consistently issues lead to timely, well-owned decisions. This sets the direction for the remainder of the chapter, which focuses on how these decision conditions can be designed and applied in practice.

TABLE 14.1 Oversight vs intervention operating model

Dimension	Oversight-oriented	Intervention-oriented
Thresholds	Reporting markers	Decision triggers
Escalation	Hierarchical	Ownership-based
Governance forums	Review and alignment	Decision and action
CRO role	Reporter of risk	Designer of decision conditions
Outcome	Visibility	Timely intervention

Why decisions stall under pressure

The conditions under which leaders operate have changed materially. Decision-making is no longer episodic or contained within stable structures[1]. It is continuous, distributed and shaped by overlapping strategic, operational and regulatory demands. Three forces define this environment.

Decision velocity has increased. Strategic, operational and technology decisions now interact in real time. A product change affects customer behaviour immediately. A system constraint alters execution within hours. Regulatory developments reshape priorities before governance cycles can respond. Decisions overlap rather than follow a sequence.

Complexity has expanded alongside speed. Interdependencies across functions, platforms and third parties mean cause and effect are not always visible. Local issues can propagate before they are fully understood, requiring leaders to act with incomplete information.

Regulatory expectations have evolved. Supervisors focus on resilience, accountability and decision traceability, placing emphasis on how decisions are taken, who owns them and how quickly they translate into action.[2]

These pressures interact with a structural reality inside most organizations where ownership is fragmented. Transformation, technology and operations operate across different layers with distinct priorities, while risk, compliance and audit provide oversight across all three. Alignment relies on coordination rather than predefined decision rules, which performs adequately in stable conditions but begins to strain as pressure increases.[3]

As coordination becomes the primary mechanism for decision-making, action depends on alignment across functions. Authority becomes conditional and the time required to act extends. Reporting expands to maintain visibility, while the ability to respond early remains uneven.

At the same time, teams closest to the problem adapt to maintain delivery. Workarounds and informal solutions emerge where formal structures cannot respond quickly enough.[4] These actions sustain performance in the short term, yet they remain outside governance and are rarely integrated into the broader system.

Individually, each response is rational. Together, they create a consistent pattern. Visibility increases, decision ownership weakens and adaptation occurs outside the system. The organization continues to function, though coherence begins to erode.

The result is a divergence between local agility and system-wide resilience. Teams respond quickly to immediate constraints, while the organization struggles to translate these responses into coordinated action at scale.

This interaction between competing demands, fragmented ownership and behaviour constrains leadership capacity. As demands increase, the time available to interpret signals, assign ownership and act with clarity reduces, while coordination requirements expand.

This dynamic explains why improvements in oversight alone do not strengthen resilience. The organization becomes more capable of observing its conditions while remaining constrained in its ability to act.

For leadership, the implication is structural rather than incremental. Resilience depends on restoring clarity of ownership, aligning decision authority with where action is required, and ensuring that local adaptation is recognized and integrated into the broader system.

This defines the operating context for the CRO. The role extends beyond coordination across fragmented structures to shaping the conditions under which decisions are taken, so that the organization can act with speed and coherence.

The CRO as an architect of agility

Resilience at scale depends on how consistently organizations translate signals into decisions with speed and clarity. Achieving this requires deliberate design. The CRO is uniquely positioned to provide that design.

Traditionally, the role has been defined through oversight. The CRO ensures that risks are identified, measured and reported. This remains essential. Visibility and governance depend on it. It does not determine how the organization acts when conditions change. Agility depends on what happens next.

When issues arise, the organization must interpret them consistently, assign ownership without delay and act within defined boundaries. In many organizations, these steps remain fragmented. Functions interpret the same issue differently, ownership shifts as alignment is sought, and governance processes introduce delay at the moment speed is required.

In this context, the CRO's role evolves from observing these constraints to defining how signals are interpreted, who is expected to act and how decisions are taken when issues arise. This shift can be understood through the agility architecture model, shown in Figure 14.1.

The CRO shapes organizational agility through three interconnected roles. As a signal integrator, they ensure that issues are interpreted consistently across functions, creating a shared understanding as they emerge. As a

FIGURE 14.1 The agility architecture model

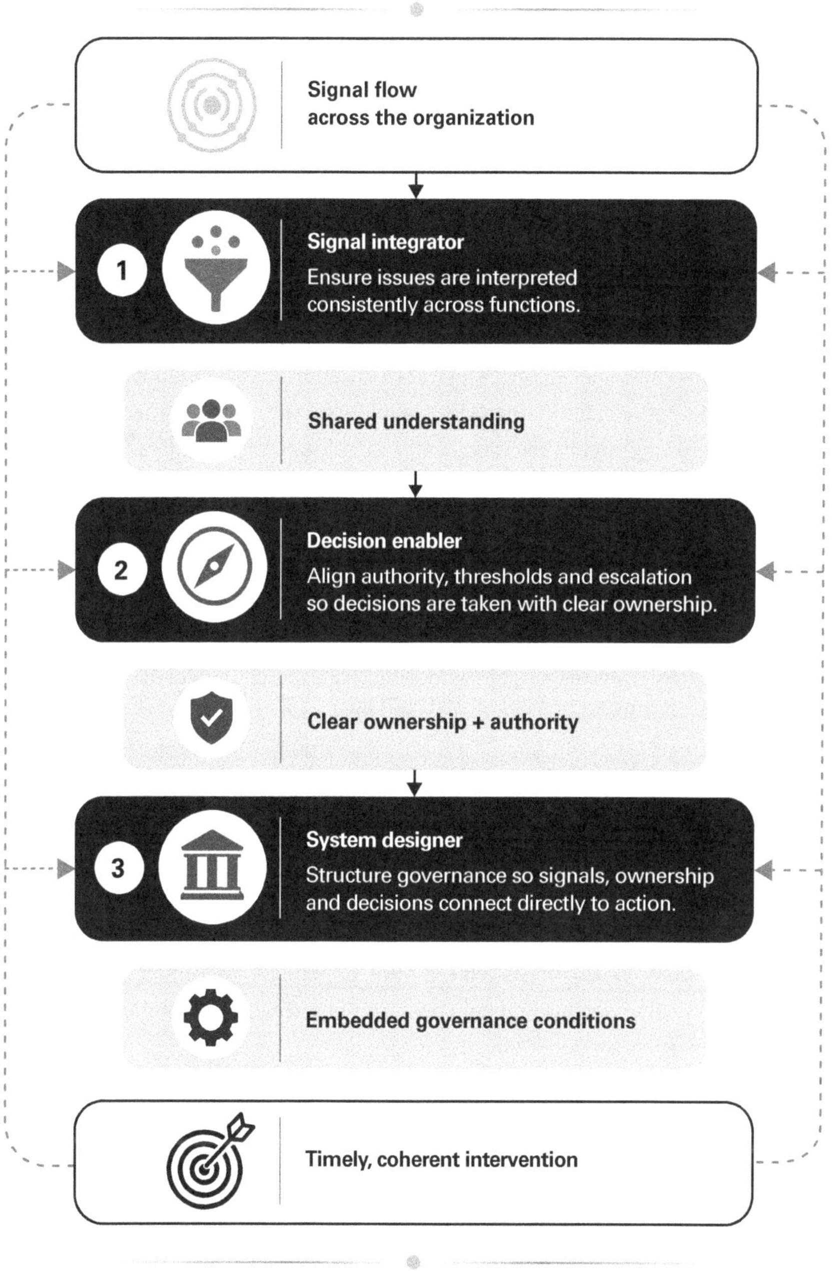

Agility is achieved when signals are consistently interpreted, decisions are clearly owned and governance enables action under pressure.

decision enabler, they align authority, thresholds and escalation so that decisions are taken with clear ownership at the point of signal. As a system designer, they structure governance so that signals, ownership and decisions connect directly to intervention. Operational ownership remains with the business. The CRO's role is to define how decisions are taken, ensuring that governance supports timely intervention while maintaining control.

REAL-WORLD EXAMPLE

EDP (Portugal): Decision alignment in renewable transition

The transition to renewable energy requires organizations to operate under sustained uncertainty. Market volatility, regulatory evolution and capital intensity create conditions where investment decisions carry long-term consequences while being shaped by short-term fluctuations.

Organizations, such as EDP (Energias de Portugal),[5] operate at a scale where these tensions are structural. EDP committed to a €25 billion gross investment plan between 2023 and 2026, equivalent to approximately €6.2 billion annually. Around 85 per cent of this capital is directed towards renewable generation, with the remainder allocated to electricity networks. Decisions on allocation, timing and execution carry material implications for both performance and resilience.

This scale creates a continuous decision requirement. The organization targets approximately 4.5 GW of new renewable capacity each year, requiring coordination across project development, financing, regulatory approval and operational integration. Decisions cannot be deferred without affecting delivery and accelerating them without alignment increases exposure.

Scenario design has traditionally supported strategic planning in this context. It provides structured views of possible future conditions, informing investment decisions and risk assessments. In many organizations, this activity remains periodic, informing planning cycles rather than live decisions.

At EDP, the role of scenario design has evolved. Rather than producing scenarios as stand-alone outputs, they are embedded directly into capital allocation and investment committee discussions. When decisions are taken on project prioritization, funding allocation or timing, alternative scenarios are presented alongside the base case. This creates a shared frame of reference across strategy, finance and operations at the point where trade-offs are made.

This approach reflects the CRO's role as a signal integrator and system designer. Scenario inputs are treated as decision inputs, ensuring that different functions operate with a consistent interpretation of uncertainty. Governance forums incorporate these inputs directly into decision-making, reducing the need for sequential validation and enabling clearer ownership at the point of action.

Alignment is achieved within the decision itself. Differences in interpretation are surfaced early when options remain open. The need for repeated validation across governance structures reduces, as assumptions are tested in real time. The effect is not an increase in decision speed; it is a reduction in decision friction.

Decisions require fewer iterations; assumptions are challenged earlier and ownership remains clear. Signals related to market shifts, regulatory changes or project constraints are interpreted consistently and acted upon without extending governance timelines.

This alignment is visible in how EDP manages exposure to market volatility. Over 70 per cent of planned renewable capacity is secured through long-term power purchase agreements, providing revenue stability while supporting continued investment at scale. In this context, de-risking is achieved through decisions taken with clarity on timing, counterparties and market conditions. The broader implication extends beyond the energy sector.

In capital-intensive environments, resilience depends less on the volume of analysis and more on how that analysis is integrated into decision-making. Understanding uncertainty improves foresight. Its impact depends on how it shapes decisions when they are taken.

Trust, dissent and controlled tension

Structures define how decisions are expected to be taken. Leadership behaviour and governance design determine whether they occur in practice. Leaders reinforce ownership by supporting decisions when issues arise, while the CRO defines decision boundaries, aligns authority with thresholds, and ensures that escalation supports action rather than delaying it. Resilience depends on how these elements operate together so that decisions are taken with clarity and ownership at the point where issues emerge.

Leading with trust and clarity

Trust and clarity depend on what leaders reward and how decision authority is designed. Leaders establish trust by reinforcing decision ownership in practice. When issues arise, they expect individuals to act within their remit and support those decisions rather than reopening them for validation. This reduces the need for repeated confirmation and allows decisions to be taken with confidence when information is incomplete.

Clarity is created through design. The CRO defines decision boundaries, aligns authority with thresholds and ensures that escalation provides support without transferring ownership. This establishes who decides, when they decide and under what conditions.

Resilience strengthens when leadership behaviour and governance design reinforce each other. Decisions remain close to the point where issues emerge, supported by clear ownership and consistent authority.

Creating space for dissent and challenge

Dissent functions as a control[6] when it is reinforced through leadership behaviour and governance design. Leaders create space for challenge by expecting assumptions to be tested and by supporting those who raise concerns early.

Leaders create space for dissent by encouraging assumptions to be tested and by supporting those who raise concerns early. The CRO embeds this into governance by defining how challenge is raised, evaluated and incorporated into decisions, ensuring that differing views strengthen decision quality rather than delay it. When these conditions are in place, emerging risks are surfaced and addressed before they become embedded in ongoing activity.

Escalation as a decision mechanism

Escalation supports resilience when it enables decisions and constrains it when it replaces them. Leaders influence this through how they respond to early signals, reinforcing ownership rather than encouraging deferral.

The CRO shapes escalation by aligning it with decision authority, so that support is provided without transferring accountability. When escalation is structured in this way, decisions remain close to the point where issues emerge and action occurs without unnecessary delay.

Controlled Jugaad

Chapter 5 introduced the concept of Jugaad as the practical improvisation that emerges when formal structures cannot respond quickly enough. In this chapter, the focus shifts from why these adaptations occur to how organizations use them.

Repeated workarounds signal where the system cannot absorb current conditions. They indicate capability gaps, structural inefficiencies and risks that remain outside formal governance. The issue is not the initial adaptation; it is whether the organization recognizes and responds to the pattern.

Leaders influence how these signals are treated. When recurring adaptations are ignored or discouraged, risks accumulate outside the system. When they are surfaced and examined, they provide early insight into where processes and governance require adjustment.

The CRO integrates these signals into the system. Recurring workarounds are identified, assessed and either formalized, redesigned or removed. Improvisation is not eliminated. It is channelled so that local adaptation strengthens the organization rather than fragmenting it.

Improvisation becomes a signal for system design, not a deviation from it. Leadership behaviour and governance design reinforce these mechanisms.

KEY PRINCIPLE

Resilient organizations define how behaviour supports decision-making in practice.

Trust encourages ownership. Challenge improves judgement. Escalation supports action. Adaptive learning ensures that local solutions strengthen the wider system.

When these elements are aligned, behaviour reinforces resilience. When they are not, structure alone cannot sustain it.

The next section translates these principles into leadership actions and board-level implications.

REAL-WORLD EXAMPLE

DHL Group (Germany): Escalation clarity and local decision ownership at scale

Global logistics networks operate under continuous disruption. Route closures, regulatory changes and capacity constraints require immediate decisions at the point of execution. In distributed organizations, these conditions test not only systems but behaviour.

Organizations, such as DHL Group,[7] operate at a scale where this challenge is structural. With approximately 600,000 employees across more than 220 countries and territories, decisions are taken continuously across locations, time zones and operating environments. Under these conditions, the distinction between escalation and ownership becomes critical.

In traditional escalation models, local teams identify issues and seek direction from central functions. This approach provides alignment. Under disruption, it increases dependency on coordination and extends the time required to act.

DHL's approach has focused on redefining how escalation operates in practice. Rather than treating escalation as a transfer of responsibility, the organization has clarified the conditions under which local teams act and when central coordination is required. Thresholds are linked to operational impact, customer commitments and network dependencies. Within these boundaries, local teams retain authority to re-route shipments, adjust capacity and prioritize delivery in response to real-time conditions.

This approach reflects the CRO's role as a decision enabler and system designer. Escalation is structured to support action rather than transfer ownership, with thresholds defining when local teams act and when coordination is required. Governance is aligned with decision authority at the point of execution, reducing reliance on central validation. This shift changes behaviour at the moment ownership is tested.

Local teams act without waiting for validation when conditions fall within defined limits. Escalation is used when decisions carry network-wide implications, not as a default response to uncertainty. Ownership remains with the point of execution, supported rather than replaced by central functions.

As a result, decisions are taken closer to where issues emerge and resolved within a single operating cycle. Coordination remains available, though it no longer defines the pace of response.

This behavioural shift is supported by system design. The group invests approximately €3.0 to €3.4 billion annually to modernize infrastructure and digitalize operations. These investments enable flexible network planning, allowing capacity to be adjusted dynamically as demand fluctuates. Local action is grounded in a system capable of absorbing and scaling adaptation.

Local adaptation remains essential. Teams continue to adjust routes, processes and capacity in response to disruption. These adaptations occur within defined boundaries and are captured to identify recurring constraints across the network. This creates a feedback loop between behaviour and system design.

Patterns of escalation highlight where decision boundaries require refinement. Recurring adaptations reveal structural constraints that can be addressed through changes in governance, capacity planning or network configuration. The result is a system where escalation supports decision-making rather than replacing it.

This model supports resilience at scale. In 2024, DHL Group generated €84.2 billion in revenue while maintaining performance across segments despite sustained disruption, including record earnings in Supply Chain and stable throughput in Global Forwarding under constrained conditions.

Board and executive implications

Boards receive assurance through governance structures that define roles, thresholds and escalation paths, with reporting confirming that these operate as intended. This provides a clear view of how decisions are expected to be taken, yet it does not show whether those decisions occur early enough to influence outcomes.

Oversight shifts from the presence of governance to whether it enables timely, well-owned decisions in practice. This changes how leadership interprets organizational performance.

Clear structures indicate that escalation and reporting are possible. Their value depends on whether they reduce decision friction, preserve ownership and support action when issues arise. Governance is effective when it enables decisions rather than delaying them.

At board level, this requires a move from reviewing resilience to testing decision readiness. Boards are not positioned to take operational decisions. They assess whether the organization is prepared to take them. This involves examining how decisions are made, how ownership is exercised and whether escalation supports or replaces action.

The focus shifts to observable decision patterns, as detailed in Table 14.2:

- issues discussed without resolution
- escalation used in place of action
- decisions requiring repeated validation.

These patterns indicate whether resilience exists in practice.

For boards, this interpretation brings oversight closer to behaviour. The focus moves from confirming that governance exists to understanding how it operates in practice. The central question becomes whether decision ownership is maintained when it matters most.

For executive leadership, the same shift requires precision in how decision-making is structured. Executives define who decides, what triggers

TABLE 14.2 From governance structures to decision readiness

Governance view	Traditional interpretation	Decision-focused interpretation
Clear escalation paths	Issues can be escalated effectively	Ownership may be transferred rather than exercised
Defined decision forums	Decisions are reviewed at the right level	Decisions may be delayed by coordination requirements
Comprehensive reporting	Leadership has full visibility	Visibility may not translate into intervention
Distributed accountability	Responsibilities are clearly assigned	Authority may remain unclear under pressure
Increased escalation volume	Risks are being surfaced	Decisions are not resolved at the point of origin

action and where authority sits across functions. When these elements are unclear, escalation fills the gap. When they are defined, decisions remain close to the point of action.

Executives strengthen this by aligning authority with the point where issues arise, defining thresholds as decision triggers, and ensuring that escalation provides support without transferring ownership.

Resilience depends on the interaction between these domains. Structure without behavioural alignment creates visibility without intervention. Behaviour without structural clarity creates inconsistency and reliance on individual judgement. Resilience emerges when both operate together.

For boards and executives, the clearest indicator of maturity is how consistently decisions are taken when issues arise. This determines whether the organization acts while outcomes can still be influenced.

Practical playbook

Improving resilience depends less on adding tools and more on changing how decisions are taken. Most organizations already possess the data, forums and escalation mechanisms required to act. The constraint lies in how these elements operate together when a signal emerges. This playbook focuses on a small number of targeted interventions that reshape decision conditions, reduce friction and preserve ownership.

Ten boardroom-ready actions

Boards and executives strengthen resilience by aligning ownership, thresholds and behaviour in practice.

1. **Define decision ownership at the point of risk**
   Ensure ownership is explicit where signals emerge so decisions are taken with context and without delay.
2. **Align escalation thresholds with action triggers**
   Use thresholds to prompt action, not reporting, with a defined response for each breach.
3. **Assess escalation behaviour through targeted surveys**
   Understand how individuals act under pressure and whether escalation supports or replaces decisions.
4. **Integrate scenario outputs into live decisions**
   Use scenario analysis at the point of decision rather than within periodic planning cycles.
5. **Simplify dashboards to highlight decision signals**
   Retain indicators that prompt action and remove metrics that add visibility without impact.
6. **Track decision latency**
   Measure the time between signal identification and decision to assess responsiveness.
7. **Embed structured challenge in governance forums**
   Ensure dissent is expected and improves decision quality.
8. **Surface repeated local workarounds**
   Treat recurring adaptations as signals of structural constraints.
9. **Make cross-functional dependencies visible**
   Clarify where coordination is required to avoid delays in ownership.
10. **Align authority with accountability**
    Ensure individuals responsible for outcomes are empowered to act.

These actions define the conditions under which signals lead to decisions and decisions lead to action.

Targeted CRO interventions (action asymmetry)

A small number of CRO-led interventions can disproportionately influence how decisions are taken across the organization.

- **Resilience dashboards**
  Shift dashboards from reporting outcomes to highlighting decision triggers. Indicators should show where action is required, not only what has occurred.
- **Escalation surveys**
  Capture how escalation operates in practice. Patterns of delay, over-escalation or avoidance reveal where ownership is unclear.
- **Scenario design**
  Use scenarios to test decision pathways under pressure. The objective is to understand how decisions are taken, not to predict outcomes.

These interventions operate with asymmetry. They require limited structural change while influencing behaviour across multiple levels.

Managing 'controlled Jugaad'

As discussed earlier, improvisation emerges when formal structures cannot respond quickly enough. The objective is not to eliminate it but to manage it deliberately.

- **Allow** when local constraints require immediate adaptation.
- **Escalate** when repetition signals structural weakness.
- **Institutionalize** when a workaround consistently improves performance.

This approach treats improvisation as a signal for system improvement rather than a deviation from it.

Barbell and OODA in practice

Resilience depends on balancing stability with adaptability. The barbell approach combines a strong protective core with targeted flexibility at the edges. Controls, capital discipline and governance provide stability, while controlled adaptation enables response to changing conditions.

The OODA loop[8] focuses on decision cycles. Shortening the cycle improves responsiveness by enabling earlier decisions and timely action.

For the CRO, the role is to align these dimensions. Boundaries define how decisions are taken, and decision cycles determine how quickly they occur. Resilience emerges when both operate together.

Closing principle

The effectiveness of this playbook is determined by whether it changes how decisions are taken.

Resilience strengthens when:

- signals trigger action
- ownership remains clear
- decisions occur while outcomes can still be influenced.

KEY TAKEAWAYS

- **Resilience depends on decision conditions, not governance structures alone**. Structures provide visibility and define accountability. Their effectiveness depends on whether signals translate into timely, well-owned decisions. Organizations strengthen resilience when governance enables intervention rather than delaying it.
- **The gap between visibility and action is a leadership challenge**. Reporting, escalation paths and governance forums improve understanding. Decisions slow when ownership becomes unclear and coordination replaces action. Resilience depends on reducing decision friction and preserving authority where issues emerge.
- **The CRO acts as an architect of agility**. The role extends beyond reporting risk. Effective CROs integrate signals across functions, align authority with thresholds and design governance that supports timely intervention. Their contribution lies in shaping how decisions are taken rather than owning decisions themselves.
- **Behaviour determines whether governance works in practice**. Trust supports ownership. Dissent improves judgement. Escalation either enables decisions or replaces them. Local adaptation reveals where systems require adjustment. Resilient organizations channel these dynamics deliberately so that behaviour reinforces rather than undermines governance.
- **Boards and executives strengthen resilience by testing decision readiness**. Maturity is reflected in how consistently decisions are taken when issues arise. A small number of targeted interventions, including clear ownership, decision-based thresholds, integrated scenarios and measures of decision latency, can significantly improve the organization's ability to act while outcomes can still be influenced.

Reframing forward

Resilience is often described as a capability developed through frameworks, controls and governance structures designed to withstand disruption. In practice, it is expressed through decisions.

Structures define how the organization is intended to operate. Behaviour determines how it responds when conditions change. Most organizations already possess the necessary components: governance frameworks, defined escalation paths and extensive data. What varies is how consistently these elements translate into action. The constraint is not structural; it is how decisions are taken.

Closing this gap depends on how leadership shapes decision conditions. Authority must be aligned with where action is required, and governance must support decisions rather than delay them. The CRO contributes by designing these conditions so that frameworks and structures enable action in practice.

Resilience becomes a consequence of how the organization decides when conditions change.

This chapter has focused on the internal conditions that enable those decisions. The next chapter extends this logic beyond the organization, examining how resilience operates across interconnected systems where coordination, dependency and collective response determine outcomes.

Endnotes

1. Snowden, D J and Boone, M E (2007) A leader's framework for decision making, *Harvard Business Review*, 85 (11), 68–76
2. Bank of England (2021) *Operational Resilience: Impact tolerances for important business services*, Bank of England, London
3. Beer, S (1972) *Brain of the Firm*, Allen Lane, London
4. Taleb, N N (2012) *Antifragile: Things that gain from disorder*, Random House, New York
5. EDP (2024) *Annual Report 2023*, EDP, Lisbon
6. Edmondson, A (1999) Psychological safety and learning behavior in work teams, *Administrative Science Quarterly*, 44 (2), 350–83
7. DHL Group (2025) *Annual Report 2024*, DHL Group, Bonn
8. Boyd, J (1995) *The Essence of Winning and Losing*

PART FIVE

Towards resilient futures

15

Collective agility

Expanding resilience beyond the individual

CHAPTER OBJECTIVES

- Reframe resilience as a collective organizational capability rather than an individual responsibility.
- Examine how sustained pressure and governance design influence adaptive capacity.
- Understand how resilience asymmetry creates hidden organizational fragility.
- Strengthen coordination, recovery capability, trust and distributed decision-making to support sustainable adaptation under pressure.

Many organizations seek to strengthen resilience through wellbeing programmes, resilience training and leadership messaging focused on adaptability. These interventions can support individuals during periods of uncertainty and pressure but do not necessarily address the structural conditions that determine whether resilience remains sustainable across the organization over time.

Performance can remain strong even as the effort required to sustain it increases. Programmes continue to move forward and reporting provides reassurance, creating the impression that the organization is adapting successfully. Over time, however, continuity becomes increasingly dependent on people compensating for the limitations of structures, processes and priorities.

What initially appears as commitment and flexibility gradually becomes a substitute for organizational capacity. Resilience weakens when adaptation depends more on human endurance than on the system itself. At this stage, burn-out eventually becomes visible, although exhaustion was rarely the original problem.

This chapter explores how collective agility emerges through coordination, recovery capability, trust, distributed decision-making and ecosystem resilience. Collective agility describes an organization's ability to adapt coherently under sustained pressure without progressively exhausting the people, relationships and systems on which performance depends. It examines why organizations that overemphasize endurance can unintentionally create structural fragility even while operational performance continues to meet expectations.

Resilience is not ultimately determined by how much pressure individuals can absorb. It depends on whether organizations preserve the structures, relationships and recovery capacity required to sustain adaptation as uncertainty, interdependence and operational complexity continue to expand.

Resilience does not reside solely in individuals

Resilience is often maintained operationally by consuming human adaptability.[1] The prevailing organizational narrative treats resilience as a personal attribute. Individuals are encouraged to become more adaptable, more resilient and more capable of coping with uncertainty and sustained pressure. Under this model, resilience becomes closely associated with endurance. Employees who continue performing despite exhaustion are viewed as resilient. Managers who absorb increasing complexity without escalation are perceived as dependable. Teams that sustain delivery under constrained conditions are often celebrated as evidence of organizational strength.

That framing becomes problematic when organizations interpret sustained endurance as evidence of resilience. In practice, teams often continue delivering through increasing coordination effort, reduced recovery time and growing operational strain long before deterioration becomes formally visible. Human adaptability becomes the mechanism through which organizations absorb structural pressure that governance systems, operating models or transformation structures can no longer manage efficiently themselves.[2]

Human adaptability often becomes the cheapest and fastest way to preserve continuity. It is easier to rely on experienced individuals to bridge gaps than to redesign structures, simplify governance or invest in new capabilities. The immediate costs remain low and performance appears stable. The longer-term costs are less visible. Recovery capacity contracts, dependency on key individuals increases and resilience becomes progressively harder to sustain.

Endurance and resilience are not interchangeable concepts.[3] Endurance allows organizations to absorb pressure temporarily through sustained human effort. Resilience depends on whether the organization can continue adapting without progressively degrading coordination quality, recovery capability, decision effectiveness or trust across the system.

In governance terms, this creates a form of resilience asymmetry, where the demands placed on adaptation grow faster than the organization's ability to recover and replenish capacity. Table 15.1 highlights the structural conditions through which this imbalance becomes visible and the governance implications that accompany them.

These structural conditions often escape attention because they do not fit neatly within traditional governance mechanisms. Most organizations maintain indicators for incidents, outages, regulatory breaches and delivery

TABLE 15.1 The systemic friction checklist

Structural condition	Governance implication
Escalating demand: operational and transformation pressure increase continuously against constrained resources	Adaptive capacity is consumed faster than it is replenished
Governance expansion: additional oversight layers are introduced to improve control and visibility	Coordination burdens increase and decision velocity weakens
Decision centralization: authority moves upward during uncertainty	Frontline adaptability declines as escalation pathways lengthen
Transformation overlap: multiple change initiatives operate simultaneously	Recovery cycles and operational slack become compressed
Dependency concentration: experienced individuals compensate informally for structural gaps	Key-person dependency and unquantified operational exposure increase
Recovery erosion: sustained pressure reduces reflection, learning and regeneration capacity	Long-term resilience deteriorates beneath stable short-term performance

delays. Far fewer monitor the factors that sustain adaptation itself. Coordination fatigue, shrinking recovery margins and growing dependence on discretionary effort rarely appear in dashboards or board packs, even though they can weaken resilience long before operational performance begins to deteriorate.

From a governance perspective, this represents an unquantified dependency embedded across the organization. Much of the capacity that sustains performance sits outside formal measures of resilience, leaving boards and executives with limited visibility into how much continuity depends on discretionary effort, institutional memory and informal coordination.

The challenge is whether the organization itself can regenerate coordination quality, recovery capability and decision effectiveness as uncertainty, interdependence and operational strain continue to expand. A resilient individual may function temporarily inside an unhealthy system. A resilient organization preserves the conditions that allow people, teams and networks to adapt sustainably over time.

Continuous pressure is replacing episodic disruption

Historically, resilience was associated primarily with recovery from discrete shocks. Organizations prepared for incidents, responded when disruption occurred, stabilized operations and gradually returned to steady-state conditions. That model assumed recovery periods existed between crises. However, in many sectors, those intervals have narrowed substantially or disappeared altogether. Most institutions no longer experience disruption as isolated events[4] separated by periods of stability. Instead, they operate inside continuous adaptation cycles shaped by technological acceleration, AI integration, geopolitical instability, supply chain volatility, regulatory expansion, workforce transformation, cost pressure and growing reputational scrutiny. This changes the nature of resilience itself.

Transformation now operates continuously alongside normal delivery expectations. Adaptation is no longer episodic: it becomes part of the operating environment. Under these conditions, the critical constraint is no longer operational capability alone. The deeper issue is whether organizations retain sufficient adaptive capacity to sustain coordination, judgement, learning and recovery while pressure remains persistent.

This creates a significant governance challenge because traditional resilience indicators often fail to capture organizational strain early enough.

Boards typically maintain visibility over financial performance, delivery milestones, operational incidents, regulatory metrics and programme execution. These indicators remain necessary, yet do not always reveal whether the organization's underlying adaptability is strengthening or deteriorating over time.

Continuity of delivery does not equate to resilience. Changes in behaviour and ways of working frequently provide earlier signals that collective agility is becoming constrained. Table 15.2 summarizes some of the indicators that organizations should monitor.

These indicators are often interpreted individually rather than systemically. Attrition may be viewed as a workforce issue. Escalation delays may be attributed to process inefficiency. Delivery friction may be treated as temporary transformation disruption. In practice, they frequently indicate that collective agility is becoming constrained across the organization.

The pressure intensifies further because modern institutions now operate inside highly interconnected dependency networks. Organizations depend extensively on suppliers, regulators, technology providers, outsourced delivery

TABLE 15.2 Early indicators of collective agility erosion

Observable signal	Underlying structural issue	Potential organizational consequence
Rising attrition among experienced staff	Recovery capacity and organizational trust weakening	Loss of institutional memory and increased execution risk
Slower escalation cycles	Governance friction and decision overload	Delayed response to emerging operational threats
Increased informal coordination	Formal structures no longer operating at required speed	Hidden dependency on discretionary effort
Declining cross-functional collaboration	Competing priorities fragmenting operational alignment	Reduced organizational adaptability
Reduced willingness to challenge decisions	Psychological safety weakening under pressure	Strategic blind spots and weaker governance challenge
Recurring delivery friction	Continuous transformation exceeding adaptive capacity	Programme delays and operational instability

partners, communities and distributed operational ecosystems that sit beyond direct managerial control.

This interdependence changes the structure of organizational vulnerability. Cyber incidents, geopolitical escalation, infrastructure failures, reputational events or supply chain disruption can now propagate rapidly across organizational boundaries because operational continuity depends on multiple interconnected systems functioning coherently under pressure. In that context, resilience increasingly depends not only on internal controls but also on the adaptability of relationships between institutions operating under simultaneous strain.

Yet many organizations continue governing as though periods of stability will naturally return once major programmes conclude. Increasingly, continuous adaptation has become the operating norm. Under these conditions, resilience depends less on the scale of control frameworks and more on the ability to preserve recovery capacity, judgement and coordination while pressure remains persistent. Collective agility therefore becomes a strategic leadership issue rather than an operational resilience issue alone.

The five conditions of collective agility

Unlike individual resilience, which focuses primarily on personal coping capability, collective agility operates at the level of interaction, coordination, decision quality and shared adaptation. The framework shown in Figure 15.1 identifies five interdependent conditions that shape collective agility.

The conditions reinforce one another. Situational awareness weakens when trust deteriorates. Decision quality declines when recovery capacity contracts. Ecosystem resilience becomes fragile when coordination across institutions slows under pressure. With that, collective agility depends less on isolated capability and more on the quality of interaction between these conditions over time.

1. Shared situational awareness

Collective adaptability depends on shared understanding. Teams must identify where pressure is accumulating, which priorities matter most, what trade-offs are emerging and how risks are evolving across the system.

In resilient organizations, operational signals are integrated across functions before escalation becomes necessary. In fragile systems, fragmentation

FIGURE 15.1 The five conditions of collective agility

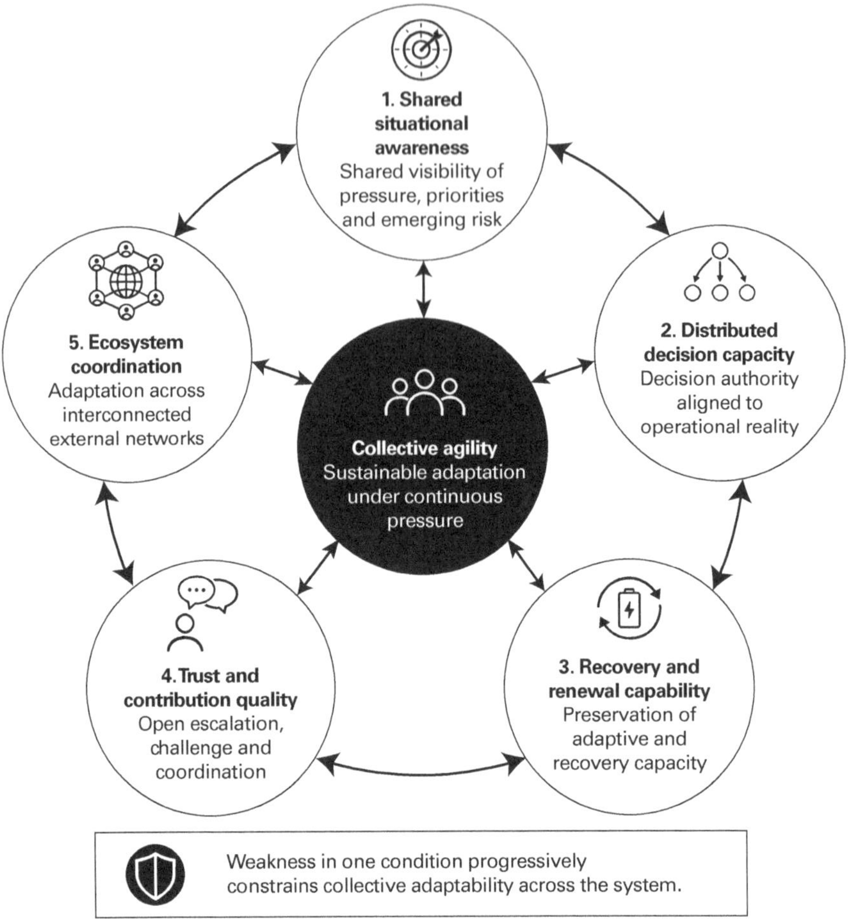

emerges early. Different parts of the organization begin operating with conflicting assumptions about priorities, capacity or risk exposure.

Boardroom warning sign: risks are repeatedly identified locally but fail to trigger coordinated cross-functional response until operational disruption occurs.

2. Distributed decision capacity

Organizations adapt more effectively when decisions can move close to operational reality while remaining aligned to governance intent. This does not mean reducing oversight. It means reducing unnecessary decision travel.

Where escalation pathways become excessively layered, responsiveness deteriorates. Frontline teams become dependent on distant approvals while leadership teams lose proximity to operational realities. Over time, decision latency replaces agility.

Boardroom warning sign: operational teams increasingly rely on informal workarounds because formal decision pathways cannot operate at the required speed.

3. Recovery and renewal capability

Many organizations associate resilience with maintaining performance under pressure. Collective agility depends equally on the organization's ability to regenerate cognitive, operational and leadership capacity after sustained strain.

Without recovery mechanisms, judgement quality, escalation effectiveness, learning capability and coordination strength progressively weaken over time.

Boardroom warning sign: delivery metrics remain stable while attrition, fatigue and coordination friction steadily increase.

4. Trust and contribution quality

Trust determines whether people contribute openly under pressure. In resilient systems, challenge travels safely across organizational boundaries. Escalation occurs early. Mistakes become learning opportunities rather than political liabilities. In fragile systems, individuals begin filtering information before escalating it upward, reducing organizational visibility precisely when situational awareness matters most.

Trust is an operational resilience variable that directly affects escalation quality, transparency and adaptive coordination under pressure.

Boardroom warning sign: meetings become increasingly performative while meaningful challenge and escalation reduce over time.

PRACTITIONER PULSE

Ownership and trust shape resilience most

In a LinkedIn poll[5] of risk and governance professionals, 47 per cent identified ownership as the cultural factor with the greatest influence on resilience. Trust received 40 per cent of responses, while energy and signal flow accounted for 11 per cent and 3 per cent respectively.

> The results suggest that resilience depends less on individual effort and more on the quality of shared responsibility and trust across the organization. Respondents placed significantly greater emphasis on ownership and trust than on communication mechanisms or organizational energy. This reinforces the chapter's argument that collective agility strengthens when people can act with confidence, challenge constructively and contribute without relying excessively on a small number of individuals.

5. Ecosystem coordination

Modern resilience increasingly extends beyond organizational boundaries into third-party and fourth-party dependency networks. Suppliers, regulators, technology providers, outsourced partners, public agencies and communities often become part of the adaptive response during disruption.

Resilience depends not only on internal controls but also on how effectively interconnected institutions coordinate under simultaneous pressure. For boards and CROs, ecosystem coordination increasingly becomes a question of systemic concentration risk rather than supplier oversight alone.

Boardroom warning sign: critical operational dependencies remain understood contractually but not operationally across the wider ecosystem.

The burn-out trap and the hidden transfer of resilience obligations

Burn-out is rarely caused by workload alone.[6] It reflects a sustained imbalance between pressure and recovery. Employees can tolerate periods of high intensity when effort still produces progress and renewal remains possible. Exhaustion accelerates when adaptation continues while opportunities for recovery steadily diminish. Teams may continue delivering and transformation programmes may remain on track, although the effort required to sustain continuity becomes progressively harder to replenish.

Over time, the burden of adaptation can shift away from formal structures and towards people and relationships that sit largely outside governance mechanisms. Figure 15.2 illustrates how resilience obligations gradually migrate from systems to individuals and teams.

FIGURE 15.2 The hidden transfer of resilience obligations

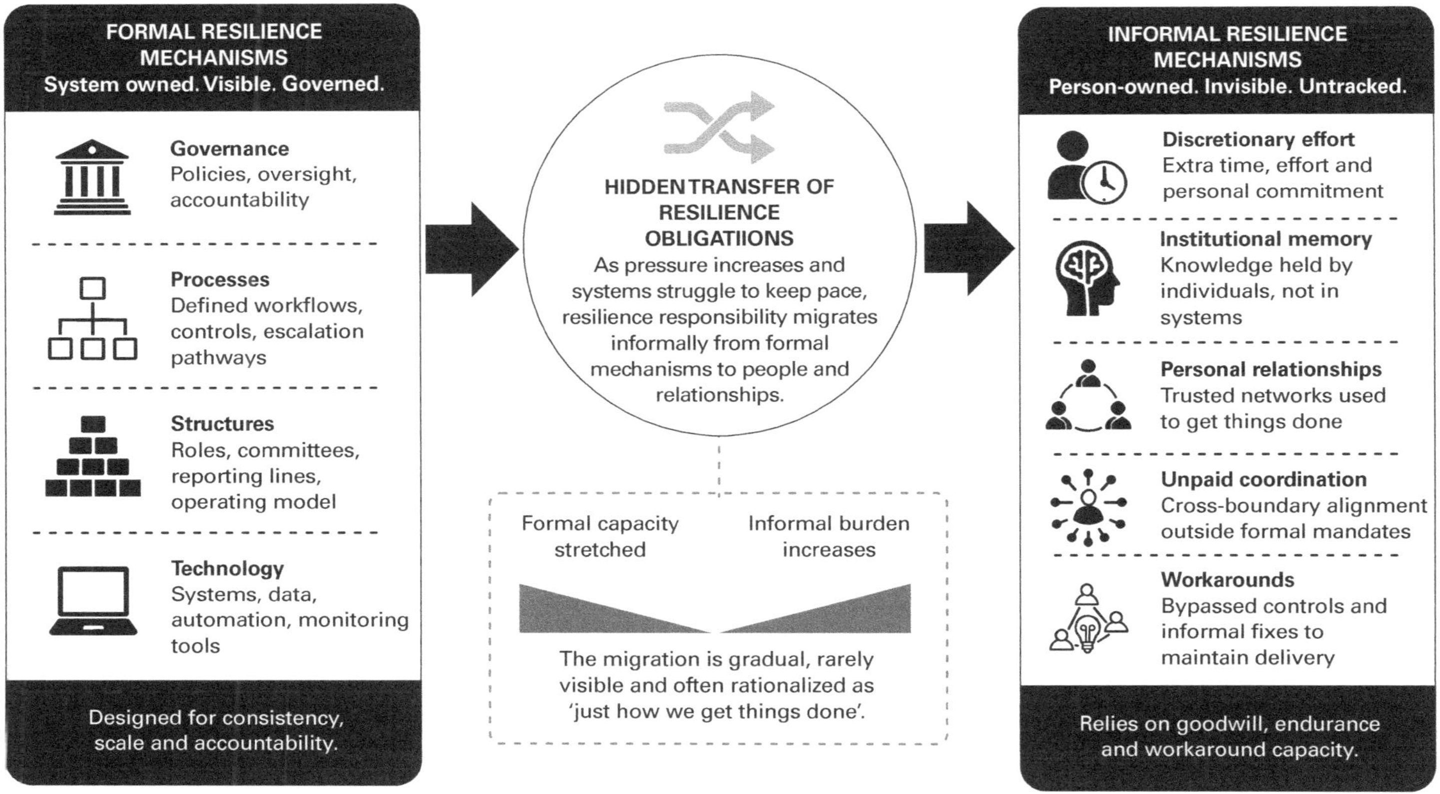

TABLE 15.3 Informal resilience networks in adaptive systems

Adaptive behaviour	Immediate organizational benefit	Long-term structural risk
Experienced managers bypass formal escalation delays	Faster issue resolution	Governance blind spots expand
Cross-functional relationships coordinate informally	Delivery continuity maintained	Key-person dependency concentration
Teams absorb additional workload voluntarily	Short-term operational stability	Systemic capacity depletion
Employees avoid escalation to preserve momentum	Reduced operational friction	Delayed risk crystallization
Mission-driven commitment sustains performance	Organizational continuity preserved	Burn-out and disengagement accumulation

Prolonged transformation programmes often make this transfer visible because operational delivery and change activity compete for the same organizational capacity. Informal workarounds and discretionary effort preserve momentum in the short term, although they can gradually concentrate resilience within a narrowing group of highly adaptive individuals and relationships. What initially appears as flexibility can evolve into dependency. Table 15.3 highlights how behaviours that support continuity temporarily may simultaneously increase longer-term fragility.

RESILIENCE SHOULD NOT DEPEND ON HEROES

Experienced individuals often bridge gaps that formal structures struggle to absorb. Problems are resolved, priorities are coordinated and work continues despite increasing complexity.

This form of resilience creates hidden dependency. Over time, adaptability becomes concentrated within a small number of individuals rather than distributed across the organization.

Collective resilience strengthens when decision-making, coordination and problem-solving continue even when key individuals are unavailable. Resilience becomes more sustainable when it belongs to the system rather than to its heroes. (Adapted from insights shared during interviews conducted for this book.)

The mechanics of this resilience transfer are not unique to corporate environments. They appear consistently across complex adaptive systems operating under sustained pressure.

REAL-WORLD EXAMPLE

Community resilience networks (Spain and UK): Collective adaptation under sustained pressure

The limits of resilience as individual endurance become most visible when formal systems alone can no longer absorb sustained disruption.

This has become increasingly apparent in parts of Spain exposed to recurring wildfire conditions.[7] Prolonged drought, rising temperatures, rural depopulation and constrained public resources have increased both the frequency and intensity of fires across several regions. During severe wildfire periods, adaptation often depended less on centralized response structures and more on how quickly communities could coordinate locally as conditions changed.

Resilience emerged through relationships that already existed before the crisis escalated. Farmers shared information on shifting fire conditions through local networks. Volunteer groups coordinated equipment and evacuation support across neighbouring communities. Local authorities, agricultural cooperatives and residents adapted continuously as roads closed, conditions shifted and resource constraints intensified. Decisions remained close to operational reality because situational awareness was distributed across the community rather than concentrated within a distant command structure.

The difference between communities became visible quickly. Areas with stronger local trust, clearer shared ownership and faster coordination adapted more effectively under pressure. Information travelled earlier. Resource gaps were identified faster. Response efforts mobilized before conditions became critical rather than after local capacity had already been exceeded.

A similar pattern appears across UK charity resilience networks operating under sustained financial and social strain. Many charities, including networks, such as Trussell[8] and British Red Cross,[9] continue delivering critical services despite rising demand, funding uncertainty, workforce fatigue and increasing regulatory pressure. On paper, these organizations often appear remarkably resilient. In practice, continuity is frequently sustained through a fragile mix of unpaid overtime, informal collaboration, personal commitment and long-standing relationships between volunteers, donors, local authorities and community groups.

Burn-out is fundamentally a wellbeing issue. In some organizations, however, it reflects the environment people work within rather than the resilience of the individuals experiencing it. Management effectively substitutes people's wellbeing for structural resilience. Pressure continues to rise while investment in recovery, simplification, prioritization and adaptive capacity is not prioritized. Short-term performance is preserved, though increasingly, by consuming the human capacity on which long-term resilience depends.

Boardroom warning sign: high-performer attrition, delivery instability and recurring project delays are treated as isolated workforce or recruitment issues rather than systemic indicators that adaptive demand has exceeded the organization's structural recovery capacity.

Board and executive implications

Collective agility changes how boards and executives interpret resilience indicators. Traditional resilience oversight has focused primarily on operational continuity, financial resilience, technology recovery, regulatory compliance and incident metrics. These remain important but they do not fully reveal whether the organization's adaptive capacity is strengthening or deteriorating under sustained pressure.[10]

Increasingly, the governance challenge is whether organizations can continue making sound decisions, coordinating effectively and maintaining recovery capacity while transformation, operational delivery and external pressures compete for the same resources.

Boards require visibility into dimensions of organizational performance that traditional resilience reporting often captures only indirectly:

- horizontal coordination quality
- recovery sustainability
- transparent escalation behaviour
- contribution and challenge dynamics
- systemic ecosystem dependency
- structural reliance on discretionary effort.

The focus moves from confirming that resilience structures exist to understanding whether they remain operationally effective under sustained strain.

In that context, several governance questions become increasingly important:

- Where is discretionary effort compensating for structural weakness?
- Where are informal workarounds increasingly replacing formal escalation pathways?
- Where is escalation treated as friction rather than adaptive intelligence?
- How dependent is resilience on informal relationships rather than formal structures?
- Where could third-party or fourth-party disruption create systemic concentration risk?
- Are leaders rewarding sustainable adaptability or continuous overextension?
- Does leadership communication encourage visibility of strain or concealment of pressure?

These questions shift governance closer to observable organizational behaviour. Resilience becomes less about confirming the existence of frameworks and more about understanding how the organization adapts under sustained pressure. Table 15.4 reframes common resilience indicators through the lens of collective agility.

TABLE 15.4 From resilience oversight to collective agility oversight

Traditional resilience view	Conventional interpretation	Collective agility interpretation
Stable operational delivery	The organization is adapting effectively	Performance may depend on unsustainable adaptive labour
Increased escalation activity	Risks are being surfaced appropriately	Decision friction may be increasing across governance layers
Low incident volumes	Control environment remains effective	Emerging strain may remain operationally concealed
High employee commitment	Culture remains strong and engaged	Recovery capacity may be deteriorating beneath performance stability
Extensive governance reporting	Leadership has sufficient visibility	Visibility may not translate into coordinated adaptation
Third-party resilience reviews	Contractual compliance has been verified	Ecosystem interdependencies may still create systemic exposure

Traditional resilience indicators often confirm that structures, controls and reporting mechanisms exist. They do not necessarily reveal whether the organization retains sufficient adaptive capacity to sustain resilience under continuous pressure.

For executive leadership, this creates a more direct responsibility for how adaptability is designed operationally.

Executives influence:

- where authority sits
- how quickly decisions move
- how escalation operates under pressure
- how recovery capacity is preserved
- whether coordination becomes easier or more fragmented during transformation.

When these conditions weaken simultaneously, organizations become increasingly dependent on discretionary effort and informal resilience networks to preserve operational continuity.

For the CRO, the implications extend beyond oversight into organizational influence. They are increasingly positioned between two interconnected domains:

1. **Structural resilience** – risk appetite, thresholds, escalation design and resilience governance
2. **Adaptive resilience** – coordination quality, escalation behaviour, recovery sustainability and organizational strain indicators.

Within structural resilience, the CRO defines mechanisms that support visibility, escalation and response. Within adaptive resilience, the CRO increasingly influences how those mechanisms operate under real-world pressure.

For boards and executives, the clearest indicator of collective agility is not whether disruption occurs. It is whether the organization can continue adapting without progressively exhausting the human, structural and relational conditions on which sustainable performance depends.

Boardroom warning sign: stable delivery metrics, low incident volumes and strong transformation reporting coexist with rising attrition, slower escalation, increasing coordination fatigue and growing dependency on informal operational workarounds.

Practical playbook

Strengthening collective agility requires organizations to preserve the conditions that allow coordination, recovery, escalation and adaptation to remain effective under sustained pressure. The objective is to prevent resilience from becoming dependent on unsustainable discretionary effort, hidden coordination networks or continuous overextension.

Boards

Boards oversee whether the organization can sustain adaptation without progressively weakening recovery capacity, coordination quality or decision effectiveness. They should:

1. **Monitor recovery capacity alongside performance**
   Stable delivery metrics should be assessed alongside indicators such as attrition, escalation delays, coordination fatigue and workload concentration. Performance stability does not always indicate sustainable resilience.
2. **Assess organizational absorption capacity**
   Boards should evaluate whether the cumulative intensity of transformation exceeds the organization's ability to absorb change while maintaining effective coordination and operational judgement.
3. **Evaluate ecosystem resilience operationally**
   Third-party oversight must extend beyond contractual compliance. Boards should evaluate systemic concentration risk and assess how external ecosystems coordinate during simultaneous, multi-party disruption.

Executives

Executives determine how adaptability operates in practice through decision structures, prioritization and coordination mechanisms. They should:

1. **Reduce unnecessary decision travel**
   Decision authority should remain as close as possible to operational reality during periods of elevated uncertainty. Excessive escalation layers slow responsiveness and weaken adaptability.
2. **Make trade-offs explicit**
   Executives strengthen collective agility when trade-offs between delivery, risk, cost and transformation are surfaced transparently rather than absorbed informally by teams.

3 **Protect challenge and recovery capacity**
Continuous pressure without meaningful recovery weakens judgement, escalation quality and learning effectiveness. Executives should ensure that uncertainty does not suppress challenge or normalize exhaustion.

Chief risk officers and risk leaders

Risk leaders provide visibility into how resilience operates behaviourally as well as structurally. They should:

1 **Expand resilience reporting beyond operational continuity**
Risk reporting should include indicators reflecting coordination quality, escalation behaviour, recovery sustainability and organizational strain alongside traditional resilience metrics.

2 **Identify hidden dependency on adaptive labour**
Risk leaders should assess where delivery continuity depends disproportionately on discretionary effort, key individuals or informal coordination networks operating outside formal governance structures.

3 **Assess resilience asymmetry explicitly**
Risk functions should examine where adaptive demand expands faster than the organization's ability to regenerate sustainable recovery capacity, coordination effectiveness and decision quality.

KEY TAKEAWAYS

- **Resilience is a collective capability, not an individual attribute**. The ability to absorb pressure depends less on personal endurance and more on whether organizations preserve the conditions that allow people, teams and networks to adapt together. Sustainable resilience emerges through interaction rather than isolated capability.
- **Resilience asymmetry develops when adaptive demand grows faster than recovery capacity**. Organizations can maintain performance for extended periods while simultaneously weakening the conditions that support effective adaptation. Pressure accumulates when recovery, coordination and decision capacity fail to keep pace with growing demands.
- **Short-term performance can be maintained by consuming long-term resilience**. Discretionary effort, institutional memory and informal

coordination often preserve delivery in the short term. Over time, these mechanisms can create hidden dependencies and transfer resilience obligations away from structures and towards people.

- **Collective agility depends on five interconnected conditions.** Shared situational awareness, distributed decision capacity, recovery and renewal capability, trust and contribution quality, and ecosystem coordination determine whether organizations can adapt sustainably. Weakness in one condition progressively constrains the others.
- **Burn-out is a wellbeing issue with organizational causes.** In some environments, management effectively substitutes people's wellbeing for structural resilience. Persistent pressure combined with insufficient recovery gradually transfers the cost of adaptation to individuals and teams.
- **Modern resilience extends beyond organizational boundaries.** Suppliers, technology providers, regulators and wider ecosystems increasingly influence resilience outcomes. Coordination across dependencies becomes as important as the effectiveness of internal controls.
- **Boards and executives must look beyond traditional resilience indicators.** Controls, reporting and continuity plans confirm that structures exist. Collective agility requires leaders to understand whether those structures remain effective under sustained pressure and whether performance increasingly depends on hidden adaptive labour.
- **The clearest indicator of resilience is the ability to adapt without exhausting the conditions that make adaptation possible.** Long-term resilience depends on preserving the human, structural and relational capacity required to sustain performance under continuous change.

Reframing forward

Resilience increasingly depends on whether organizations can sustain adaptation without progressively weakening the human, structural and relational conditions on which performance depends. This changes the leadership challenge fundamentally.

Traditional resilience models focused primarily on surviving disruption and restoring stability after impact occurred. Many organizations now operate in environments where recovery periods are shorter, transformation is continuous and coordination extends across highly interconnected ecosystems. Under these conditions, resilience depends less on endurance and more on the ability to preserve recovery capacity, decision quality, trust and coordinated adaptability while pressure remains persistent. Therefore, the challenge facing leaders is evolving.

It is no longer sufficient to build organizations capable of absorbing disruption episodically. Leaders must now design systems capable of adapting continuously without fragmenting the relationships, governance structures and contribution networks that allow collective agility to function over time.

This becomes even more significant as artificial intelligence reshapes decision-making, operational coordination, escalation dynamics and organizational judgement. Intelligent systems will increasingly influence how signals are interpreted, how decisions are prioritized and how operational responses are coordinated across complex environments.

The future of resilience will depend not only on technology itself but on the quality of interaction between human judgement, intelligent systems, adaptive governance and collective decision-making under pressure.

The next chapter explores how resilience must evolve in the age of AI and examines how organizations can preserve human foresight, accountability and adaptive coordination as intelligent systems become increasingly embedded within operational and governance structures.

Endnotes

1 Hollnagel, E, Woods, D D and Leveson, N (2006) *Resilience Engineering: Concepts and precepts*, Ashgate, Aldershot
2 Dekker, S (2011) *Drift into Failure: From hunting broken components to understanding complex systems*, Ashgate, Farnham
3 Woods, D D (2015) Four concepts for resilience and the implications for the future of resilience engineering, *Reliability Engineering & System Safety*, 141, 5–9
4 Uhl-Bien, M and Arena, M (2018) Leadership for organizational adaptability, *Human Resource Management Review*, 28 (1), 89–104
5 Haye, J (2025) Which cultural factor shapes resilience most? LinkedIn, 24 August, www.linkedin.com/feed/update/urn:li:activity:7430180174224052224
6 Maslach, C and Leiter M P (2016) *Burnout*, Wiley, Hoboken, NJ

7 OECD (2023) *Building Resilience to Wildfire Risk*, OECD Publishing, Paris, www.oecd.org

8 Trussell (2024) Emergency food support and community resilience across the UK. www.trussell.org.uk

9 British Red Cross (2024) UK emergency response and community resilience, www.redcross.org.uk/about-us/what-we-do/uk-emergency-response

10 Vogus, T J and Sutcliffe, K M (2007) Organizational resilience: Towards a theory and research agenda, in IEEE International Conference on Systems, Man and Cybernetics, Montreal, Canada, 3418–22

16

Resilience in the age of AI

> CHAPTER OBJECTIVES
>
> - Examine how AI reshapes organizational resilience through accelerated decision-making and automated escalation.
> - Understand how dependency develops across intelligent systems, shared infrastructure and common models.
> - Explore how governance, oversight and human judgement must evolve as AI becomes embedded in decision-making.

AI is becoming a core capability to support forecasting, monitoring, customer interaction, operational coordination and decision-making. Intelligent systems improve processing speed, expand analytical capability and accelerate how signals move across the organization. These changes strengthen operational capability. They also reshape how resilience develops under pressure.

Governance systems were historically designed around human limitations, including coordination delays, fragmented visibility and operational friction. AI reduces many of these constraints. Decision cycles accelerate, escalation pathways become more automated and operational responses increasingly depend on systems that prioritize and interpret information before human review occurs.[1] This creates new forms of resilience exposure.

Dependency develops across shared infrastructure providers, common models, data environments and automated decision processes embedded across multiple operational activities simultaneously. Organizations gain responsiveness while reducing the time available for challenge, interpretation and oversight before decisions scale across the enterprise.

This chapter examines how AI reshapes resilience through decision speed, dependency, governance concentration and behavioural adaptation. Resilience increasingly depends not only on technological capability but also on whether organizations retain sufficient judgement and visibility as intelligent systems become more deeply embedded within decision-making itself.

AI is changing organizational judgement, not just automation

Many organizational conversations about AI begin with efficiency. Boards discuss productivity gains, predictive analytics, operational acceleration and workflow automation. Executives focus on faster processing, broader monitoring capability, sharper forecasting and lower operational cost. These benefits are real. They also capture only part of the organizational shift underway.

AI increasingly influences how organizations interpret signals, prioritize information, escalate concerns, allocate resources and coordinate responses under pressure. Intelligent systems now shape parts of the decision environment itself rather than simply supporting operational execution.[2] This changes how resilience develops across the organization.

Historically, governance systems evolved around human limitations. Decision-making was constrained by fragmented visibility, coordination delays, limited analytical capacity and operational friction. These conditions slowed organizations down, though they also created space for review, escalation and challenge before decisions propagated across the enterprise. Recommendations were debated. Assumptions encountered scrutiny. Escalations moved through management layers before action scaled operationally.

AI changes this balance significantly. Intelligent systems can process vast quantities of information in real time, identify patterns invisible to human teams and support decisions at a scale few organizations could previously sustain. Organizations gain faster processing, broader monitoring capability, accelerated analysis and forms of responsiveness that would historically have required substantial increases in staffing, coordination or cost. AI is experienced initially as an operational advantage. The governance implications emerge much later.

As intelligent systems become more embedded within operational and strategic processes, organizations begin adapting around them. Teams rely more heavily on machine-generated prioritization. Escalation increasingly follows system-defined logic. Managers become accustomed to recommendations appearing analytically rigorous and operationally precise. Over time, confidence shifts gradually away from human interpretation towards machine-supported judgement. This transition rarely occurs consciously. It develops through gradual behaviour adaptation.[3]

Consider a bank using AI-driven credit monitoring to identify deteriorating customer exposures. Initially, the system strengthens oversight by detecting emerging patterns faster than manual review processes. Relationship managers still retain authority to challenge recommendations or escalate concerns independently. Over time, however, teams begin relying more heavily on model outputs because the system consistently appears accurate and data-driven. Exceptions receive less scrutiny. Decisions increasingly follow algorithmic scoring patterns. Then, when economic conditions begin shifting outside the assumptions embedded within the historical training data, the organization may continue operating with high confidence precisely when interpretive judgement becomes most necessary. The risk is that confidence persists beyond the reliability of the underlying assumptions. This creates an important governance shift.

AI systems do not remove ambiguity, bias or uncertainty. They relocate them into layers of data selection, optimisation logic, historical assumptions and contextual interpretation that become progressively harder to observe as system complexity increases. Decision confidence can strengthen at the same moment visibility over how recommendations are formed begins to weaken.[4]

Under stable conditions, the tension may remain manageable for long periods, but during volatility or disruption, the consequences become more significant. Resilient organizations depend partly on challenge, escalation, second review and interpretive debate. These activities often appear operationally inefficient because they slow coordination and complicate execution. However, in practice, they function as governance mechanisms that help organizations recognize when assumptions no longer align with changing conditions.

AI reduces friction exceptionally well. That capability creates strategic advantage, though it also introduces a resilience dilemma many organizations have not yet fully confronted: how much friction is necessary to preserve sound judgement under pressure?

The question becomes increasingly important as organizations face faster decision cycles, deeper dependency on intelligent systems and rising pressure to respond immediately to changing conditions. During uncertainty, leaders naturally prioritize speed, coordination and decisiveness. AI amplifies all three at the same time. But, as outlined earlier, without effective governance safeguards, it can also narrow challenge, reinforce dominant assumptions and accelerate exposure before leadership teams fully recognize how conditions are changing around them.

In that context, the greatest AI risk is not technological malfunction alone. It is organizational dependency combined with declining human scrutiny.

Speed vs discernment

The defining resilience tension in the AI era is whether organizations can still slow themselves down when conditions require interpretation rather than acceleration.

Historically, large institutions benefited from what appeared operationally inefficient: time. Information moved through management layers slowly enough to allow coordination, contextual interpretation and challenge before decisions propagated across the enterprise. These delays frustrated executives and slowed execution, though they also acted as stabilizing mechanisms that reduced the likelihood of weak assumptions scaling unchecked through the system. AI reduces those stabilizers dramatically.

Intelligent systems can now detect anomalies, prioritize risks, trigger operational responses and execute decisions almost instantaneously. Financial markets already illustrate the implications clearly, where algorithmic trading systems operate at speeds that compress the distance between signal and execution far beyond human intervention capability. Under stable conditions, this creates extraordinary responsiveness. Under unstable conditions, it can also accelerate the speed at which volatility propagates once underlying assumptions begin to fail. The same dynamic is increasingly emerging across organizational environments.

Fraud monitoring systems can block activity automatically. Supply-chain engines can re-route logistics dynamically. AI-supported forecasting can reshape operational priorities in real time. These capabilities strengthen responsiveness enormously, though they also alter how organizations behave under pressure. As decision cycles compress, leadership teams have less time to determine whether changing external conditions have invalidated the assumptions embedded within the systems themselves.

This creates a subtle but important shift in resilience dynamics. Years ago, organizational fragility often emerged from delayed action. Now, fragility may increasingly emerge from automated momentum that continues reinforcing outdated assumptions faster than governance systems can recognize the surrounding environment has changed.[5]

The risk becomes less about isolated model failure and more about synchronized propagation. Many organizations now depend on shared cloud providers, concentrated data infrastructures, external APIs and common foundation models embedded simultaneously across multiple operational processes, so dependency no longer sits within discrete outsourcing arrangements. It becomes distributed across the operational architecture of the enterprise itself. A disruption affecting one major provider can propagate across onboarding, customer servicing, operational reporting, fraud monitoring and internal decision workflows across multiple firms at once.

REAL-WORLD EXAMPLE

OpenAI and governance concentration risk

The governance tensions surrounding generative AI became publicly visible during the leadership crisis at OpenAI[6] in late 2023, when the temporary removal and rapid reinstatement of CEO Sam Altman exposed how quickly governance structures could come under pressure during periods of extreme technological and commercial acceleration.

The significance of the episode extended beyond the leadership dispute itself. As competitive pressure intensified across the technology sector, organizations raced to deploy increasingly powerful models into commercial environments. Larger models, faster releases, broader integration and accelerated market adoption quickly became defining measures of competitive positioning. Governance systems were required to evolve at the same pace as the technology itself while also addressing questions that remained only partially understood across the industry.

The challenge extended far beyond technical model safety. The debate increasingly centred on oversight independence, escalation authority, accountability, transparency and the practical ability of governance structures to exert meaningful challenge under conditions of extraordinary commercial acceleration. Questions that traditionally evolved over years of institutional development were compressed into months as organizations attempted to balance innovation pressure, investor expectations, geopolitical competition, public scrutiny and emerging regulatory concern simultaneously. This created a governance asymmetry.

Technological capability expanded faster than the institutional mechanisms designed to absorb the consequences of that capability. Decision-making became increasingly concentrated around a relatively small number of organizations, infrastructure providers, foundation models and leadership teams whose influence extended rapidly across multiple sectors concurrently. External oversight frameworks remained fragmented across jurisdictions while internal governance structures struggled to adapt to the pace, scale and societal implications of deployment.

The issue was never whether innovation should proceed. The issue was whether governance systems could evolve quickly enough to preserve effective challenge while commercial incentives increasingly rewarded acceleration.

Organizations often assume technological sophistication automatically strengthens institutional resilience. In practice, rapid capability expansion can weaken resilience when governance maturity, escalation mechanisms and interpretive oversight fail to evolve at a comparable pace. The resulting vulnerability rarely emerges through immediate technological breakdown. It develops more gradually through compressed decision cycles, concentration of dependency, reduced interpretive friction and declining institutional capacity to slow momentum long enough to reassess underlying assumptions.

The governance maturity surrounding the technology becomes as important as the technology itself.

The challenge is compounded by behavioural adaptation inside organizations. As intelligent systems become more deeply embedded within operational environments, escalation increasingly follows machine-defined prioritization logic. Recommendations arrive already filtered, ranked and interpreted before discussion begins. Over time, organizations risk developing what might be described as algorithmic deference: a gradual reduction in independent challenge because machine-generated outputs acquire greater perceived credibility than individual interpretation.

The aviation sector offers a useful parallel.[7] Increased cockpit automation improved operational safety dramatically while creating concerns around manual recovery capability when systems failed unexpectedly. Pilots retained formal authority throughout. What changed was the frequency with which independent intervention and recovery judgement were actively exercised under pressure.

A pattern beginning to emerge organizationally is one of employees remaining formally accountable for decisions while progressively losing the organizational habit of slowing systems down long enough to reassess whether conditions themselves have changed.

This is where the tension between speed and discernment becomes most important. AI increases organizational responsiveness enormously, though resilience depends on more than responsiveness alone. Under pressure, resilient organizations must still retain the capacity to interrupt automated momentum, challenge embedded assumptions and reintroduce interpretive judgement before instability scales across the system – like pilots can.

The strongest organizations will not necessarily be those operating at the greatest speed. They will be those capable of recognizing when resilience requires deliberate interpretive restraint.

AUTOMATION CHANGES ACCOUNTABILITY MORE THAN IT CHANGES DECISIONS

Many discussions about AI focus on whether machines make better decisions than humans. The more significant governance challenge is often determining how accountability evolves when recommendations, prioritization and escalation pathways are increasingly shaped by automated systems.

Formal accountability structures may remain unchanged. Decision committees still meet, executives retain approval authority and governance frameworks continue to operate. Yet independent challenge can become less frequent as confidence in automated outputs increases.

Over time, organizations can reach a point where responsibility remains clearly assigned, while the reasoning behind important decisions becomes progressively harder to trace and question. The resilience challenge is not who owns the decision; it is whether enough scrutiny remains to recognize when automated recommendations should be challenged before exposure scales across the organization.

Board and executive implications

Boards increasingly face a governance challenge that traditional technology oversight structures were not designed to address.

AI is now embedded across operational processes, analytical workflows, customer interaction and organizational coordination in most large institutions. Oversight increasingly depends on understanding how deeply resilience and decision-making rely upon systems whose assumptions, dependencies and escalation logic may not remain fully visible across the organization.

Technology governance used to be concentrated on implementation risk, cyber exposure, operational stability and regulatory compliance, and those issues remain important. Yet, AI now introduces an additional governance challenge because intelligent systems increasingly influence how organizations prioritize activity, interpret signals, allocate resources and coordinate responses under pressure.

This changes how resilience should be interpreted at board and executive level. Operational processes may appear distributed while the underlying infrastructure, models, and decision logic become increasingly concentrated beneath the surface.[8] Reporting may remain stable even as dependency deepens across shared providers, common data environments and automated decision processes embedded across various operational activities simultaneously.

The governance implications are also behavioural. As machine-generated recommendations become more embedded operationally, escalation patterns and decision dynamics often begin changing gradually across the organization. Teams rely more heavily on system-generated prioritization, while recommendations increasingly arrive already filtered and interpreted before discussion begins. Organizations can retain formal accountability structures while reducing the frequency with which assumptions are independently challenged under pressure.

This also changes the role of the CRO. Technology governance has focused heavily on controls, validation, security and compliance. While those capabilities remain necessary, risk leaders increasingly need visibility over where dependency is concentrating, where governance responsiveness is weakening, and where automated environments may be reinforcing assumptions faster than organizations can reassess them under changing conditions.

Now, the most effective CROs will act less as technical reviewers and more as interpreters of organizational conditions within accelerated decision environments.

REAL-WORLD EXAMPLE

SoftBank and strategic AI dependency

SoftBank's[9] long-term positioning around artificial intelligence illustrates a different resilience tension: concentration through conviction.

For more than a decade, Masayoshi Son consistently positioned AI as the organizing infrastructure of future economic systems. Through the Vision Fund and major investments across semiconductors, telecommunications, robotics and AI-enabled platforms, including its strategic focus on Arm Holdings, SoftBank concentrated capital around the assumption that increasingly intelligent systems would reshape global decision-making and industrial coordination.

The strategy delivered substantial strategic advantage. Large-scale AI ecosystems can accelerate insight generation, strengthen coordination and improve forecasting capability across complex environments. The resilience challenge emerges when conviction begins driving convergence.

As organizations rely on similar models, shared infrastructure and concentrated semiconductor architectures, diversity in how risks are interpreted gradually narrows. Under stable conditions, this can create extraordinary efficiency and alignment. Under stressed conditions, it can amplify synchronized exposure across markets and industries.

Financial markets have demonstrated similar dynamics before. Quantitative trading models built on comparable assumptions often improved liquidity during normal conditions while amplifying volatility when market behaviour diverged sharply from historical expectations. The issue was not the sophistication of the models themselves. It was the concentration of dependence on similar interpretive logic across multiple participants at the same time. (Note that AI ecosystems create the possibility of a comparable dynamic at a much broader scale).

The resilience lesson extends beyond technology adoption. Organizations require more than analytical capability. They require sufficient diversity of interpretation, challenge and strategic perspective to prevent convergence from gradually weakening the system's adaptive capacity under pressure.

Practical playbook

AI increasingly shapes how organizations interpret signals, prioritize activity and coordinate decisions. Strengthening resilience requires visibility over where dependency is accumulating, where decision cycles are accelerating, and where governance structures may struggle to adapt under changing conditions.

Boards

Boards oversee whether resilience and accountability remain effective as AI adoption expands across the organization.

1 **Monitor concentration of dependency**
Boards should understand where critical processes rely on common infrastructure providers, foundation models, external APIs or shared data environments. Operational dependency may appear distributed while remaining structurally concentrated.

2 **Assess how AI shapes decision-making**
Oversight should examine where machine-generated outputs materially influence prioritization, escalation, customer outcomes or strategic interpretation. This provides visibility over where automated environments increasingly shape organizational decisions.

3 **Monitor governance and escalation dynamics**
Boards should assess whether escalation patterns, review processes and decision forums are changing as AI adoption expands. Stable reporting does not necessarily indicate stable assumptions.

Executives

Executives determine how AI capability is integrated into operational coordination and decision-making.

1 **Maintain recovery flexibility**
Operational efficiency should not eliminate the organization's ability to intervene manually when systems fail or conditions change unexpectedly. Resilience depends on retaining sufficient operational flexibility under stress.

2 **Clarify override and escalation responsibilities**
AI-supported decisions should operate within clear accountability structures. Teams need clarity over when recommendations can be challenged, escalated or overridden.

3 **Assess accelerated decision environments**
Executives should identify where AI compresses the distance between signal, interpretation and action. Faster response can reduce the time available for coordination and contextual review under pressure.

Chief risk officers and risk leaders

Risk functions provide visibility over how AI changes dependency, governance conditions, and organizational behaviour in practice.[10]

1 **Map concentration exposure**
Risk leaders should identify dependency across providers, infrastructure, models and operational processes. This includes understanding where correlated exposure could affect multiple services at the same time.

2 **Monitor behavioural adaptation**
Risk oversight should examine how escalation, review and independent challenge evolve as machine-generated recommendations become more embedded operationally.

3 **Test governance responsiveness**
Scenario exercises should assess whether governance structures can still absorb accelerated decision cycles during periods of instability and changing conditions.

KEY TAKEAWAYS

- **AI changes governance conditions as much as it changes technology capability**. Intelligent systems increase speed, scale and analytical capacity. They also compress the time available for interpretation, challenge and judgement before decisions are propagated across the organization.
- **Resilience exposures increasingly emerge through dependency and concentration**. Shared infrastructure providers, foundation models, data architectures and external APIs create interconnected dependencies that can affect multiple organizations simultaneously. The resulting exposure often extends beyond traditional technology risk and into strategic, operational and systemic resilience.
- **Human judgement remains a critical resilience capability**. As AI-generated recommendations become embedded in daily operations, there is a risk that challenge, escalation and independent review gradually weaken. Effective governance requires organizations to preserve the ability to question assumptions, interpret context and intervene when conditions change.
- **Accountability must evolve alongside automation**. Automated decision environments do not remove responsibility. Boards, executives and CROs need visibility over how decisions are formed, challenged, escalated and coordinated to ensure governance remains effective as technology adoption expands.

- **Resilient organizations preserve interpretive capacity.** AI can strengthen foresight, coordination and decision-making when supported by effective governance. Long-term resilience depends on maintaining the organizational capability to recognize when assumptions no longer hold, reassess emerging conditions and adapt before exposure scales across the system.

Reframing forward

The organizations that succeed in the AI era will not necessarily be those with the most advanced automation. They will be those capable of integrating intelligent systems without weakening accountability, escalation quality, independent challenge and strategic foresight.

The next chapter builds on this foundation. It examines how organizations evolve from resilience as protection, towards adaptability as an institutional capability embedded across leadership, governance, culture and decision-making itself.

Endnotes

1 Brynjolfsson, E and McAfee, A (2014) *The Second Machine Age: Work, progress, and prosperity in a time of brilliant technologies*, W W Norton & Company, New York

2 Shrestha, Y R, Ben-Menahem, S M and von Krogh, G (2019) Organizational decision-making structures in the age of artificial intelligence, *California Management Review*

3 Parasuraman, R and Riley, V (1997) Humans and automation: Use, misuse, disuse, abuse, *Human Factors*

4 Burrell, J (2016) How the machine 'thinks': Understanding opacity in machine learning algorithms, *Big Data & Society*

5 Taleb, N N (2012) *Antifragile: Things that gain from disorder*, Random House, New York

6 Hao, K (2023) The messy, secretive reality behind OpenAI's boardroom crisis, *The Atlantic*, 22 November

7 Woods, D D and Hollnagel, E (2006) *Joint Cognitive Systems: Patterns in cognitive systems engineering*, CRC Press, Boca Raton, FL

8 NIST (2023) *AI Risk Management Framework (AI RMF 1.0)*, National Institute of Standards and Technology, Gaithersburg, MD

9 The Economist (2024) Why the AI boom is concentrating power in a handful of firms, The Economist, 13 April

10 European Union (2024) EU Artificial Intelligence Act, European Commission, Brussels

17

The future of resilient organizations

CHAPTER OBJECTIVES

- Understand how resilience evolves from recovery towards adaptability and organizational learning.
- Explore how organizations build antifragility under conditions of uncertainty and interdependence.
- Strengthen the capabilities required to adapt, learn and evolve as conditions change rapidly.

Resilience preserves performance. Adaptability preserves relevance.

Resilience determines whether organizations can adapt before changing conditions force disruption, restructuring or strategic decline. Traditionally, resilience focused on continuity, recovery and stability under pressure. That approach emerged in environments where disruption was comparatively episodic, operationally contained and easier to isolate within specific systems or events.

Operating conditions are now more interconnected, fast-paced and exposed to continuous external pressure. Decision cycles shrink faster than governance structures can respond. Dependencies spread across technology, supply chains, expertise and operational ecosystems. Leadership credibility can deteriorate rapidly when escalation weakens, coordination fragments or communication becomes inconsistent under pressure.

Under these conditions, resilience extends beyond recovery capability alone. It shapes how organizations allocate authority, govern uncertainty, preserve flexibility and sustain execution quality as conditions evolve.

Leadership teams face a persistent tension. Stability remains essential because investors, regulators, customers and employees continue expecting consistency, accountability and disciplined execution. At the same time, organizations optimized excessively around efficiency, centralization and predictability often struggle once conditions move beyond the assumptions supporting operational performance. Therefore, adaptability is critical.

This chapter examines how organizations need to evolve from traditional resilience towards agility, adaptive capacity and ultimately antifragility. It explores how leadership, governance, culture and organizational design evolve when uncertainty is treated not simply as disruption to withstand but as a condition that continuously reshapes organizational capability itself.

The adaptive enterprise: Resilience beyond recovery

Resilience is often constrained by the way organizations continue to define it. Many institutions still position resilience primarily as a protective capability activated during disruption through business continuity, crisis coordination, recovery planning and operational stabilization. These capabilities remain essential, though they no longer address the full organizational challenge because resilience now extends across the conditions shaping the organization before, during and after disruption.

Pressure develops continuously across interconnected systems rather than through isolated operational events, while dependencies accumulate across technology, suppliers, operational ecosystems and specialized expertise simultaneously. Workforce fatigue weakens escalation discipline as overloaded teams defer challenge, normalize delay and narrow decision-making under sustained pressure. AI reduces the distance between signal, interpretation and action. Regulatory intervention, geopolitical instability and supply chain disruption reshape priorities across the enterprise at the same time rather than sequentially through discrete operational failures.

Under these conditions, the defining resilience question changes. The issue is no longer limited to whether organizations can recover from disruption. The issue is whether governance, leadership and decision-making remain sufficiently adaptive as conditions evolve.

Traditional resilience focused too heavily on preservation. Adaptability now becomes equally important.

Many organizations strengthen efficiency while simultaneously reducing flexibility. Decision-making centralizes to preserve consistency, escalation thresholds rise to reduce reporting volume, and transformation programmes remove redundancy to optimize cost. Governance structures often add further review layers intended to strengthen oversight, though the cumulative effect can slow responsiveness once conditions begin changing under pressure.

These dynamics often reinforce short-term performance because delivery accelerates, reporting stabilizes and governance appears controlled and disciplined. Organizations calibrated too tightly around efficiency, however, can gradually lose the flexibility required once conditions move beyond the assumptions supporting operational performance.

Adaptive organizations respond differently. They preserve optionality intentionally and maintain sufficient flexibility to redistribute coordination and respond effectively as conditions evolve.

Strategic shifts reshaping resilience

Three structural shifts are reshaping resilience:

1. Accelerating decision velocity
2. Deepening systemic interdependence
3. Rising expectations around institutional trust.

Together, these forces are changing how organizations interpret pressure, govern uncertainty and sustain effective decision-making under stress.

Accelerating decision velocity

Artificial intelligence, automation, digital platforms and real-time analytics compress organizational decision cycles dramatically. Decisions that once unfolded across weeks or months can now propagate across the enterprise within hours or minutes.

Most governance structures evolved for slower environments where escalation moved through management layers and reporting remained retrospective by design. Organizational friction once slowed coordination, though those delays also created space for challenge, reassessment and escalation before momentum scaled across the system.

As decision cycles accelerate, resilience requires sufficient capacity to reassess assumptions before operational momentum propagates across the system.

Deepening systemic interdependence

Resilience no longer depends solely on the strength of individual institutions. It also depends on interconnected ecosystems built upon shared providers, concentrated supply chains, common data environments, external platforms and embedded third-party services.

Dependencies build up beneath operational convenience, scalability and integration. Organizations optimize around efficiency while concentration exposure becomes progressively harder to observe. A disruption affecting one infrastructure layer or provider can propagate rapidly across multiple organizations because operational architectures converge around common dependencies. Exposure becomes structurally correlated rather than operationally isolated.

Rising expectations around institutional trust

Stakeholders evaluate organizations through leadership behaviour during uncertainty rather than through performance outcomes alone. Transparency, escalation discipline, adaptability and decision clarity now influence institutional credibility as directly as operational delivery itself.

Under pressure, governance behaviour becomes highly visible. Delayed escalation, fragmented accountability, inconsistent messaging or defensive communication can erode trust rapidly even when underlying operational issues remain manageable. Organizations that demonstrate clarity, coordination and transparency during instability often strengthen stakeholder confidence despite difficult conditions.

Resilience extends beyond continuity capability alone. It shapes institutional legitimacy and long-term trust.

From resilience to agility to antifragility

The progression from resilience towards antifragility reflects a fundamental shift in organizational design. For decades, institutions optimized primarily for stability, predictability, efficiency and control, while variability was treated as operational weakness to be reduced through standardization, tighter coordination and governance discipline.

That model functioned effectively in relatively stable environments. It becomes more constrained once volatility itself becomes persistent rather than episodic.

In that context, the distinction between robustness, resilience, agility and antifragility becomes strategically important. Robust organizations resist disruption and prioritize stability. Resilient organizations absorb disruption, recover and learn from failure. Agile organizations adapt as conditions evolve. Antifragile organizations strengthen through exposure to volatility, stress and uncertainty.

Many organizations confuse efficiency with resilience. Systems that appear resilient are often highly optimized forms of robustness: efficient, consistent and effective within tight expected operating conditions, though less capable of adapting once the broader environment moves outside predefined tolerances.

The challenge for organizations is not efficiency itself. The challenge is preserving sufficient adaptability once conditions move beyond the boundaries the organization was designed to absorb.

With that, the greatest resilience threat of the next decade may not be disruption itself. It may be organizations becoming exceptionally efficient at operating under assumptions that are no longer true.

That tension often becomes visible under pressure. Systems calibrated for precision struggle with ambiguity. Governance structures designed for control slow adaptation when responsiveness becomes necessary. Leadership teams accustomed to stable conditions can interpret structural change as temporary disruption requiring correction rather than evidence that underlying assumptions no longer align with reality.

Antifragile organizations respond differently because they treat stress as information rather than interruption. Volatility exposes concentrated dependency, weak assumptions, governance rigidity and emerging constraints that frequently remain hidden during stable periods. The advantage comes from the organization's ability to interpret changing conditions early and adapt before fragility becomes embedded across the system.

Antifragility does not imply instability or permanent improvisation. Sustainable adaptability still depends on governance clarity, operational coordination, disciplined oversight and organizational trust. Adaptation without sufficient structure can fragment coordination, while excessive rigidity gradually weakens organizational flexibility.

Resilience evolves beyond recovery and operational continuity alone. Organizations capable of adapting effectively preserve learning capacity while maintaining governance discipline, accountability and strategic coherence. Controlled experimentation exists within defined boundaries. Insight remains distributed closer to operational reality rather than concentrating exclusively within senior leadership layers. Escalation pathways remain active because challenge strengthens adaptation rather than obstructing execution.

Adaptive organizations balance two conditions continuously: stability sufficient to preserve trust and execution quality, alongside flexibility sufficient to adapt before rigidity constrains organizational response. That balance becomes one of the defining leadership challenges of the coming decade. Organizations will differentiate themselves through their ability to interpret uncertainty early, adapt under pressure and strengthen through learning before disruption forces transformation upon them.

Adaptive capability also creates widening organizational asymmetry over time. Practically, relatively small differences in learning speed, coordination flexibility and decision responsiveness can produce disproportionately large differences in long-term performance. Institutions capable of learning, redistributing coordination and adapting under pressure strengthen progressively through changing conditions, while less adaptive organizations become increasingly constrained by rigidity, dependency and slower decision responsiveness. The gap between adaptive and non-adaptive organizations therefore compounds structurally rather than incrementally.

Behaviour, pressure and organizational adaptation

The future of resilience depends less on static control structures and more on how organizations interpret, escalate and respond to pressure collectively. Governance frameworks, reporting structures and operational controls remain necessary, yet resilience ultimately operates through human behaviour under changing conditions.

People determine whether organizations adapt effectively. Employees decide which signals are escalated and which remain suppressed. Leaders influence whether uncertainty is acknowledged openly or reframed defensively to preserve confidence and momentum. Middle management shapes whether challenge is rewarded, tolerated or discouraged through delivery pressure and performance expectations. Governance forums determine whether visibility produces intervention and adaptation or simply additional reporting activity.

Culture shapes resilience operationally rather than symbolically, particularly during sustained pressure where behavioural conditions often deteriorate before major operational issues emerge. Escalation slows as teams attempt to manage problems locally before creating organizational disruption.

Reporting language softens as pressure becomes normalized. Workarounds evolve into accepted operating practice. Decision-making narrows around immediate delivery priorities while broader strategic consequences receive less attention.

These behaviours are frequently reinforced because they continue supporting short-term delivery objectives. Deadlines are achieved, operational performance remains acceptable and visible disruption is avoided. Over time, organizations can become conditioned to operating under elevated pressure while gradually losing the space required for reflection, challenge and reassessment.

In that context, the core challenge of resilience is whether the organization still retains sufficient capacity to recognize how sustained pressure is reshaping behaviour, coordination, escalation and decision-making across the system.

This creates a persistent asymmetry in resilience leadership. Organizations often reward visible execution while under-recognizing the conditions supporting long-term adaptability. Teams that effectively absorb pressure are frequently viewed as high performing precisely when coordination fatigue, narrowing challenge and weaker escalation discipline are already taking hold across the organization. But this is not sustainable.

Adaptive organizations strengthen cultures differently. Escalation is treated as contribution rather than disruption. Psychological safety exists alongside accountability rather than replacing it. Operational challenge strengthens execution quality instead of being interpreted as resistance to progress or lack of alignment. Most importantly, these organizations recognize that resilience is collective rather than individual.

The myth of the endlessly resilient individual becomes dangerous in complex organizations because sustained performance cannot depend indefinitely on discretionary effort, informal heroics, hidden coordination burdens or exhausted teams compensating for structural weakness. Organizations that rely excessively on exceptional individuals often mistake personal sacrifice for institutional resilience.

Adaptive resilience requires something more durable: organizational systems capable of supporting people under pressure, preserving escalation quality during uncertainty, maintaining challenge under delivery strain and sustaining learning capacity when conditions become difficult. Strong organizations do not rely on absorbing unlimited pressure indefinitely. They recognize when adaptation, redistribution or structural change becomes necessary before exhaustion hardens into systemic fragility.

Governance as adaptive infrastructure

Governance models designed for relatively stable environments often struggle under continuous uncertainty because they were built primarily around control, oversight and accountability through structured reporting cycles. These mechanisms remain essential, though they become less effective once governance grows detached from the operational conditions shaping organizational resilience in practice.

Boards frequently receive highly structured reporting while remaining distant from the behavioural and coordination dynamics influencing adaptability across the organization. Operational strain, weaker escalation discipline, concentrated dependency and decision bottlenecks do not always appear clearly through traditional governance metrics because most reporting frameworks remain heavily outcome-oriented. Financial performance may remain stable while the conditions supporting resilience become progressively constrained.

Adaptive organizations redesign governance around visibility rather than retrospective reporting alone, strengthening leadership's understanding of how changing conditions influence behaviour, escalation effectiveness, coordination quality and organizational adaptability across the system.

Oversight evolves as a result. Governance expands beyond confirming whether controls operated correctly towards understanding whether organizational conditions continue supporting sound decision-making, effective escalation and adaptive capacity under pressure.

Adaptive governance also strengthens organizational learning capability. Organizations capable of learning rapidly from operational friction, weak signals, near misses and coordination breakdowns strengthen faster because insight travels more effectively across the system. Organizations that suppress uncomfortable information, narrow challenge or over-prioritize reporting stability often reinforce the same conditions that weaken adaptability under pressure.

Governance becomes more than a mechanism for retrospective validation. It functions as organizational infrastructure for interpretation, escalation, learning and adaptation under changing conditions.

Board and executive implications

Resilience requires interpretation as much as control. Historically, leadership authority was reinforced through decisiveness, escalation hierarchy and directional certainty. These capabilities remain important, yet they become less effective once organizations operate under persistent uncertainty, compressed decision cycles and interconnected operational conditions.

Leadership increasingly operates within environments where coordination, escalation and decision-making evolve faster than traditional governance structures were designed to absorb. Leadership consequently becomes less about directing stable systems and more about interpreting changing conditions across interconnected environments.

Boards require greater visibility over whether the organization retains sufficient flexibility under pressure. Traditional reporting often prioritizes short-term performance, delivery stability, efficiency and financial outcomes while providing less visibility over the organizational conditions supporting long-term resilience. Weaker escalation discipline, narrowing challenge, concentrated dependency and compressed decision-making can therefore develop alongside strong operational performance and acceptable financial results. Boards also need to distinguish between performance supported by sustainable adaptability and performance maintained through constrained organizational flexibility under pressure.

Executive leadership faces a related tension. Under sustained pressure, organizations naturally centralize decision-making to preserve coordination and delivery consistency. Initially, this can improve responsiveness. Over time, however, information becomes filtered before reaching executive forums, while assumptions are challenged less frequently across the organization. Leadership teams may therefore receive greater volumes of reporting while losing visibility over how conditions are evolving in practice.

Maintaining sufficient diversity of interpretation becomes critical once operational momentum accelerates. Organizations that discourage challenge or reinforce assumptions too quickly can embed outdated conclusions before changing conditions are fully understood.

The expectations placed on CROs and resilience leaders are evolving in parallel. Risk leadership relies on recognizing how pressure reshapes escalation, coordination and decision-making as conditions evolve across the organization.

Effective CROs maintain visibility over how dependency, escalation quality, coordination and decision-making evolve under sustained pressure. Their value depends on identifying when organizational conditions are beginning to constrain adaptability before traditional reporting reflects the shift.

Adaptive organizations rely less on concentrated leadership control and more on distributed organizational interpretation. Local expertise influences decisions earlier. Escalation pathways remain active under pressure. Challenge remains possible even during periods of accelerated execution, reducing the distance between operational reality and executive visibility while strengthening organizational adaptability under changing conditions.

Leadership ultimately depends less on controlling complexity directly and more on preserving the organizational capacity to adapt continuously as conditions evolve.

Practical playbook

These shifts carry direct implications for leadership, governance and risk oversight. Resilience requires organizations to preserve adaptability, escalation quality and effective coordination under sustained pressure.

Boards

Boards oversee whether resilience and adaptive capacity remain effective as operating environments become more interconnected and accelerated.

1. **Assess whether governance cycles remain aligned to operational conditions**
   Boards should evaluate whether reporting, escalation and oversight structures continue operating at a pace consistent with how decisions are formed and executed across the enterprise. Stable reporting does not necessarily indicate stable operating conditions.
2. **Monitor concentration risk**
   Boards should understand where resilience relies upon concentrated technology providers, suppliers, operational expertise, platforms or shared infrastructure. Operational independence may appear stronger than the underlying dependency structure supporting it.
3. **Expand resilience oversight beyond continuity capability**
   Oversight should examine workforce sustainability, escalation effectiveness, decision conditions and adaptability alongside traditional continuity and recovery planning.

Executives

Executives determine how enterprises preserve adaptability while operating under sustained delivery pressure and transformation intensity.

1 **Preserve adaptive flexibility during transformation**
Efficiency and transformation programmes should not weaken escalation discipline, operational flexibility, learning capacity or cross-functional coordination under pressure.

2 **Reduce organizational friction that delays escalation**
Executives should assess where governance complexity, fragmented accountability or excessive coordination layers slow responsiveness or discourage challenge.

3 **Strengthen learning capability**
Operational insight, weak signals, coordination friction and near misses should translate into structural adaptation before pressure becomes embedded operationally across the business.

Chief risk officers and risk leaders

Risk functions provide visibility over how changing conditions influence behaviour, escalation quality and resilience sustainability in practice.

1 **Integrate resilience indicators into strategic visibility**
Risk leaders should incorporate escalation effectiveness, dependency concentration, workforce conditions, coordination pressure and adaptability into resilience oversight alongside traditional risk indicators.

2 **Monitor behavioural adaptation under pressure**
Risk oversight should examine how sustained pressure influences escalation pathways, challenge dynamics, reporting behaviour and decision-making across the enterprise.

3 **Test governance responsiveness under changing conditions**
Scenario exercises should assess whether governance structures can still absorb accelerated decision cycles and sustained operational pressure while preserving effective escalation and decision quality.

KEY TAKEAWAYS

- **Resilience evolves from recovery to adaptation.** Continuity and recovery remain important, though long-term resilience increasingly depends on an organization's ability to learn, adjust and evolve as conditions change.

- **Resilience erodes gradually before it fails visibly**. Dependency, coordination friction, constrained challenge and compressed decision-making often weaken adaptive capacity long before performance indicators deteriorate.
- **Behavioural and cultural conditions determine adaptive capacity**. Escalation quality, organizational learning and the willingness to challenge established assumptions influence whether institutions adapt effectively or become progressively constrained by outdated ways of operating.
- **Antifragile organizations treat stress as information**. Volatility and disruption reveal hidden dependencies, weak assumptions and structural constraints. Organizations that learn from these signals strengthen their capabilities while maintaining governance discipline and accountability.
- **The future belongs to organizations that adapt before they are forced to transform**. Boards, executives and CROs require visibility not only over performance outcomes but also over the organizational conditions that shape adaptability, learning and long-term resilience.

Conclusion: The journey from *The Risk Within* to organizational agility

An organization's capacity to survive a disruption is decided long before the pressure intensifies. True resilience does not show up in how a crisis team responds but in how an enterprise governs uncertainty during moments of stable performance.

This book began with a simple proposition: resilience is not a defensive capability operating at the edge of strategy. It is part of how organizations sustain execution, preserve trust and continue creating value under pressure. Many organizations still approach resilience through fragmented initiatives: stronger controls, improved continuity planning, enhanced cyber capability, expanded oversight or workforce wellbeing programmes. Each contributes value independently. Resilience weakens when these efforts remain disconnected from the broader leadership system shaping how decisions are made, challenged, escalated and acted upon.

Organizations often optimize for efficiency, speed and growth while assuming resilience will emerge naturally from scale or process maturity. Under stable conditions, that assumption can appear justified. The difficulty emerges when operating conditions change faster than coordination mechanisms can absorb. Decision pathways lengthen, escalation slows and informal workarounds become embedded within normal operations. Recovery margins narrow even as operational pressure continues to intensify.

The Risk Within, my other book, explored how psychological safety, leadership behaviour and culture shape organizational risk. This book extends that argument further. Organizational agility does not emerge from frameworks alone. It develops through the interaction between culture, governance, decision-making, trust and adaptability under pressure. Resilient organizations are shaped by the conditions leaders create every day, long before resilience is tested directly.

Several themes have remained consistent throughout this book.

Resilience is relational

Organizations adapt because people share information early, raise concerns without fear and make decisions with sufficient clarity and authority. When fear suppresses escalation, resilience weakens regardless of how sophisticated frameworks appear on paper.

Governance shapes adaptability

Governance shapes adaptability through the quality and speed of organizational decision-making. It is not measured by the number of committees, controls or reporting packs an organization maintains. It is measured by whether signals travel effectively, whether accountability remains clear under pressure, and whether decisions can be made early enough to prevent manageable issues from becoming systemic events.

Resilience requires trade-offs

Strategic resilience is ultimately an organizational design challenge. Organizations cannot maximize growth, efficiency, optionality, redundancy and speed simultaneously. Resilience depends on deliberate architectural choices about how authority, coordination, flexibility and recovery capacity are distributed across the enterprise. Because these capabilities are interconnected, resilience cannot be strengthened effectively through piecemeal initiatives or fragmented control improvements alone.

Resilience cannot rely on human endurance alone

Many organizations appear resilient because people compensate continuously for structural weakness through discretionary effort, informal coordination and sustained personal commitment. Leaders cannot transfer responsibility for structural resilience onto individuals and teams. Over time, performance may remain stable while recovery capacity weakens beneath the surface through growing exhaustion, burn-out and attrition. Resilient organizations reduce unnecessary friction and preserve sustainable adaptability. They leave space for their people to recover and enable them to act under stress. Fragile organizations increasingly depend on human endurance to absorb structural strain until exhaustion becomes institutionalized as resilience.

Learning capacity determines longevity

Organizations that adapt effectively do not avoid stress. They absorb pressure, interpret signals and evolve faster than conditions destabilize them. This is where resilience begins to move towards agility and ultimately, towards antifragility. The objective is not permanent stability. It is the ability to strengthen through disruption without losing coherence, trust or strategic direction.

The operating environment is becoming increasingly interconnected, accelerated and difficult to interpret. Technological dependency, geopolitical instability, supply chain concentration and AI-driven decision velocity are reshaping how pressure develops across the enterprise. As machine-generated insight accelerates operational tempo, preserving the human capacity to interpret ambiguity, challenge assumptions and escalate concerns becomes increasingly critical before automated confidence outpaces governance oversight. Under these conditions, resilience becomes inseparable from leadership credibility.

Sustainable resilience can no longer depend primarily on certainty, control or heroic intervention. It depends on distributed capability: leaders who create clarity without oversimplifying complexity, governance structures that preserve challenge under pressure and cultures that allow uncomfortable information to surface before conditions deteriorate further.

The strongest enterprises are rarely those with the largest balance sheets or the most detailed control environments. More often, they are the ones that recognize changing conditions earlier, preserve decision quality under pressure and continue learning while competitors become consumed by stabilization.

This capability cannot be delegated to specialist functions. Boards shape resilience through the trade-offs they incentivize and the questions they choose to ask. Executives shape resilience through operating rhythms, escalation dynamics and resource allocation choices. Culture determines whether these layers strengthen one another or gradually fragment under pressure.

Throughout this book, the focus has been on patterns leaders can recognize within their own environments: delayed escalation, narrowing recovery margins, invisible coordination burdens, governance fatigue, dependency concentration and cultural silence disguised as alignment. In most cases, the underlying signals already exist. The challenge is rarely informational alone. As operational friction becomes normalized, governance delays become embedded. Workarounds become embedded until short-term adaptation begins silently weakening long-term resilience.

One of leadership's most important responsibilities is interpretive clarity: recognizing when operational stability is masking the gradual deterioration of resilience beneath the surface.

What leaders must do next

Boards should challenge whether governance structures surface deteriorating conditions early enough to influence decisions before exposure compounds. Executive teams should assess whether speed, efficiency and transformation targets are unintentionally narrowing adaptive capacity elsewhere across the enterprise. Risk leaders should determine whether escalation thresholds drive meaningful intervention or simply produce additional reporting. Managers should recognize when performance pressure begins suppressing challenge, escalation, transparency and recovery capacity within teams.

Attention must also shift towards organizational conditions that are easy to normalize: repeated workarounds becoming accepted practice; coordination burdens hidden behind strong short-term delivery; fatigue interpreted as commitment; delayed decisions reframed as diligence; concentration risk disguised as efficiency and silence mistaken for alignment.

Strategic ambition without adaptive capacity eventually becomes fragility. Over the next decade, leaders will need to recognize deterioration long before performance visibly declines. They will need to challenge the normalization of structural vulnerabilities within their organizational blueprint and strengthen resilience across the system rather than through siloed initiatives.

A call to action

This is why resilience matters so profoundly today. The ability to absorb pressure, adapt intelligently and sustain coherent decision-making increasingly determines whether meaningful ambition remains achievable under volatile conditions.

Whether in corporations, public institutions or civil society, leadership increasingly depends on the ability to operate through uncertainty without losing alignment, trust, coordination or strategic coherence as conditions continue to evolve.

That responsibility extends beyond protecting performance metrics or maintaining operational continuity. Institutions shape livelihoods, markets, communities and public confidence. When resilience deteriorates, the consequences extend far beyond internal disruption. They affect the reliability of essential services, the stability of supply chains, the confidence of customers and citizens, and the trust societies place in institutions expected to operate responsibly through disruption.

Leadership carries a broader stewardship responsibility. Resilience is no longer a supporting capability sitting behind strategy. It is part of the organizational architecture determining whether strategy remains executable as complexity, pressure and uncertainty continue to intensify.

Resilient risk management sustains the organizational conditions that allow value, trust, adaptability and coordinated execution to continue under pressure.

Ultimately, resilience is not built during disruption.

By then, your choices have already determined the outcome.

AFTERWORD: A PERSONAL REQUEST

Thank you for taking the time to read *Resilient Risk Management*.

Writing this book has been both a privilege and a responsibility. My hope is that it has challenged your assumptions, offered practical insights and provided a fresh perspective on how resilience, governance and risk leadership can help organizations navigate uncertainty with confidence.

If these ideas have been useful, I would be deeply grateful if you could take a few minutes to leave a review on Amazon or another online retailer. Reviews are invaluable. They help other leaders discover the book and decide whether it will be useful to them. Even a brief review of just a few sentences can make a genuine difference.

If your organization has policies governing external communications or public commentary, Amazon allows you to use a display name when publishing reviews, helping you protect your privacy while still sharing your perspective.

I would also love to hear how you have applied these ideas in practice. Please connect with me on LinkedIn, visit www.aevitium.com, or listen to the *RiskMasters* podcast, where I continue these conversations with risk leaders, board members and executives from around the world.

Thank you once again for your support and for being part of a community committed to building organizations that are not only resilient but ready for whatever comes next.

With my sincere thanks
Julien Haye

GLOSSARY

The following definitions provide a common language for the concepts explored throughout this book. They are intended to establish clarity across governance, leadership, culture, resilience and risk management discussions. The definitions combine regulatory practice, organizational theory, resilience research and practical leadership application.

Adaptive capacity: The ability of an organization to adjust behaviours, structures, decisions and operating models in response to changing conditions while maintaining strategic coherence and operational effectiveness.

Agility: The organizational capability to sense change, make timely decisions and adapt execution rapidly without losing strategic direction, governance integrity or operational stability.

Antifragility: A condition in which systems, teams or organizations strengthen through volatility, stress, disruption or disorder rather than merely resisting or recovering from them.

Board oversight: The collective responsibility of the board to provide direction, challenge, accountability and assurance over strategy, risk, resilience, governance and organizational performance.

Black swan event: A rare, high-impact event that is difficult to predict using conventional assumptions or historical models and that often appears obvious only in hindsight.

Business continuity: The capability of an organization to continue delivering critical products, services and operations during and after a disruption.

Collective agility: The ability of teams, functions and leadership groups to coordinate, adapt, escalate and respond effectively under changing conditions through shared awareness and distributed decision-making.

Control environment: The combination of governance structures, leadership behaviours, accountability mechanisms, cultural norms and operational practices that influence how control operates across an organization.

Culture: The shared behaviours, assumptions, incentives, norms and decision patterns that shape how work is performed, how risks are interpreted and how accountability operates in practice.

Decision velocity: The speed at which decisions are made, communicated and acted upon across the organization.

Deep uncertainty: This happens when decision makers do not know or cannot agree on the appropriate model that relates action to consequences, the probability distributions used to represent uncertainty or which consequences to consider.

Escalation: The process through which issues, risks, concerns or emerging signals are transferred to higher levels of authority, coordination or oversight for decision-making or intervention.

Foresight: The structured capability to anticipate emerging developments, assess future uncertainty, identify weak signals and prepare for plausible disruptions before they materialize.

Governance: The structures, responsibilities, oversight mechanisms, decision processes and behavioural expectations used to direct and control an organization.

Grey rhino: A highly probable, visible and potentially high-impact threat that is frequently neglected, delayed or under-addressed despite clear warning signs.

Human risk: Risk arising from human behaviour, decision-making, incentives, communication, capability limitations or cultural dynamics.

Meta-capability framework: A meta-capability framework is a high-level strategic model used to organize and integrate various individual competencies into a unified system that drives organizational performance.

Operational resilience: The ability of an organization to prevent, adapt, respond, recover and learn from operational disruptions while continuing to deliver important business services.

Organizational agility: The capacity of an organization to adapt strategy, operations, governance and decision-making in response to changing internal and external conditions.

Organizational resilience: The integrated capability of an organization to anticipate, absorb, adapt to, recover from and strengthen through disruption while sustaining strategic objectives, operational performance and stakeholder trust.

Psychological safety: A shared belief that individuals can speak up, challenge, escalate concerns, admit mistakes and contribute ideas without fear of blame, humiliation or retaliation.

Recovery capacity: The organizational ability to restore performance, capability, coordination and decision effectiveness following disruption or sustained stress.

Resilience: This is the dynamic capability of an organization to navigate volatility and pivot its strategy without fracturing its core identity. It is a generative design that surfaces latent strain, enabling leaders to make asymmetric trade-offs before pressure crystallizes into crisis. Truly resilient organizations evolve through disruption by design, strengthening coherence rather than merely surviving shock.

Resilience maturity: The extent to which resilience capabilities are embedded, integrated, measured and sustained across leadership, governance, operations, culture and decision-making.

Risk: This is formally defined by ISO 31000:2018 as the 'effect of uncertainty on objectives', typically characterized by reference to potential events and consequences. In decision theory, following the Knightian tradition, risk refers to situations where the set of possible future outcomes is known and can be assigned a reliable probability distribution based on historical data or statistical modelling.

Risk appetite: The amount and type of risk an organization is willing to accept in pursuit of its strategic objectives.

Risk capacity: The maximum level of risk an organization can absorb without threatening its viability, strategic sustainability, financial stability or operational integrity.

Risk culture: The behaviours, attitudes, norms and decision patterns that shape how individuals and groups identify, discuss, escalate and manage risk.

Risk governance: The framework through which boards and executives direct, oversee and monitor risk-related decision-making, accountability and organizational behaviour.

Risk tolerance: The defined variation or deviation from objectives, thresholds or performance expectations that an organization is prepared to accept within its broader risk appetite.

Scenario analysis: A structured process used to examine how organizations may perform under different future conditions, disruptions or combinations of events.

Strategic resilience: The ability of an organization to sustain strategic direction, competitiveness and long-term value creation under changing market, geopolitical, technological or societal conditions.

Systemic risk: Risk capable of spreading across interconnected systems, organizations, sectors or markets, creating cascading consequences beyond the original source of disruption.

Three lines model: A governance model that clarifies accountability for risk ownership, oversight and assurance across management, risk functions, compliance functions and internal audit.

Uncertainty: Or 'Knightian uncertainty' occurs when the possible future states of the world can be identified but there is no valid basis for assigning probabilities to those outcomes. According to the Intergovernmental Panel on Climate Change (IPCC), uncertainty involves a lack of information or even 'disagreement about what is known or even knowable', making it impossible to use traditional probabilistic tools for long-term planning.

VUCA: An environment characterized by volatility, uncertainty, complexity and ambiguity.

Weak signals: Early indicators, anomalies, behavioural shifts or emerging patterns that may suggest developing risks, disruptions or structural changes before they become fully visible.

Workaround: An informal adjustment, bypass or operational adaptation developed by individuals or teams to maintain delivery under constraints, pressure or system limitations.

INDEX

The main index is filed in alphabetical, word-by-word order. Acronyms are filed as presented; numbers are filed as spelt out. Locators in italics denote information within figures and tables.